# DOLLS

## A GUIDE FOR COLLECTORS

by

**CLARA HALLARD FAWCETT**

WITH

ILLUSTRATIONS BY THE AUTHOR

Copyright © 2013 Read Books Ltd.
This book is copyright and may not be
reproduced or copied in any way without
the express permission of the publisher in writing

British Library Cataloguing-in-Publication Data
A catalogue record for this book is available from the
British Library

# Dolls

A doll is a model of a human being, often used as a toy for children. Dolls have traditionally been used in magic and religious rituals throughout the world, and dolls made of materials like clay and wood have been found in the Americas, Asia, Africa and Europe. The earliest documented dolls go back to the ancient civilizations of Egypt, Greece and Rome. Such dolls – specifically used as toys for girls, with moveable limbs and clothing, were notably documented in ancient Greece, created both as rudimentary playthings, but also as elaborate art. Today's doll manufacturing has its roots in Germany though, dating back to the fifteenth century. With industrialisation and the appearance of new materials like porcelain and plastic, dolls were increasingly mass-produced, and from this point onwards, right until the present day, dolls have become increasingly popular as simple toys and expensive collectibles.

The earliest dolls were made from available materials like clay, stone, wood, bone, ivory, leather and wax. Archaeological evidence places dolls as the foremost candidate for the world's oldest toy! Wooden paddle dolls (a type of female figurine found in burials) have been discovered in Egyptian tombs which date to as early as 2000 BCE. Dolls with movable appendages and removable outfits date back to at least 200 BCE. Greek dolls were made of clay and articulated at the hips and shoulders, and there are clear stories, dating from around

100 AD that describe such dolls being used by little girls as playthings. The modern dolls predecessors, the German models, have been documented as far back as the thirteenth century, with wooden dolls dating from the fifteenth century. From this point onwards, increasingly elaborate dolls were made for Nativity scenes, especially in Italy, and dolls with detailed, fashionable clothes were sold in France from the sixteenth century.

The German and Dutch 'peg wooden dolls' (using a jointing technique where the arms and/or legs are attached to the body with pegs), were cheap and simply made and were popular toys for poorer children in Europe. Wood continued to be the dominant material for doll construction until the nineteenth century, when it became increasingly combined with other materials such as leather, wax and porcelain. This allowed for doll construction to be far more intricate. It is unknown when dolls' glass eyes first appeared, but brown was the dominant eye colour for dolls up until the Victorian era when blue eyes became more popular, inspired by Queen Victoria. Interestingly, up until the middle of the nineteenth century, European dolls were predominantly made to represent grown-ups. Childlike dolls and the later ubiquitous baby doll did not appear until the 1850s, but by the late century, childlike dolls had overtaken the market.

The earliest celebrity dolls were 'Paper dolls'; dolls usually made of cardboard like materials, with separate clothes usually held onto the dolls by folding tabs. The nineteenth century ballerina paper dolls were among the earliest celebrity dolls, and the 1930s Shirley Temple doll sold in the millions, becoming one of the most successful celebrity dolls. A similar genre of doll, 'fashion dolls', were primarily designed to be dressed, and reflect fashion trends – usually modelled after teenage girls or adult women. Contemporary fashion dolls are typically made of vinyl, the most famous example of which, is the 'Barbie doll'. Barbies were made from 1959 onwards, by the American toy company Mattel, and have dominated the market from their inception. The only doll to challenge Barbie's dominance was the 'Bratz' make, reaching forty percent of the market share in 2006.

Despite their construction for children, some dolls, such as the nineteenth century bisque dolls, made by French manufacturers such as Bru and Jumeau, may be worth over £22,000 today. Dolls have also made it into the political and artistic spheres, with artists such as Hans Bellmer, who made surrealistic dolls with interchangeable limbs in the 1930s and 1940s, in opposition to the Nazi party's idolisation of the perfect Aryan body. East Village artist Greer Lankton became famous in the 1980s for her theatrical window displays of drug addicted, anorexic and mutant dolls, reflecting the deteriorating social conditions of America's 'cultural capital.' Many books (mostly aimed at children) have also dealt with dolls, for example tales such as *Whilhelmina. The Adventures of a Dutch Doll*, by Nora Pitt-Taylor and the *Raggedy Ann* books by Johnny

Gruelle, first published in 1918. Our fascination with dolls is showing no signs of waning in the present day, and it is hoped that the reader enjoys this book.

*DEDICATED*

*to*

*MY HUSBAND AND OUR DAUGHTER*

*and to the*

*MEMORY OF MY MOTHER*

# CONTENTS

| Chapter | | Page |
|---|---|---|
| 1. | WHAT IS A DOLL? | 1 |
| 2. | ON COLLECTING DOLLS—WHERE TO BUY; WHAT TO PAY; DOLLS WORTH COLLECTING | 4 |
| 3. | EARLY TOY DOLLS | 10 |
| 4. | DOLLS OF THE NINETEENTH CENTURY | 17 |
| 5. | CHINA-HEADED DOLLS AND THEIR MARKS | 35 |
| 6. | BISQUE DOLLS AND THEIR MARKS | 55 |
| 7. | DOLLS OF PAPIER MÂCHÉ AND COMPOSITION | 71 |
| 8. | HAND-MADE DOLLS | 81 |
| 9. | THE CHRISTMAS CRIB | 87 |
| 10. | THE CLOTH DOLL | 90 |
| 11. | WOODEN DOLLS | 100 |
| 12. | THE WAX DOLL | 106 |
| 13. | METAL DOLLS | 112 |
| 14. | LEATHER DOLLS | 115 |
| 15. | RUBBER DOLLS | 118 |
| 16. | CELLULOID DOLLS | 121 |
| 17. | OLD PAPER DOLLS | 124 |
| 18. | PUPPETS AND HOW THEY ARE MADE | 133 |
| 19. | EXHIBITING DOLLS FOR FUN AND PROFIT | 143 |
| 20. | RESTORING THE OLD DOLL | 146 |
| 21. | COLLECTORS' DOLLS PATENTED IN AMERICA | 151 |

# CONTENTS [Continued]

| Chapter | | Page |
|---|---|---|
| 22. | SHOPS IN AMERICA SELLING ANTIQUE DOLLS | 154 |
| 23. | MUSEUMS WHERE DOLLS MAY BE SEEN | 159 |
| 24. | BIBLIOGRAPHY—DOLLS | 164 |
| 25. | MUSIC COMPOSED FOR DOLLS | 171 |
| 26. | LITERATURE ON PUPPETS | 173 |

# ILLUSTRATIONS

| Illustration Number | | Page Number |
|---|---|---|
| 1. | DOLLS IN ANTIQUITY. GERMAN, BRONZE; GREEK, TERRA-COTTA; EGYPTIAN, WOOD (BEAD HAIR) | 11 |
| 2. | ALASKAN WOODEN DOLL | 12 |
| 3. | WOODEN BREAD KNEADER. EGYPTIAN, CIRCA 2000 B. C. | 13 |
| 4. | WOODEN BREAD KNEADER. GERMAN, 18th CENTURY | 13 |
| 5. | COPTIC "STUFF" DOLLS, ABOUT 500 AND 600 A. D. | 13 |
| 6. | GERMAN CLAY DOLL, 12th CENTURY | 14 |
| 7. | A GREEK CLAY BABY DOLL FROM ANTIQUITY; 19th CENTURY WOODEN BABY DOLL FROM OBERAMMERGAU, GERMANY | 14 |
| 8. | GOTHIC CLAY DOLL FROM NUREMBERG | 14 |
| 9. | GUSTAVUS ADOLPHUS OF SWEDEN. WOOD. CIRCA 1650 | 14 |
| 10. | 17th CENTURY BABY DOLL IN WHEEL CHAIR | 14 |
| 11. | TWO WOODEN QUEEN ANNE DOLLS, CIRCA 1700, AND AN 18th CENTURY FRENCH FASHION DOLL | 15 |
| 12. | CHINA DOLL LEGS AND ARMS | 18 |
| 13. | DOLL LEG OF COTTON WITH STITCHED-ON STOCKING AND BOOT | 19 |
| 14. | AMERICAN-MADE DOLL BODIES | 20 |
| 15. | BROWN-EYED DOLL OF 1840 WITH TYPICAL CLOTH BODY | 23 |
| 16. | "PUMPKINHEAD" CIRCA 1850 | 25 |
| 17. | TINY BISQUE DOLLS 90 YEARS OLD | 26 |
| 18. | DRESSED AND UNDRESSED BISQUE WALKING DOLL. FRENCH, LATE 19th CENTURY. COURTESY MRS. Wm. KNOBLOCH, WASHINGTON, D. C. | 28 |
| 19. | CREEPING DOLL OF 1871 | 30 |
| 20. | WALKING DOLL, CIRCA 1869. CHINA HEAD | 30 |
| 21 | PATENT DRAWING FOR WALKING DOLL OF 1869 | 30 |
| 22. | PATENT DRAWING FOR WALKING DOLL OF 1873 | 31 |
| 23. | GERMAN BISQUE-HEADED, KID-BODIED DOLL. LATE 19th CENTURY. COURTESY MRS. FRANKLIN HILL DAVIS, WASHINGTON, D. C. | 33 |
| 24 | FRENCH DOLL OF THE 1860's WITH UNUSUAL JOINTS | 33 |
| 25. | CHINA-HEADED PEDDLER DOLL, CIRCA 1840 | 33 |
| 26. | "THE WORKING DOLL" | 33 |
| 27. | JUMEAU DOLL OF 1870. COURTESY MRS. HENRY A. DIAMANT | 33 |
| 28. | FRENCH BISQUE-HEADED DOLL, CIRCA 1890 | 33 |
| 29. | DOLL WITH BISQUE HEAD, ARMS AND LEGS, CIRCA 1880's | 33 |
| 30, 31, 32. | THREE COMMON VARIETIES OF LATE 19th CENTURY CHINA HEADS | 36 |
| 33, 34. | MORE COMMON LATE CHINA-HEADS | 37 |
| 35. | DOTTER DOLL WITH PATENTED CORSETS | 38 |

## ILLUSTRATIONS [Continued]

| Illustration Number | | Page Number |
|---|---|---|
| 36. | GOLDSMITH DOLL WITH PATENTED CORSETS | 38 |
| 37. | CHINA-HEAD CIRCA 1880 | 39 |
| 38, 39. | BROTHER-SISTER CHINA HEADS, CIRCA 1880's | 39 |
| 40, 41. | BROTHER-SISTER CHINA HEADS OF THE LATE 1880's | 39 |
| 42. | CHINA HEAD WITH ITS FOOT AND ARM, 1885 | 40 |
| 43. | UNUSUAL CHINA HEAD OF THE LATE 1870's | 40 |
| 44. | CHINA HEAD WITH ITS FOOT AND ARM COMMON DURING THE 1870's | 40 |
| 45. | GERMAN BLOND CHINA-HEAD OF 1868 | 40 |
| 46. | CHINA-HEAD OF THE 1850's-1860's | 41 |
| 47. | PINK LUSTER CHINA-HEAD OF THE 1840's | 41 |
| 48. | CIVIL WAR BENEFIT CHINA-HEADED DOLL | 41 |
| 49. | UNUSUAL CHINA-HEADED DOLL OF THE 1850's | 42 |
| 50. | CHINA HEAD WITH BRUSH MARKS AT TEMPLE AND BROWN EYES, CIRCA 1865 | 42 |
| 51 | "WINNIE DAVIS," A CHINA-HEADED SURVIVAL OF 1870. CONFEDERATE MUSEUM, RICHMOND, VA. | 42 |
| 52. | THREE RARE CHINA-HEADED DOLLS | 43 |
| 53. | CHINA-HEADED DOLL, CIRCA 1860 | 44 |
| 54. | CHINA HEAD CALLED MARY TODD LINCOLN | 44 |
| 55. | CHINA HEAD OF THE EARLY 1870's | 44 |
| 56, 57. | "CHILD" AND "LADY" CHINA HEADS OF THE COVERED WAGON ERA | 44 |
| 58. | BEAUTIFUL RINGLETTED CHINA HEAD OF ABOUT 1860, SUPPOSED TO REPRESENT ADELINI PATTI | 45 |
| 59. | CHINA HEAD OF THE LATE 1850's AND EARLY '60's WITH ARM AND LEG | 45 |
| 60, 61. | PRE-CIVIL WAR CHINA HEADS WITH ARM AND LEG | 45 |
| 62. | UNUSUAL CHINA HEAD OF THE 1850's. COLLECTION MRS. WILLIAM GARRISON, WASHINGTON, D. C. | 45 |
| 63. | CHINA HEAD SOMETIMES CALLED "DAGMAR" | 46 |
| 64. | UNUSUAL CHINA HEAD, CIRCA 1850's. COLLECTION MRS. GEORGE R. HUNT, AUX VASSE, MO. | 46 |
| 65. | JENNY LIND. COURTESY THE MUSEUM OF THE CITY OF NEW YORK | 46 |
| 66. | MID-19th CENTURY BALD CHINA HEAD WITH NATURAL HAIR GLUED ON; CHINA ARMS AND LEGS. COURTESY THE NEW YORK HISTORICAL SOCIETY MUSEUM | 46 |
| 67. | EARLY 19th CENTURY WOODEN PEG-JOINTED DOLL WITH GLAZED PINK LUSTER HEAD | 46 |
| 68. | CHINA HEAD WITH GOLD LUSTER SNOOD. 1850's-1860's | 46 |
| 69 | FINE CHINA HEAD, CIRCA 1830. COURTESY MRS. FRANKLIN HILL DAVIS | 47 |
| 70. | MISS VERYWORN, A CHINA-HEADED DOLL OF 1832. UNUSUAL HAIRDRESS | 47 |

# ILLUSTRATIONS [Continued]

| Illustration Number | | Page Number |
|---|---|---|
| 71. | "EUGENIE," 1850, WITH LEG AND ARM | 47 |
| 72. | CHINA HEAD OF 1850. COURTESY MRS. VIRGIL WILSON HALL | 49 |
| 73. | CHINA HEAD OF UNUSUAL INTEREST, CIRCA 1860. COURTESY MRS. GEORGE WICHELOW | 50 |
| 74-78. | UNUSUAL TINY CHINA-HEADED DOLLS, AND A "FROZEN CHARLOTTE" | 51 |
| 79. | OLD MARKS | 52 |
| 80. | FULPER BISQUE HEAD | 56 |
| 81. | LATEST 20th CENTURY JUMEAU FRENCH DOLL | 56 |
| 82. | EARLY "CHILD" JUMEAU | 56 |
| 83. | JUMEAU "LADY" DOLL OF THE 1860's | 56 |
| 84. | UNUSUAL SMILING JUMEAU. COURTESY MRS. FRANKLIN HILL DAVIS | 56 |
| 85. | JUMEAU FRENCH DOLL, CIRCA 1860. THE MARYLAND HISTORICAL SOCIETY | 56 |
| 86. | M. BRU FRENCH DOLL OF 1868. COURTESY MRS. ELSIE JACHOWSKI, WASHINGTON, D. C. | 56 |
| 87. | SIMON & HALBIG GERMAN DOLL, CIRCA 1890 | 57 |
| 88. | DOLL COMMEMORATIVE OF BATTLESHIP MAINE. COURTESY MRS. FRANKLIN HILL DAVIS | 57 |
| 89. | GIBSON GIRL. BISQUE HEAD, NATURAL HAIR, KESTNER KID BODY | 57 |
| 90. | A KESTNER BABY DOLL HEAD | 57 |
| 91. | ROSE O'NEILL'S BISQUE-HEADED KEWPIE | 57 |
| 92. | BYE-LO BABY DESIGNED BY GRACE S. PUTNAM. MADE IN GERMANY | 57 |
| 93. | BABY DOLL HEAD DESIGNED BY GEORGENE AVERILL | 57 |
| 94. | LATE GERMAN ALL-BISQUE HEAD | 57 |
| 95. | NINE GERMAN "FAMILY" DOLLS, 1890-1920's | 58 |
| 96. | ARMOND MARSEILLE BISQUE-HEADED BALL-MOUNTED DOLL, 20th CENTURY | 59 |
| 97. | ARMOND MARSEILLE FLAPPER GIRL, 1920's | 59 |
| 98. | ARMOND MARSEILLE CHILD DOLL WITH PAINTED STOCKINGS AND SHOES | 59 |
| 99. | SIMON & HALBIG CLOWN DOLL, CIRCA 1930's | 59 |
| 100. | EARLIER GERMAN BISQUE-HEADED CLOWN DOLL | 59 |
| 101. | GERMAN BISQUE HEAD WITH MODELLED HAIR AND INSET GLASS EYES | 59 |
| 102. | SIMON & HALBIG CHINESE HEAD OF BISQUE | 59 |
| 103. | GERMAN BISQUE-HEADED BOY DOLL OF 1927 | 59 |
| 104. | WILLOBY. GERMAN-MADE GEBRUDER HEUBACH BISQUE HEAD MADE FOR EXPORT TO FRANCE | 59 |

## ILLUSTRATIONS [Continued]

| Illustration Number | | Page Number |
|---|---|---|
| 105-111. | FANCY PARIAN BISQUE HEADS FROM 1875-1881. COURTESY MRS. GEORGE R. HUNT | 60 |
| 112, 113. | FANCY PARIAN HEADS, CIRCA 1870 | 61 |
| 114. | ALL-BISQUE HEAD WITH TOPKNOT. GERMAN, 1880's | 61 |
| 115. | ALL-BISQUE BOY HEAD, CIRCA 1870 | 61 |
| 116. | PARIAN HEAD, CIRCA 1870. COURTESY THE LITTLE MUSEUM, HILLCREST, WASHINGTON, D. C. | 61 |
| 117. | PARIAN "BOY" HEAD, CIRCA 1860 | 61 |
| 118. | FANCY PARIAN WITH ROSES IN HAIR, CIRCA 1870 | 62 |
| 119. | THE "BLUE SCARF DOLL" | 62 |
| 120. | BOY DOLL WITH BRUSHMARKS AT TEMPLE | 62 |
| 121. | "MME. LE BON" | 62 |
| 122. | "LADY VALENTINE." BISQUE, CIRCA 1865 | 62 |
| 123. | "FREDDIE." PARIAN BISQUE BOY, CIRCA 1880 | 62 |
| 124. | ALL-BISQUE HEAD, CIRCA 1885. GLAZED RIBBON BAND. COLLECTION MRS. GEORGE WICHELOW | 63 |
| 125. | PARIAN HEAD WITH SNOOD AND TASTLED TIARA, CIRCA 1860. COLLECTION MRS. GEO. R. HUNT | 63 |
| 126. | FRENCH ALL-BISQUE HEAD, CIRCA 1880 | 63 |
| 127. | WHITE BISQUE HEAD, CIVIL WAR PERIOD | 63 |
| 128. | ALL-BISQUE HEAD, CIRCA 1860's | 63 |
| 129. | PARIAN HEAD WITH INSET GLASS EYES, CIRCA 1850's | 63 |
| 130. | "PRINCESS PARIAN," CIRCA 1860 | 64 |
| 131. | PARIAN DOLL, CIRCA 1855 | 64 |
| 132. | PARIAN DOLL WITH BAND IN HAIR, LONG RINGLETS. COURTESY MRS. FRANK C. DOBLE, CAMBRIDGE, MASS. | 64 |
| 133. | UNUSUAL FRENCH BISQUE-HEADED DOLL WITH CORONET BRAID, CIRCA 1880 | 64 |
| 134. | "DAGMAR" | 64 |
| 135. | "LADY BALTIMORE," A RARE DRESDEN | 65 |
| 136. | FOUR SMALL ALL-BISQUE DOLLS, 1850-1900 | 65 |
| 137. | FINE GRADE STONE BISQUE WITH SHIRRED BLOUSE, CIRCA 1890. COURTESY MRS. KATHRYN RODGERS, WASHINGTON, D. C. | 65 |
| 138. | LATE STONE BISQUE BONNET DOLL | 67 |
| 139. | NINE BONNET-HEADS FROM 1880-1914 | 67 |
| 140, 141, 142. | UNUSUAL STONE BISQUE BONNET-HEADS, CIRCA 1880. COURTESY MRS. WM. GARRISON | 67 |
| 143. | LATE 19th CENTURY BONNET DOLL | 67 |
| 144. | MARKS AND NAMES FOUND ON BISQUE-HEADED DOLLS, AND BRU JNE. MEDAL | 69 |
| 145. | PAPIER-MÂCHÉ HEAD OF 1810 | 72 |
| 146. | INEXPENSIVE DOLLS OF THE FIRST EMPIRE PERIOD | 72 |
| 147. | EARLY 19th CENTURY PAPIER-MÂCHÉ-HEADED DOLLS | 72 |

## ILLUSTRATIONS [Continued]

*Illustration Number* — *Page Number*

148. BLUE-EYED BRUNETTE PAPIER-MÂCHÉ HEAD, CIRCA 1830. COURTESY MRS. GEORGE WICHELOW .................... 72
149-153. GREINER'S PATENT HEADS .................... 73
154. UNUSUAL GREINER HEAD .................... 74
UNNUMBERED "NINA," PAPIER-MÂCHÉ COMPOSITION. A DOLL WHICH PLAYED A PART IN THE CIVIL WAR. CONFEDERATE MUSEUM, RICHMOND, VA. .................... 75
155. DEWEES COCHRAN CHILD PORTRAIT DOLL, 1937 .................... 75
156. SHIRLEY TEMPLE DOLL SANS HAIR .................... 75
157. MME. ALEXANDER MODERN COMPOSITION DOLL SANS HAIR .................... 75
158. PEGGY, THE McCALL FASHION MODEL. COMPOSITION. MODERN .................... 75
159-162. 20th CENTURY GERMAN COMPOSITION "FLIRTING EYE" DOLLS .................... 76
163. BILLIKEN, 1909 .................... 78
164. PARSONS-JACKSON BABY DOLL, 1914 .................... 78
165. "ALICE IN WONDERLAND." HAND-MADE DOLL BY MURIEL ATKINS BRUYERE .................... 83
166, 167. SKETCHES FROM DOLLS SCULPTURED BY GERTRUDE FLORIAN, DETROIT, MICH. COURTESY MRS. WM. KNOBLOCH .................... 83
168. HAND-MADE DOLL HEAD OF PAPIER-MÂCHÉ BY MRS. D. L. BOYER, TAKOMA PARK, MD. .................... 83
169. HAND-CARVED WOODEN DOLL BY CLAIRE HALLARD FAWCETT, WASHINGTON, D. C. .................... 83
170. "JO" OF LITTLE WOMEN, AN AILEEN HARRIS DOLL .................... 83
171, 172. CLOTH DOLLS WITH EMBROIDERED FEATURES BY BERNARD RAVDA. COURTESY MRS. WM. KNOBLOCH .................... 85
173. POMONA (ENGLISH) HAND-PAINTED DOLLS, CIRCA 1928 .... 85
174. KATCHINE AMERICAN INDIAN DOLLS .................... 85
175. AMERICAN REDWARE DOLLS FROM THE PENNSYLVANIA POTTERIES, 1840 .................... 85
176. MADONNA. ITALIAN CRÈCHE FIGURE, 1925 .................... 88
177. 18th CENTURY ITALIAN CRÈCHE FIGURE .................... 88
178. MODERN CRÈCHE DOLL BY KATHRYN RODGERS AND EVELYN DUMBAUGH .................... 88
179. a. ROMAN RAG DOLL, 3rd CENTURY A. D. ROYAL ONTARIO MUSEUM
b. MODERN CLOTH DOLL BY DOROTHY HEIZER. COURTESY MR FRANK B. NOYES, WASHINGTON, D. C. .... 91
180. a. OLD FRENCH RAG DOLL.
b. QUEEN ANNE CLOTH DOLL WITH EMBROIDERED FEATURES .................... 93

## ILLUSTRATIONS [Continued]

| Illustration Number | | Page Number |
|---|---|---|
| 181. | A GROUP OF AMERICAN RAG DOLLS | 93 |
| 182. | THE BERNHARD WILMSEN DRESSED RAG DOLL OF 1895 | 93 |
| 183. | THE PALMER COX "BROWNIES," 1892 | 93 |
| 184. | RAGGEDY ANDY AND RAGGEDY ANN | 93 |
| 185. | AMERICAN-MADE CLOTH DOLL. MODERN. "A BLOSSOM CREATION" | 93 |
| 186. | AMERICAN-MADE CLOTH DOLL. MODERN. GEORGENE NOVELTIES INC. | 93 |
| 187. | KATIE KRUSE DOLL, 1912 | 95 |
| 188. | MARGARET STEIFF FELT CLOWN DOLL, 1908 | 95 |
| 189. | LENCI (ITALIAN) DOLL, 1921 | 95 |
| 190. | BAMBOLO REGINA, AN ITALIAN FELT DOLL, 1930's | 95 |
| 191. | NORAH WELLINGS (ENGLISH) RAG BABY WITH PAINTED HAIR. MODERN | 95 |
| 192. | TYPICAL NORAH WELLINGS DOLL | 95 |
| 193. | TWO ENGLISH CLOTH DOLLS | 95 |
| 194. | RUSSIAN CLOTH DOLL—UKRAINIAN WOMAN | 99 |
| 195. | RUSSIAN "CHILD" CLOTH DOLL | 99 |
| 196. | "VILLAGE BOY." RUSSIAN | 99 |
| 197. | GREEK FELT DOLL—SOPHOCLES OF SKYROS | 99 |
| 198. | FRENCH FELT DOLL | 99 |
| 199. | POLISH VICTIMS RELIEF FUND DOLL OF 1915 | 99 |
| 200. | "LADY RALEIGH," BACK VIEW OF FIRST KNOWN EUROPEAN DOLL TO ARRIVE IN AMERICA. DETAIL FROM RARE PRINT | 101 |
| 201. | "MISS KNOT," AN EARLY 19th CENTURY WOODEN PEG-JOINTED DOLL | 101 |
| 202. | "VICKIE," OLD-STYLE MODERN WOODEN DOLL | 101 |
| 203. | "HEIL," WOODEN DOLL FROM EUROPE, NEW IN 1925 | 101 |
| 204. | "MISS OLD," A WOODEN DOLL OF UNCERTAIN AGE | 101 |
| 205. | EAST INDIAN WOODEN PLAY DOLL OF 1874 | 101 |
| 206. | MODERN WOODEN PEG-JOINTED DOLL FROM SWITZERLAND | 101 |
| 207. | CHINESE DOLL WITH WOODEN HEAD AND HANDS, CIRCA 1930 | 103 |
| 208. | WOODEN DOLLS FROM THE COLLECTION OF QUEEN VICTORIA | 103 |
| 209. | JOEL ELLIS WOODEN DOLL OF 1873; GEORGE W. SANDERS WOODEN DOLL OF 1880 | 103 |
| 210. | HARRY E. SCHOENHUT ALL-WOODEN DOLL OF 1912 | 103 |
| 211, 212. | WAX HATTED DOLLS, CIRCA 1860. COURTESY MRS. WM. GARRISON | 109 |
| 213. | WAX-HEADED PEDDLER DOLL OF THE 19th CENTURY | 109 |
| 214, 215. | TWO-FACED WAX DOLLS | 109 |

xiv

# ILLUSTRATIONS [Continued]

| Illustration Number | | Page Number |
|---|---|---|
| 216. | D. CHECKENI'S FOUR-FACED WAX DOLL HEAD, 1866 | 109 |
| 217. | MME. MONTANARI WAX DOLL HEAD | 109 |
| 218. | WAX OVER PAPIER-MÂCHÉ, WOODEN ARMS AND LEGS. 1850's. COURTESY MRS. WM. GARRISON | 109 |
| 219. | WAX OVER PAPIER-MÂCHÉ COMPOSITION. LIMBS OF SAME MATERIAL. LATE 1860's | 109 |
| 220. | "GERALDINE," TYPICAL WAX-OVER-PAPIER-MÂCHÉ OF THE 1870's-'80's | 109 |
| 221. | WAX CIVIL WAR BENEFIT DOLL. RED CROSS MUSEUM. WASHINGTON, D. C. | 109 |
| 222. | 1⅛" CHARM DOLL OF WHITE AND GOLD METAL, PERFECTLY JOINTED | 113 |
| 223. | SWISS METAL BALL-JOINTED DOLL | 113 |
| 224, 225, 226. | MINERVA AND JUNO METAL DOLL HEADS, 1894 TO MODERN TIMES | 113 |
| 227, 228. | METAL-HEADED DOLLS, CIRCA 1850, WITH WOODEN ARMS AND LEGS, CLOTH BODY. WAX OVER THE METAL. COURTESY MRS. FRANKLIN HILL DAVIS | 113 |
| 229, 230. | MOROCCAN DOLLS, FISHERMAN AND HOUSEWIFE, FROM THE COLLECTION OF MRS. WM. KNOBLOCH | 116 |
| 231. | LEATHER BABY DOLL FROM MOROCCO | 117 |
| 232. | RUBBER-HEADED DOLL WITH PAINTED EYES, PURCHASED IN HOLLAND, 1935 | 119 |
| 233. | JENNY LIND ALL-RUBBER DOLL | 119 |
| 234, 235. | RUBBER DOLLS OLD AND NEW—GOODYEAR, 1851; NILSEN, 1941 | 119 |
| 236. | THREE RUBBER DOLL HEADS FROM THE GOODYEAR PATENT | 119 |
| 237. | THE WESLEY MILLER HOLLOW RUBBER DOLL OF 1875 | 119 |
| 238. | THE A. W. MONROE HARD RUBBER HEAD OF 1875 | 119 |
| 239. | TYPICAL SMALL RUBBER BABY DOLL | 119 |
| 240. | UNMARKED RUBBER BABY DOLL OF INTEREST | 119 |
| 241. | LEFFERTS & CARPENTER CELLULOID DOLL OF 1881; BONNETED CELLULOID DOLL OF THE 1880's | 122 |
| 242. | UNMARKED GERMAN CELLULOID HEAD OF BOY | 122 |
| 243. | UNMARKED CELLULOID HEAD, PAINTED EYES, MODELLED HAIR | 122 |
| 244. | EARLY 20th CENTURY CELLULOID HEAD. GLASS EYES INSET | 122 |
| 245. | SCHULTZ BROS. GERMAN CELLULOID BABY HEAD | 122 |
| 246. | SCHULTZ BROS. GERMAN CELLULOID BOY HEAD OF 1927 | 122 |
| 247. | FRENCH CELLULOID DOLL, HILLCREST MUSEUM, WASHINGTON, D. C. | 122 |

# ILLUSTRATIONS [Continued]

|  |  | Page |
|---|---|---|
| 248. | UNMARKED ALL-CELLULOID DOLL, CIRCA 1890 | 122 |
| 249. | CELLULOID DOLL WITH NATURAL HAIR WIG | 122 |
| 250. | GERMAN CELLULOID DOLL HEAD WITH GLASS SLEEPING EYES; INSET TEETH | 122 |
| 251. | ALL-CELLULOID DOLL, 1935; DOLL WITH CELLULOID HEAD AND HANDS, CIRCA 1930 | 122 |
| 252. | PAPER DOLL AND COSTUME OF 1822. COURTESY MUSEUM OF THE CITY OF NEW YORK | 125 |
| 253. | HAND-PAINTED BALLET DANCER, 1830. COURTESY MUSEUM OF THE CITY OF NEW YORK | 125 |
| 254, 255. | GIRL AND BOY PAPER DOLLS OF THE 1850's. COURTESY MRS. JENNY CALVERT, WASHINGTON, D. C. | 125 |
| 256. | JENNY LIND PAPER DOLL WITH SEPARATE WIG | 125 |
| 257. | JENNY LIND COSTUME WORN IN AN OPERATIC ROLE | 125 |
| 258. | MRS. TOM THUMB AND COSTUME. COURTESY MISS LENORE DE GRANGE, WASHINGTON, D. C. | 127 |
| 259. | A McLOUGHLIN BROS. PAPER DOLL OF THE 1860's | 127 |
| 260. | TOPSY AND EVA PAPER DOLLS | 127 |
| 261. | QUEEN ISABELLA OF SPAIN AND THREE COSTUMES. A RAPHAEL TUCK & SONS PAPER DOLL OF THE 1860's. COURTESY MISS LYDIA HURD, BELMONT, MASS. | 127 |
| 262. | A GENTLEMAN PAPER DOLL OF THE 1870's | 127 |
| 263. | PAPER DOLL AND COSTUME FROM ARTISTIC SERIES III, RAPHAEL TUCK & SONS, Ltd., 1894 | 129 |
| 264. | PAPER DOLL OF 1894 WITH YACHTING COSTUME. COURTESY THE MUSEUM OF THE CITY OF NEW YORK | 129 |
| 265. | FOUR PAPER DOLLS USED FOR ADVERTISING PURPOSES. a. CORDOVA COFFEE; b. NEW ENGLAND MINCE MEAT; c. CLARK'S O. N. T. COTTON; d. BARBOUR'S IRISH FLAX | 129 |
| 266. | FOUR PAPER DOLLS WITH COSTUMES. GERMAN | 129 |
| 267. | SWINGING-LIMBED PAPER DOLL, PATENTED IN 1880 | 129 |
| 268. | AN 18th CENTURY PANTIN | 129 |
| 269. | AN 18th CENTURY PANTIN | 129 |
| 270. | DIAGRAM SHOWING HOW TO MAKE A MARIONETTE | 136 |
| 271. | CONTROLLER FOR MARIONETTE & MARIONETTE DRESSED WITH STRINGS IN PLACE | 136 |
| 272. | FIST PUPPET HEAD AND BODY | 140 |
| 273. | FIST PUPPET WITH HAND IN PLACE | 140 |
| 274. | DIAGRAM FOR RECONSTRUCTING THE OLD DOLL BODY. PATTERN No. 1, PRECIVIL WAR PERIOD | 146 |
| 275. | BODY TYPE USED FOR LARGE DOLLS, No. 2 | 147 |
| 276. | PATTERN No. 3, USED EXTENSIVELY DURING THE LAST QUARTER OF THE 19th CENTURY AND IN THE 20th | 148 |

# IN APPRECIATION

TO Mrs. George Whichelow of Boston, Mass., Mrs. Franklin Hill Davis, Mrs. William Knobloch and Mrs. William Garrison of Washington, D. C., I owe special thanks for opening their doors so that I might sketch their dolls to my heart's content.

To Mrs. George R. Hunt of Aux Vasse, Mo., for the splendid photographs, from which I made some sketches, and to Miss Janet Pinney of the Museum of the City of New York for her cooperation in preparing the illustrations for the chapter on Paper Dolls, and others who gave or offered help, including my husband and our daughter, I owe a debt of gratitude.

The illustrations of dolls which are not otherwise credited are from the Clara and Claire Fawcett collections.

The hair of the dolls sketched, unless otherwise stated, is modelled of self material.

# DOLLS
# A GUIDE FOR COLLECTORS

*Chapter I*

## WHAT IS A DOLL?

WHAT is a doll? The question is often asked when a doll collector exhibits figures or figurines as "dolls." There are many definitions, from which the reader may draw his own conclusions. The Century Dictionary defines "doll" as: "A puppet representing a child, usually a little girl (but also sometimes a boy or a man, as a soldier, etc.), used as a toy by children, especially by girls."

According to the same authority, "the common explanation of 'doll' as an abbreviation of 'idoll, idol' is certainly wrong. There is nothing to connect the word with East Friesland 'dolski,' a wooden doll, 'dokke, dok,' a doll."

Puppet, the Century explains, signifies: "A doll, a little figure of a person, moved by the fingers or by cords or wires in a mock drama, a marionette."

Quoted in illustration are:

"This were a popet in arm tenbrace
For any woman, smal and fair of face."
—*Chaucer Prologue to Sir Thopas.*

"Neither can any man marvel at the play of
puppets that goeth behind the curtain,
and adviseth well of the motion."
—*Bacon, Advancement of Learning.*

The word "puppet" obviously is from the Latin "pupa," a doll, puppet, a girl—the feminine of "pupa," a boy, child.

Such terms as "pupil," "puppy" are closely associated. For instance: the "pupil" of the eye derives from "pupilla," meaning "a baby in the eye"— a small reflection in the center of the eye.

Citations offered by the Century include:

> "A maid makes conscience of half-a-crown a-week for pins and puppets." (finery).
> —*Fletcher, "Wit without Money."*

> "Behold thy darling, whom thy soul affects
> "So dearly; whom thy fond indulgence decks
> "And puppets up (dresses as a doll) in soft,
>    in silken weeds."
> —*Quarles, "Emblems."*

> "From yonder puppet-man enquire
> "Who wisely hides his wood and wire."
> —*Swift.*

> "Of whom the tale went to turn puppet-master."
> —*Ben Jonson, "New Inn."*

> "Thou profane professor of puppetry, little better than poetry."
> —*Ben Jonson, "Bartholomew Fair."*

> "A man who seldom rides needs only to get in a coach and traverse his own town, to turn the street into a puppet-show."
> —*Emerson.*

Turning to "marionette" in the Century we find: "A puppet moved by strings; one of a set of such puppets used to represent characters on a mimic stage."

The philology of the word is fascinating. It comes from the French "marionnette," little Marion, diminutive of Marion, which, itself, is the diminutive of Marie, Mary, for Mariolette, a diminutive of Mariole, the name formerly given to little figures of the Virgin Mary.

Two words in this interpretation of "marionette" are of special appeal.

"Characters" in the sense of "actors" refers back to: "A person, a personage; as, the noble characters of ancient history; a disreputable character; specifically, one of the persons represented in a drama or in fiction" and more or less directly relates to: "the combination of properties, qualities or peculiarities which distinguishes one person or thing or one group of persons or things, from others; specifically, the sum of the inherited and acquired ethical traits which give to a person his moral individuality."

"Figures" in the sense of representations of the human face and form, the human body, comes from: "A visible object or shape; especially, a human form as a whole; an appearance representing a body."

From "figure" to "figurine" is an easy step. The Century explains: "A figure or group of figures in any material, small and of ornamental character; specifically, such a figure in pottery or metal-work" properly may be so regarded. Then follows the clue for which we have been hunting: "Figurines are especially abundant among the ancient remains of Greece, Egypt, Assyria, etc. After Alexander, from whose time dates the ornamentation of the tombs with figurines, Tanagra became the flourishing center of its province."

Now at last we arrive at the goal of our inquiry. The Century describes a Tanagra figurine as "one of the small terracotta figures of divinities, of mortals, or of animals, found in various quantity and perfection throughout Greek lands. These figures were in great demand among the Greeks as household ornaments, and it was usual to present them as offerings in temples and to bury several of them with a dead body. They were, as a rule, cast in molds and then finished, often very delicately, by hand, and after the baking they were brilliantly colored. In them is preserved a charming memorial of Greek private life in its various phases, such as the games of children and the (domestic) occupations of the women. They are commonly called Tanagra figurines because those first brought into public notice, as well as some of the most beautiful examples since found, come from the cemetery of Tanagra in Boeotia."

It is difficult to draw the line between a figure and a doll. If, as has been explained, it is a figure of a person meant only as a plaything for a child, then an idol or a figurine might easily be classed as a doll, for the idol of one generation became the play doll of another; the figures representing hawksters common during the eighteenth and early nineteenth centuries are known as peddler *dolls;*" the crèche or church figures used to depict the pageant of the birth of Christ are certainly classed as *dolls.*

*Chapter 2*

## ON COLLECTING DOLLS

## Where To Buy; What To Pay;

## Dolls Worth Collecting.

SINCE doll collecting, of recent years, has become among American women a major hobby and comparatively little is known of the old doll, there has been an increasing demand for guidance along this line; also for help in attaining a better understanding of what is considered a good collector's item, where to get it, and how much to pay; to what period the old doll belongs; if incomplete, how to complete it in keeping with its period; how to care for dolls which by their nature crack or fade with the passing of time; how to mend papier-mâché; re-wax; reconstruct old doll bodies; where to get new parts for broken ones; how to find antique dolls, etc. The purpose of this book is to help doll collectors in every way possible.

A collector's doll should tell a story. It may be a story of costume, manners, customs, tastes, unusual persons or events of past and present. The Service dolls of today will become a record of World War II, just as the dolls sold at the Sanitary Fairs during the Civil War have become part of the story of that period. Regional dolls currently sold tell us of American occupations in various States; old dolls correctly costumed tell a story of the past; foreign dolls dressed in the colorful peasant costumes of their respective countries constitute a valuable record. Typical peasant costumes of Europe are fast becoming past history. No longer does one see in Europe, even in small villages, people dressed in the quaint way we have been led to expect, except in rare instances. Many have kept their beautiful old costumes, and some villagers, for a price, will don them and pose before the tourist for a picture. By far the majority of Europeans dress even as you and I. But through dolls, as well as pictures, the past is kept alive.

Teachers will discuss the educational value of the doll, but education is not the only reason for collecting; if it were, there would be fewer doll collectors. Love of the doll itself, this miniature representation of a human being at its best—for such should be the aim of every doll designer—is instinctive in the human race. It was born in a cave and nurtured in the mind of the medicine man, who knew its worth when vested with supernatural powers to capture and hold the imagination. Primitive man stood in awe of this symbol which represented the spirit of his ancestors or perhaps a god who could punish or reward its worshippers. As the mind of man grew and such superstitions faded in civilized countries, the child welcomed the image as a plaything. The relation between the doll and its owner was reversed; now the child could punish and reward and build around the doll the drama of life.

It was a long time before artists gave serious thought to the subject of beautiful dolls for children. Dolls and toys in quantity had existed in civilized Eastern countries long before the birth of Christ—in Europe as early as the thirteenth century—and fine but expensive dolls had been made to order by famous artists for royal families and persons of great means, but it was not until comparatively recent times that lovely dolls were made for the common people, not until new and improved methods of manufacture made possible their production at low cost. The eighteenth century brought fine dolls that the *middle* classes could buy; the nineteenth century produced fine dolls within the reach of almost everyone. A late nineteenth century child could have a doll of china, wax, papier-mâché, composition or what-have-you? at a price undreamed of in the early part of the century, when the poor had to be satisfied with crude home-made wooden or rag dolls.

The following pages describe only those dolls which still can be acquired. While one must search patiently for the rare ones, there still are late nineteenth century dolls which can be found with comparative ease. The variety is legion, and it must be borne in mind that age has not as much to do with valuation as one might think. A cheaply made, poorly constructed doll of 1840 is not as desirable as a fancy Dresden or a good china-head of two generations later. Collectors have been known to pay four times as much as the item warranted for a miserable specimen of the 1840's and to turn down a rare "buy" because it was of a later period. One purpose of this book is to try to prevent such errors, to give the collector an approximate valuation. However, it should be remembered that the monetary value of old dolls constantly is changing, and the rare old ones are now so difficult to find that a dealer is justified in charging as much for them as for other fine antiques of similar desirability.

Only interesting dolls will be given here, perhaps not all of them, for no one person has the whole story of dolls; a complete record has not been made, but from the thousands the writer has seen and studied in this country and abroad, a fair idea of the doll collector's hobby may be obtained. In the past, as in the present, a great deal of "junk" has appeared on the market, dolls not worth cluttering up these pages to describe when there are so many really interesting dolls which would do credit to any collection.

In starting a collection, one should give heed to the space available. If it be small, the nine-inch doll is ideal. But for exhibition purposes, large dolls make a better showing unless small dolls are accompanied by scenic backgrounds.

Finding the best commercial dolls of the present day is an easy matter. A glance at the advertisements in magazines and newspapers or visits to large department stores will give a fair idea of modern dolls and their prices. The magazine "Playthings" describes the latest. Antique, foreign, regional and hand-made dolls are advertised in *Hobbies,* and a small publication by Kimport, Independence, Mo., called *Doll Talk.* When visiting out of town, look up the antique shops, dolls' hospitals, the "Goodwill" or "Morgan Memorial" as it is called in the Boston area, and Thrift Shops ever-present in large cities and sometimes in small ones. Here, too, may be found old fabrics suitable for clothing antique dolls.

One of the best ways to obtain the unusual is to insert a "want ad" in *Hobbies,* published in Chicago. This is the best known and probably the most comprehensive publication of its kind in the world. If you do advertise, be prepared for some disappointments and some useless expense for, whether or not you purchase, you will have to pay expressage both ways, but the good results probably, in the long run, will outweigh the bad. Descriptions by dealers sometimes are misleading, but not intentionally so. They do not always know their wares. Always ask for a *full* description and the right to return if not satisfied.

One of the oldest examples we are able to find is the Queen Anne doll (See chapter on Early Dolls) usually made of wood, sometimes the head overlaid with plaster and with glass eyes set in; commonly found with painted eyes, wooden body and legs, and arms of bamboo, with forkish fingers. A Queen Anne of cloth is rare, but those of wood are more interesting. The asking price for this type of doll averages $100 for a good example with original old dress; they have been known to sell undressed for as little as $20 a few years ago, and as high as $500, a ridiculous price.

Crèche (Christmas crib) dolls centuries old likewise have been found not infrequently in American antique shops. The Thayer collection at the University of Kansas, and the Giovanni della Robbia (1489-1529) and Antonio Rossellino groups (fifteenth century) at the Metropolitan Museum in New York City are fine examples for study purposes. One also may find them in old cities. New Orleans, La., had a number at one time, brought over by the early settlers. The reason why we find so many old ones today is that they were made by the thousands from the very beginning of the Christmas festival to within comparatively recent times. The height of their popularity seems to have been from the fifteenth to the eighteenth centuries, but we have modern ones, too. Old ones usually are well preserved because they were used only at the Christmas season. The price range is from about $5 to $75 or more. It is possible to purchase a fine piece for $35.

Rare dolls with fancy hairdo, the Dresdens and fine Parians and early papier mâchés are difficult to price fairly. In the opinion of some, the rarest and finest of dolls should not cost more than $300; others think $75 should be the maximum sum paid for any antique doll however rare and lovely. There is such diversity of opinion in this matter that no one person is qualified to set a standard.

An antique china-head with fancy hair arrangement should cost more than a Parian with similar coiffeur, as the china is apt to be earlier, and it is more difficult for the potter to get fine lines in china than in Parian.

The average price of a well-preserved Greiner doll See chapter on Papier Mâché and Composition seems to be $25. Few are less than $20, and many are as high as $50, a price not warranted unless the clothes are original and unusually attractive. The price of old dolls varies in different sections of the country, higher in the far West and in Florida than in the area between the District of Columbia and Portland, Maine. Blondes are apt to be more expensive than brunettes, because they are scarcer, and small Greiners sizes 0 or 1, are more difficult to find than the large ones. As is the case with other dolls, hair arrangement counts. Those dolls with the first patent marks, the *Improved*, are the most desirable of all the Greiners. One will find them in both boy and girl hair styles; the former with short, slightly wavy hair parted in the middle, the latter with corkscrew ringlets curved to the head See sketches in the chapter on *Papier-Mâché and Composition*. A pair of these in original costume would bring top price. The original Greiner patent papers are missing from the Patent Office in Washington, but there is in the possession of Mrs. Frank C. Doble of Cambridge, Mass., a picture of the original papers with the ringletted girl doll head resting beside them.

Wooden dolls are much sought after; even the twentieth century Schoenhut See Chapter on Wooden Dolls often brings $15 or $20, and sometimes more, although it should not, for there still are many examples in this country. The Joel Ellis wooden doll rarely brings more than $35, although it goes back to 1872.

It is better to buy from an experienced rather than an inexperienced dealer. The latter may charge too little, but, on the other hand, often charges too much, the price being based upon the advice of a doll-collecting friend who is herself a novice, but wants to please. Beginners often pay to a dealer who does not intentionally over-charge four times as much for an old doll as the item warrants.

In the Chapter on China-heads, notice the illustration of the commonest type. A twelve-inch size in perfect condition, undressed, should not cost more than $6. Before the Second World War, the cost was considerably less. If trade in this commodity is resumed in this post-war period, the price will decline; if not, it will advance. It would be fair to ask upward of $10 for a common *early* china-headed doll of average size about 12 inches and a brown-eyed china-head should bring more than one with blue eyes, for one only in every hundred was given brown eyes. This does not apply to the late bisque heads, where brown eyes are abundant. Queen Victoria's preference for blue eyes ruled the market in her time.

Wax dolls are so diversified in quality, style, condition. etc., that dealers have a difficult time in pricing them. The later common variety made with cheap muslin sack-like body stuffed with straw, "pop" eyes and almost no neck, the head thinly waxed over thick, cheap composition and with too-short arms and stubby, ill-shaped hands, should not bring a great deal. Five dollars is no bargain price for such a doll, even though it may be fifty or more years old. On the other hand, a fine Montanari in good condition, appropriately dressed, easily might bring a hundred dollars or more.

One sees a great diversity in the price of the common bisque-headed ball-jointed doll manufactured in quantity from about 1870 until within the past twenty or thirty years. Dealers sometimes confuse the fine French bisque with closed mouth and "jewel" eyes with the more ordinary variety and often charge as much for the common type as for the beauties. Recently a cheaply-made ten-inch doll with bisque head and ball-jointed body sold, undressed, in the middle Atlantic States for $4, a fair price; the finer ones of the same general type for upward of $10, depending upon the size, condition. quality, clothing, etc. There is a great difference in quality among these dolls. The very finest and largest of the type with closed mouth and eyes of blown glass might bring as much as $75. Closed-mouth dolls in the larger sizes are scarcer. but not necessarily older than the open-mouthed variety. Very large ones with open mouth seldom bring more than $25, and often less than that.

Kid-bodied dolls with bisque heads are more desirable, all things considered, than those with ball joints, because they are easier to care for. Elastic in the latter wears out and the doll has to be re-strung. The kid-bodied doll is apt to be older, but, again, not necessarily so. Antiques usually are "ladies" with narrow waists.

The early Jumeau, discussed in the chapter on bisque-headed dolls, brings a good price. Forty-five dollars is not uncommonly high for a twenty-inch example and, if a trousseau comes with it, the price is much greater. This price would be entirely out of proportion for the same sized bisque-headed ball-jointed doll.

Most of the old French dolls were high in price because manufacturing costs were higher in France than in Germany, but some would bring a high price in any country, for they were beautifully and expensively made. An early doll, 30 inches high, from the old-established famous Bru factory in France recently sold in a Washington antiques show for $75. This was a Bebe Bru Jne. No. 12. An early Jumeau (unmarked) of the same size might have sold for more than a hundred dollars.

Prices quoted can only approximate the market value, which constantly is changing. An old doll should be most carefully examined to be accurately appraised, and common sense must be relied upon. Beautiful, rare and unusual dolls top the list, and the prices of these depend upon quality, condition, size, clothing and the history if such is of general interest and can be authenticated. "Grandmother's doll" means nothing except as an heirloom in the family, while "a doll Queen Victoria played with when she was a child" means everything. But be sure that a statement of this kind is backed up with proven fact. Dolls of famous persons are few and far between.

*Chapter 3*

# EARLY TOY DOLLS

THE earliest toy dolls of which we have any record were dug from graves of children in Egypt and Greece, where civilization came at an early period. There are no records of dolls from prehistoric times. The earliest example of a Greek toy doll is in the shape of a rattle with a female form, the head missing. For mention of these early dolls, we may turn to old Greek literature, and for examples to the museums both here and abroad. The ancient dolls for the regular trade were crude, but some beautiful examples of dolls made for the wealthy come to us in well-modelled clay or terra-cotta, wood, marble, alabaster, ivory, wax, gold, silver and bronze.

Excavations of these treasures were plentiful during the nineteenth century. One has only to look through old magazines to get the story. "St. Nicholas" for November, 1879, prints an interesting article on "Playthings" by Olive Thorne. It gives an idea of the doll situation in the various countries before tourist trade made it profitable to invent dolls. Miss Thorne writes:

"The first toy is said to have been a rattle-box*—a symbol, said the thoughtful ancients, 'of the eternal agitation, which is the cause of progress.' The play life of our nineteenth century babies begins with the same object and the only genuine toy to be found in all Africa (says a traveler) is a rattle-box.

"The second toy was, doubtless, a doll, for that fascinating object has been in use from the earliest times of which we have any record, by all peoples, barbarous or civilized. The English name is said by some of the wise men to be a nickname for Dorothea, while others think it a contraction of 'idol.' When we see the affection of little people for their dolls, this origin seems probable. The French call a doll a *poupée* and the Germans *puppe*. The pronounciation differs in the two languages, but both names come from the Latin *pupa*, a girl. Before the 18th century, dolls were called "little ladies" or "babies."

"The dignified science of history is too much taken up with stories of the wars and troubles of grown-up people to tell us what the little ancients used to

---

* Rattles and clappers were supposed to frighten away evil spirits.

play with; but we have found out many things in spite of the big books. Out of the ground are being dug, nowadays, ruined cities and treasures of the people of long ago, among them the precious toys of children. Thus we have found out that the little people of the island of Cyprus, in the Mediterranean, who lived three thousand years ago, had toys of terra cotta, figures of animals, of horses on platforms which ran on four terra cotta wheels, with riders of curious form, some on their knees, and others holding in each arm a large jar; donkeys with panniers, two-wheeled vehicles like our drays, and chariots with

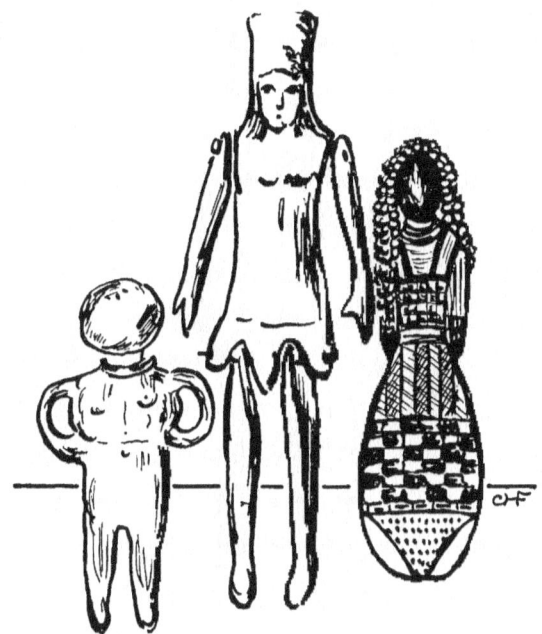

(1) Dolls in antiquity. Reading from left to right: German, bronze; Greek, terra-cotta; Egyptian, brightly painted wood with strings of beads for hair.

horses and drivers. Then they had a representation of some game,—whether of child or man,— several figures with joined hands, dancing around one standing still; perhaps some antique play of 'Oats, pease, beans.' There were also figures shaped like a jumping-jack, a mother with a baby in her arms, and, above all, dolls of all sizes and shapes, and all with smiling faces. To be sure we cannot be certain that these were the playthings of children,—the learned explorer calls them 'statuettes,' and other names,—but they are certainly very suitable for the youngsters, and all of you who live in, or visit, New York, can see them any day at the Metropolitan Museum. If they were not toys, they ought to have been.

"The ancient little Egyptians, three or four thousand years ago, had dolls, painted to represent clothes, with arms and legs moving on pins by means of strings, so that if they couldn't take off their clothes, they could move about. Some were very crude, without limbs, and for hair they had thick and long strings of beads. They also had figures washing, or kneading bread, which could be worked by pulling strings, and crocodiles which would open their

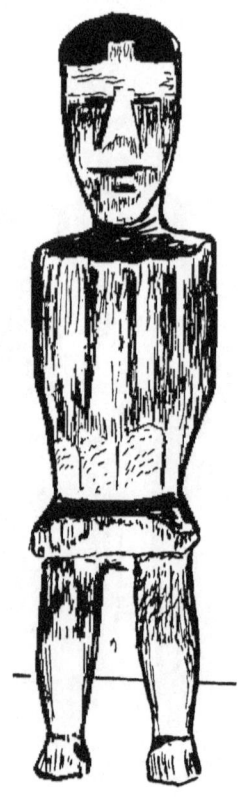

(2) Alaskan wooden doll.

mouths by the same means. The British Museum has quite a collection of ancient Egyptian toys; balls covered with leather, foot-balls, marbles, small fish, and other things. Some of the balls are stuffed with bran or husks, others are made of rushes, plaited and covered with leather, and others of painted earthenware, probably only to look at.

"The first toy of the ancient Greek baby was a rattle-box; then came—as he grew—dolls of clay (a sort of coarse china doll), figures of animals, apes, with their little ones, ducks, tortoises, and others. Then they had small wooden wagons, to which they harnessed live mice, horses and ships made of leather, chickens, and jack-stones (called by a long Greek name.) Your 'Jack-in-the-Pulpit' told you of them once in *St. Nicholas* for April, 1877. Tops were among the earliest playthings of the Greeks, and were well known in Rome in the time of Virgil. One old writer says that a woman, named Anagalia, of Corcyra, made the first ball. However that may be, we know that ladies used to play ball in those days."

(3) Wooden bread kneader; Egyptian, circa 2000 B. C.
(4) Wooden bread kneader; German, eighteenth Century.
(5) Coptic "stuff" dolls, about 500 and 600 A. D.

Miss Thorne goes on to tell of the playthings used "today" (1879) which will be quoted in a later chapter.

In Europe the toy doll came much later than in the countries of earlier civilization, and there are no extant examples of them before medieval times, although in literature mention is made of eighth and ninth century rag dolls.

The oldest extant European doll belongs in the thirteenth century, and, as in the case of the earliest Greek doll, it assumes the shape of a woman in the form of a rattle-box.

We have examples of German fourteenth century clay dolls which were made in quantity, and since the early German name for doll, *tocken*, comes from the word *tocke*, a little block of wood, it is presumed that many of the dolls were made of wood.

(6) German clay doll, 12th century. (7) Ancient Greek clay baby doll (left); 19th century wooden baby doll from Oberammergau, Germany (right). (8) Gothic clay doll from Nuremberg. (9) Gustavus Adolphus, of Sweden; wood, circa 1650. (10) 17th century baby doll in wheel chair.

From paintings and engravings we get a good idea of what the early European dolls looked like. They are dressed, for the most part, as women, which was natural, as children at that time wore little replicas of their mothers' clothes. Some writers on the subject go so far as to say that no "baby" dolls were made before the middle of the nineteenth century. We know from concrete examples and old engravings that such is not the case. Fourteenth century graves have yielded "baby" as well as "grown-up" dolls, and there are examples of early "baby" dolls in many collections. A few are sketched in this chapter. It is true that "lady" dolls predominated, judging by general proportions rather than clothes, for, as already stated, little girls wore "grown-up" styles.

## Early Toy Dolls

Only the wealthy could afford beautiful dolls in earlier days, for they had to be hand-made. The play doll of the average child was crude, but members of the royal families exchanged gorgeous creations. It was not until the eighteenth century that factories learned to produce the beauties in any quantity, and not until the middle of the last century that improved factory methods made it possible to make them en-masse at low cost.

Most of the dolls we see in old paintings and engravings are hand-carved of wood and elaborately gowned. One can find in museums and occasionally in

(11) A and B, wooden Queen Anne dolls, circa 1700; C, an 18th century French fashion doll.

antique stores examples of the plainly-dressed wooden dolls the average child played with in the seventeenth and eighteenth centuries. A few have glass eyes, but most of them are painted. The "Queen Anne" doll, as we call it, was in vogue at this period. Sometimes it was made of linen and the features embroidered, but mostly it was of wood.

The most famous early doll factories in Europe were at Sonneberg, where they started in the fourteenth century, and at Nuremberg, places that held their own in the doll world for centuries, even up to the Second World War.

Early European dolls were used both as portrayers of fashion, and as gifts between members of one royal family and another. No expense was spared in making and costuming the doll. In 1391 the king of France sent to the queen of England dolls to show the new styles that his wife, Isabella of Bavaria, had introduced into his court. The wardrobe alone cost 549 *livres*, 16 *sols*, and were made to the measurements of the figure of the English Queen. In 1497 Queen Isabella of Spain received from Anne of Brittany a large doll richly dressed. In 1517 Henry II brought six dolls to Paris "for Mesdames."

Other instances are on record. But the dolls were not always for women. Royal children, too, received expensively gowned dolls. In 1455 Madeleine de France, the young daughter of Charles II, received a present of "a doll dressed like a young girl on horseback, and a footman." In 1571 Claude de France, Duchess de Lorraine, ordered from a celebrated goldsmith six dolls "the best dressed that are possible to find" for the child of the Duchess of Bavaria. Boys, too, received dolls to play with. Louis XIII of France, when a small boy, had a number of fine dolls, and a chariot to draw them. A magnificent doll was given Mademoiselle de Bourbon at this period. The fine early dolls were so highly prized that even kings played with them, or at least had them on display in palace and castle. Louis XIV had not only dolls, but a doll's house, nine market shops with small enamelled figures, two little wooden theatres, a sedan-chair with accompanying lackeys, a vine-dresser with his wheelbarrow; a knife-grinder with his wheel, and other miniatures of the sort.

Grown-ups of centuries gone by took their dolls as seriously as do adult collectors of today. The sixteen dolls of Catherine de Medici (1519-1589) we are told were so real to her that she dressed them in mourning on occasion. While Catherine was a character not greatly to be admired, she had imagination and a fine art sense.

Marie Antoinette and later Eugenie were generous in their gifts of dolls dressed in the latest Parisian styles. Eugenie had dolls made in her own likeness and dressed in replicas of her own clothes. Our "portrait doll" artists are doing the same thing today.

History repeats. We think of animated dolls as recent inventions. They were made in Egypt two thousand years before the birth of Christ. Note sketch of doll which kneads bread when a string is pulled. This was the forerunner of all our motion dolls.

Someone has said: "Dolls are so much more beautiful now than they were in early days." That is certainly true of dolls as a whole, but wealthy persons of the past had just as beautiful dolls, and they were far more gorgeously dressed than most of our present-day products. Whenever the artist comes to the fore in doll making we have fine examples of the craft; so it was in the past, so it is in the present and will be in the years to come. Fine dolls are ageless.

*Chapter 4*

# DOLLS OF THE NINETEENTH CENTURY

COLLECTORS of old dolls, of course, are more familiar with those of the nineteenth century than the earlier ones. They are, especially the later ones, still available to the patient searcher. But if anyone should make the statement: "I know all about antique dolls" take it with the proverbial grain of salt, for none of us has the whole truth; no adequate records have been made. However, much can be learned through careful study of individual specimens in large collections. old pictures and engravings, the age of the materials used in their manufacture, and what written material is available in literature of the past. Accurate sketching of an undressed doll with careful attention to detail is one of the best ways to know that doll. Private collectors usually are willing to show their treasures to an enthusiastic dollologist, and museums throughout the country have collections. A list is given in the back of the book.

A study of the chapters on the various kinds of dolls, especially the one on the China-head, will give an idea of what characteristics to look for in the different periods. As stated, earlier dolls usually represented ladies or half-grown girls with the oval rather than the round eyes of the late nineteenth century, although the child doll was far more common in the early part of the century than is generally supposed. We see dolls of 1800-1830 with ankle-length dresses and suppose these to represent adults, forgetting that children of twelve years in that period wore just such dresses. If the doll in question has a childish face and short stature, it was in all probability meant to represent a juvenile. The "grown-up" doll of the period is unquestionably a grown-up. Adult height is exaggerated if anything. A long, slender neck, arms and legs and a tiny waistline are characteristic. Until about 1880, long deep shoulders prevailed for even the "child" doll. This is one way to distinguish between the early and the late doll, although both may have short hair.

In general, features as well as figure of the early nineteenth century doll were in better proportion than during the closing decades. Unnatural-looking bulgy arms and legs with tiny extremities came in the last thirty years of the century. Women crammed their poor feet into tight shoes with high heels to make them look as small as possible, and a tiny hand was highly desirable. In the doll, small hands and feet could be exaggerated, and were. Fat arms and legs were pleasing because they accentuated by comparison the tiny extremities.

Most of the late nineteenth century dolls have short shoulders and squat necks if we except the Parians and Dresdens and a few others such as the *Gibson Girl,* modelled by an artist. The common china-head with short curly or wavy hair was meant to represent the young girl, and old ones found with original clothes, usually testify to that fact, although collectors use them to typify the lady of the Godey period. The dolls have almost adult proportions,

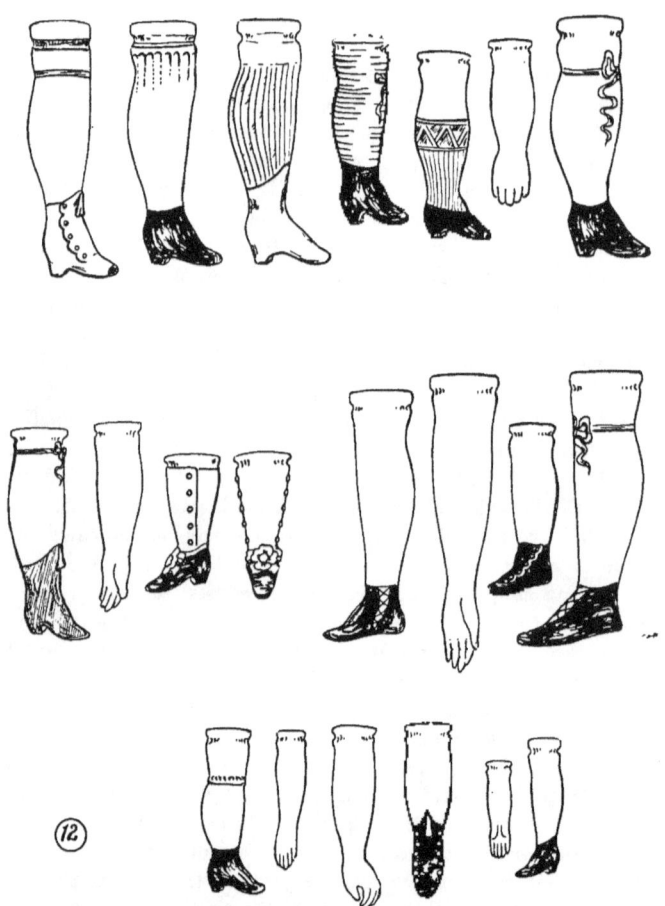

(12) China doll legs and arms. Flat soled shoes (middle row, right,) denote period between the First Empire and 1860; high heels, after 1860.

and lend themselves nicely to grown-up fashions. Women prefer dressing "lady" dolls, and authentic "ladies" of the past are difficult to find.

Different styles in doll bodies of a given period form an interesting study. The French doll sketched with one arm outstretched, in existence for eighty years, is unusual in that it has slot-and-tendon wooden joints covered with kid. The body itself is of sawdust-stuffed kid, and so are the lower legs. The turning head, bust, lower arms and hands are of bisque, the upper arms of wood covered with kid. Note the ancient crude body of the armless wooden doll of the American Indian and the old Roman rag doll sketched in the chapter on early dolls. Until the nineteenth century, not much serious thought was given

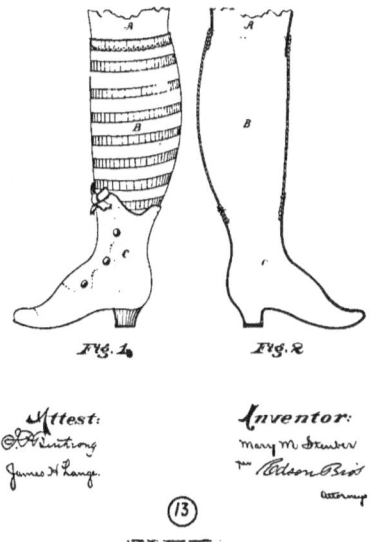

(13) Doll leg of cotton with stitched-on stocking and boot.

to the play doll for the average child. Early in the century, there were many wooden peg-jointed dolls; also dolls with kid body, a waist so tiny that it often caved in the middle despite extra hard stuffing at that point, and wooden arms and legs (sometimes this type had a cloth body). Most of them had papier mâché composition heads, but a few boasted china or wax; these are rare. Some of the papier mâché-headed dolls of about 1800 came with a body made completely of kid. hand-sewn, of course, for the sewing machine was a later invention.

After the foregoing came the various body types illustrated throughout the book. Our own country showed great activity in this field, for if we had to import most of our doll heads, we could at least make bodies for these heads.

It is claimed that the Cinderella sitting doll designed by Mrs. Irene W. Gibson of Marlboro, New Hampshire, came some time before 1860 (see P. 20, American Made Dolls and Figurines—the Supplement) but the first patent granted for kid boots stitched to the legs of a doll was issued to Mary M. Steuber of Philadelphia, Pa., in 1878. The cloth body patented by Sarah C. Robinson in 1883 was a more ambitious affair. See sketch.

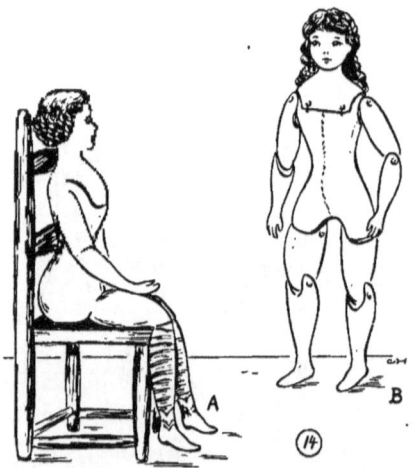

(14) American-made doll bodies. A—Designed by Irene W. Gibson, Marlboro, N. H., date uncertain; B—Cloth body patented by Sarah C. Robinson, 1883.

Charles T. Dotter of Brooklyn, New York, used (1880) the time-honored method of constructing a cloth doll body, but added the novelty of corsets printed on. Five years later, Philipp Goldsmith of Covington, Ky., used the printed corset idea, but added ornamental stitching, and the construction of the body was different, as illustrated.

Stuffing has always varied according to the material at hand, and the selling price. Cheap dolls were stuffed with cheap material. We find sawdust, bran, grass, straw, horsehair, cotton-batting, cork, etc., used throughout the nineteenth century, but the preferred stuffing in the twentieth century seems to be kapok for rag dolls and sawdust for dolls with modelled heads of composition and china; that is, when cloth is used for the body. Most of our 20th century dolls are made entirely of composition.

There is no available record of the first doll to have glass eyes, but we know that it happened at an early date, for they come with crèche dolls centuries old, and have been found in crude wooden dolls of the Queen Anne period.

The discovery of glass goes back to a dim past in history. Pliny says it took place in Syria. Glass window panes dating from before the year 79 were unearthed in the ruins of Pompeii. Transparent glass is believed to have existed about 750 B. C. in Egypt. England manufactured it in 1557, but in this country the first real glass business did not start until 1621. Glassboro, N. J., boasts the earliest bottle glass factory. One of our first interests in this line was the making of glass beads to use as a medium of exchange with the Indians.

It would be interesting to watch glass blown for dolls eyes. Compton's Pictured Encyclopedia says: " 'Spun glass,' a Venetian invention is usually made by melting the end of a glass rod, drawing a thread from it as one would draw taffy, and fastening the thread to the rim of a wheel. The rod is held in a flame to keep the glass soft while the wheel revolves rapidly, drawing out the fine thread and winding it up at the same time. The Venetians obtained beautiful designs by entwining many threads of glass, sometimes of varying colors, into bundles and twisting the bundles into many shapes. Spun glass can even be woven into cloth, and it makes the bright golden hair of the best china dolls.''

A good way to distinguish between a pre-Civil War and a post-Civil-War doll is by the feet, when the latter are modelled, for the earlier ones (1790-1860) had flat-soled shoes. See sketches.

Collectors who think "play" dolls the only real dolls, will be interested in the many references to dolls in the article entitled *Playthings* (from which quotation was made in chapter 3) written by Olive Thorne for St. Nicholas, 1879, a time when dolls were not made just for the tourists, but were playthings for the child. Although other items besides dolls are included, the whole article is so interesting that it is worth quoting in its entirety:

"Begin with the 'Cradle of Nations,'—Asia. It is said that the religion of Mohammed forbids toys, but, if so, it does not prevent little Mohammedans of Central Asia from having balls and tops, and even rag dolls, which travellers say are not very pretty, by the way. Also of terra cotta they have horses, cattle, dogs, fish, chickens, lions, and donkeys with pack saddles. In Western Asia, dolls with arms and legs moved with strings, like a jumping-jack, comic figures, whistles, marbles, and other things.

"The children of India fare better than many Asiatics about toys. The girls have dolls made of wood cut out all dressed, and painted in gay colors, as though they wore real clothes. They have them of all sizes, and, indeed, the doll is a very important member of the family. 'In many houses dolls have a room to themselves, and enjoy as much attention as children. Feasts and garden parties are given in their honor. The death of one involves a great show of mourning, and the marriage of one is a public event.' A Bengal paper gives an account of the wedding of two dolls belonging to very wealthy Hindu families.

There was a grand procession through the streets as though they were two people, followed by an expensive feast to the friends and the poor.

"Besides dolls, curiously dressed in paint and gilt, with ears of some bright color, spots on nose and chin, and a head that 'comes off,'—though the clothes do not,—the Hindu children have elephants and other animals of wonderful shapes and colors, with stripes and dots and stars of various colors and gilt, with ears that come off!

"To speak of China makes one think of lanterns, fire-works, and kites. though perhaps no one of them belongs exclusively to the children. The men fly kites, let off fire-works, and light lanterns. The lanterns of China are really wonderful. They are of every shape, color and design—round, square, flat; some in the shape of animals, and some of men, some roll on the ground and keep burning; others, shaped like horses, run on wheels; some whirl like a top; some gallop like a horse; there are ships that sail, soldiers that march, and people that dance. The power that works them is the current of hot air from the light. Some lanterns are made of red paper, with patterns made by holes; others are covered with painted gauze; some are carried in the hand, and some are made so as to stick on the wall.

"The real 'Paradise of Babies' is Japan,—as has been said many times,—for not only do the children have every imaginable toy, but many persons get their living by amusing them. Men go about the streets and blow soap bubbles for them with pipes that have no bowls as ours have. These young Japs have tops, stilts, pop-guns, magic lanterns, kaleidoscopes, wax-figures, terra cotta animals, flying-fish and dragons, masks. puzzles, and games; butterflies and beetles that flutter about; turtles that move their legs and pop out their heads; birds that fly about, and peck the fingers and whistle; paste-board targets that, when hit, burst open and let a winged figure fly out; and—most wonderful of all, perhaps—little balls looking like elder pith, which, thrown into bowls of warm water, slowly expand into the shape of a boat, or a fisherman. a tree, flower, crab, or bird.

"The girls of Japan have dolls' furniture and dishes, and, of course, dolls. They have dolls that walk and dance; dolls that put on a mask when a string is pulled; dolls dressed to represent nobles, ladies. minstrels, mythological and historical personages. Dolls are handed down for generations, and in some families are hundreds of them. They never seem to get broken or worn out. as yours do; and, in fact, they can hardly be the dear playmates that yours are. They are kept as a sort of show; and, though their little owners play with them, they do not dress and undress them and take them to bed, as you do. A good deal of the time they are rolled up in silk paper and packed away in a trunk. On the great festival day of the Japanese girls,—the Feast of Dolls—there is a great show of dolls and toys, and it is the event of the year for the queer little black-eyed maidens. The Feast of Flags is the boys' great day, and they have banners, flags, figures of warriors and great men, swords, and other toys for boys.

"But the finest toy of Japan—as no doubt you youngsters will all agree—is carried about the streets by a man or woman, for any child to play with who is the owner of the hundredth part of a cent, or one 'cash.'

"This is a small charcoal stove with hot coals, a copper griddle, spoons and cups; and, above all, ready-made batter and sauce. The happy child who

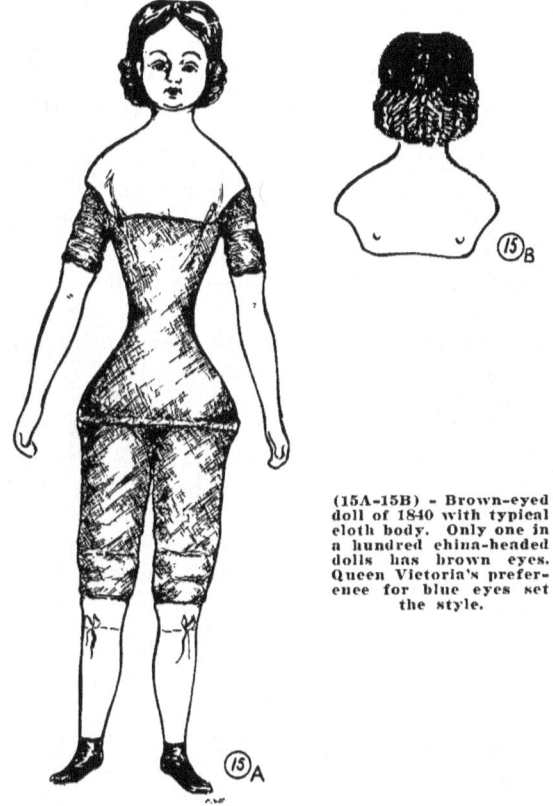

(15A-15B) - Brown-eyed doll of 1840 with typical cloth body. Only one in a hundred china-headed dolls has brown eyes. Queen Victoria's preference for blue eyes set the style.

hires this outfit, can sit down on the floor and cook and eat 'griddle cakes' to its heart's content. Could anything be nicer?

"Perhaps you boys would prefer to patronize the 'Bug Man,' who fastens paper carts to the backs of beetles with bits of wax, and a half-dozen of them will draw a load of rice up quite a hill—made of a board.

"The unfortunate babies of Africa have very few playthings, except what they make themselves. One traveler did see a rattle-box which a baby could not have made, as I said above. It was formed of a kind of fruit that has a tough rind and hard seeds, by squeezing the pulp out while green, and leaving the seeds to dry inside the hard skin. The solemn-faced black baby shook his toy with as much gravity as our babies shake theirs. Mr. Wood tells of leather dolls made by the Kaffirs; but they were made for the white man's museum, and not for Kaffir children to play with.

"The girls of Damaras are fond of dolls; but they like them best alive, so they take puppies for the purpose, and carry them about tied to their backs, as their mothers carried babies. The clumsy puppy faces look funny enough sticking out of the bandages.

"New Zealand girls have a still stranger taste; they 'play baby' with little *pigs!* They don't need your sympathy; they are fond of them, and carry them about from morning to night, under their mantles. The boys of the same country have tops, and three-cornered kites made of leaves, and they always sing while the kite flies. Besides, they play 'cat's cradle,' in which they make many more figures than we do, such as huts, men and women, and others.

"The Wezee boys play shoot with a gun made to imitate the 'white man's gun.' Two pieces of cane tied together make the barrels, the stock is made of clay, and the smoke is a tuft of loose cotton.

"In one African tribe the youngsters have spears made of reeds, shields, bows and arrows, with which they imitate their fathers' doings; and they make animals out of clay, while their sisters 'jump the rope.' Besides, Africans, like children all over the world, enjoy themselves 'making pretend.' They imitate the life around them, as you do; not playing 'keep house,' 'go visiting,' or 'give a party,' to be sure, because they see none of this in their homes; they pretend building a hut, hoeing a garden, making clay jars, and crushing corn to eat.

"What do the native South-American babies do for toys? Do without, I was going to say; but they do have blow-pipes of reeds, and they, too, mimic the various doings of grown-ups.

"Now for Europe. A list of toys made in that continent would read like an inventory of a toy shop. It is curious that even there, where there is so much interchange between the people, each nation makes its peculiar toys. Our shops bring toys from several of them, and they are quite different. From Germany we get our 'box toys,'—sets of stiff wooden soldiers, villages, farm-yards, tea-sets, and everything that comes in an oval wooden box. The patient German workmen make wooden dolls and hobby-horses, Noah's arks, spotted horses on wheels, toys that go by the dropping of sand, such as wind-mills, ships that rock, and men that dance. Above all they make marbles. In one place the very roads are paved with marbles not quite round. Toys of lead—soldiers and horses, camels, chariots and ships of war, locomotives, and others —nearly all come from Nuremburg, while tin toys—horses, steam-engines, steamers, etc.—come from another city.

"Toys are very cheap in Germany because of the division of work. A peasant will make one or two things all his life, and, of course, he comes to do his special work very rapidly. A traveler visited an old German woman, who had learned from her mother to cut out six animals from wood. They were a cat, dog, wolf, sheep, goat, elephant. She had cut these all her life, and could not cut anything else. It was her trade, and she had taught her daughter and her granddaughter, as a life work, to cut these six animals. In one house, they will perhaps do nothing but paint gray horses with black spots; in another, only red horses with white spots.

"Glass beads, or many of them, come from Venice. France sends us, first of all, wonderful young-lady dolls, with various accomplishments and the completest wardrobes and outfits; then clock-work toys, masks, sabers, muskets, and all kinds of warlike toys.

(16) "Pumpkinhead" circa 1850.

"England is scarcely behind Japan in variety of playthings. To begin with the best known and widest spread of all toys—the doll. England makes the most beautiful wax dolls in the world, though I must say the most marvelous doll I ever heard of was owned by Vasilissa the Fair, of Russia, and was able to help her mistress out of trouble by doing the hard tasks set for her, while she rested herself. But this doll, I fear, never lived out of the fairy tale books. To return to England's dolls: they have real hair, set in the scalp, and not a paltry wig; they have glass eyes, each of which is made separately, and is a work of art. There are sixteen manufacturers of dolls in London alone.

"The London doll *special* is the rag-baby, and a very pretty thing it is, just beginning to come over to our babies. The head is of wax covered with very thin muslin, which gives it a peculiarly soft and babyish look, and makes it strong enough for a live baby to play with. Dolls' boots and shoes are also an English trade.

"Next to the doll, in that busy island, comes the boat. These are made of all sizes and prices, from one costing a dime up to six or eight dollars. At one house are used eight tons of lead in one year for keels alone. England makes, also, mimic theatres, with characters and plays all ready, rubber toys of many kinds, toy picture-books, and thousands of other things.

"There are some ancient English toys told about in books. They were in the days when men-at-arms fought on horseback and the toys consisted of knights on horseback completely armed and equipped, and fastened to plat-

(17) Tiny bisque dolls 90 years old.

forms on wheels. They were of brass, and four to five inches high. To play with them, they were drawn together with force, to see which knight would be thrown off by the shock.

"In America—to begin with the natives—the Indian children living in wigwams in the far West, have their playthings, though they are somewhat crude. The boys play with bows and arrows, and the girls with dolls, or a substitute for them. The dolls are of rags, with hideous faces painted on them, and daubed with streaks of red, in the style admired by the race. To these, however, they prefer a live plaything,—or a 'meat baby,' as a little girl once said,—so they make pets of ravens, young eagles, and puppies. A young Indian girl is often seen with the wise head of one of these birds, or the fat, round face of a puppy, sticking out of her blanket behind. They also imitate the life of their mothers, and rig an arrangement with two poles crossed on the back of a dog, as the squaws do on the back of a horse, on which queer vehicle they carry jars of water, or anything they choose. The babies of the Indians, strapped into their cradles, play with the dangling string of beads or other article which is hung before their faces to make them squint, that being considered a great beauty.

"You are indebted to Mr. H. W. Ellicott, who has spent years in the Far North, and knows all about them, for a most interesting account of the playthings of the Eskimo children, who spend five or six months of every year in an underground hut, when the day is nearly as dark as the night, and all the family must find amusement within.

"Toys they have in plenty, and they are twice as useful as our toys; for, making them entertains and occupies the parents, and playing with them does the same for the children. From ivory they carve the animals of their country, —bears, wolves, foxes, geese, gulls, walrus, seals and whales. These are quite small, none more than three inches long, and many not more than one inch, but so well carved that the animal is easily recognized.

"For the boys, are made small ivory or wooden spears, arrows, lances and sleds, and, above all, toy *kyacks,* or boats, and even imitations of the 'big boat,' or ship of the stranger, with sinews, or the roots of a peculiar grass for the rigging.

"But here—as everywhere—the doll is the grand toy. No wax, china, rubber or rags will do for the Eskimo doll. It is made of ivory or wood, carefully carved as nearly like the human figure as possible, with eyes of bits of pearly shell inlaid. Some of them are twelve or eighteen inches tall, but most of them are six or eight inches only. As to the manner of playing with them, I suppose the Eskimo boys play seal-catching, bear-hunting, sledge-riding, and dog-training; and the girls keep house with their ivory dollies, get the meals and make the clothes, all in Eskimo fashion.

"It is pleasant to know that the droll little Eskimo babies have nice times, and plenty of playthings in their homes, that seem to us so dreary.

"Our own toy-shops have all the wonders of European make, but the kinds we invent ourselves are mostly mechanical toys,—creeping dolls, bears that perform, horsemen that drive furiously, boatmen that row, steam cars that go; and we have a monopoly of baseballs and bats, for no other people use them. None but English-speaking people indulge in plays so violent as to be dangerous to life and limb, as is our base ball, and the cricket of our English cousins.

"When we begin to talk of these games we reach the amusements of the grown-ups, which perhaps they wouldn't like to have called 'playthings,' though—between you and me—they are just as much toys as are dolls and tops."

So much for "playthings" the world over in 1879. It is surprising that Miss Thorne did not mention the china-headed dolls of Germany, for it was a time of great expansion in the china-head industry, when a ten or twelve-inch doll could be purchased for a dime, and tiny ones for a penny apiece. A dollar for a fine, big head was considered a good price, although the "fancies" brought more, for a greater amount of work was involved in their manufacture. It is from the period of the 1870's on that we have many of our commonest old dolls, and, at the same time, some of the best.

An interesting figure popular especially among the leisure class in England during the nineteenth (also the late eighteenth) century, was the Peddler Doll, made to represent the ever-present vendor who hawked his wares about the streets selling everything imaginable, from hand-made lace, scarfs, ribbons, pincushions, buttons, scissors, spoons, knives and kitchen utensils, to books on various subjects. Their insignia was a red cape and black hood over a small lace cap. The heads were of wax, wood, china or papier mâché, whichever material was popular at the time the doll was made. The body, clothes and accessories were hand made, and some were made entirely of cloth, with embroidered features.

—Courtesy Mrs. William Knobloch, Washington, D. C.

(18) Bisque-headed walking-talking doll of the late 19th century. Note winding key at right of the undressed doll (A), and patent symbol on soles of shoes. B shows doll dressed in old costume.

Another doll, about which little is known, is *La Poupee Travailleuse* (the working doll), mentioned in a little French book of 1864, long since out of print. Although the skirt of the "working doll" had only one door, the idea might have come from the eighteenth century wooden triptych doll, popular with Catholics in earlier days. The triptych referred to represents a monk in the form of a carved wooden doll with a door in the skirt. When the door is opened, it reveals a miniature altar with a nun at prayer. The open skirt of the working doll (treated in the same manner as the monk) discloses sewing materials, scissors, thimble, etc. (see sketch).

During the nineteenth century and earlier, Chinese "doctor dolls" of bone or ivory made their way to this country. It was long the custom for a Chinese lady in pain to point out on the anatomy of a naked reclining figure, the seat of the affliction. Modesty forbade disrobing. The average price of an ivory doll of this kind is $40.

The popularity of the china-head diminished during the "gay nineties," when bisque was "all the rage." The former was revived when women became interested in doll collecting and costuming, for the slender waist, a characteristic of the china-headed doll, lends itself to adult styling. Until World War II war, china-heads were imported from Germany in fairly large quantities, and although they are getting scarcer, some can still be found in antique shops and doll hospitals. In 1939 they sold at the Kimport Company for 35 cents for the six and one-half-inch size up to $2.50 for the eighteen-inch size, undressed. The price was considerably less in the five-and-ten-cent stores. Today the eighteen-inch size undressed brings as much as ten dollars.

Dolls which predominated during the first forty years of the nineteenth century had heads made of papier-mâché, sawdust-stuffed kid or cloth bodies, extremely narrow at the waist, and long spindley wooden arms and legs. China-heads and wooden peg-jointed dolls were also sold, and some of the latter boasted china heads. From about 1840, china, wax, then wax over papier-mâché were popular, bisque taking the lead as soon as costs decreased.

In the nineties of the last century and on into the twentieth century, bisque-headed dolls were by far the most in demand. They had come within the reach of almost everyone.

Many novelty dolls appeared at intervals during the whole of the nineteenth century. In the year 1827, Malzel made possible the first successful "mamma-papa" speaking doll (earlier experiments had been made) and at about the same time, 1826, "walking" and "sleeping" dolls were invented. Eyes were first made to open and shut by pulling a string, but after 1826, the counter-balance weight idea came into use. Since the old method continued to be followed for some time, one is apt to think that the counter-balance weight was a later invention. It has even been stated that the latter was not in general use until the 1890's, a statement easily disproved by many examples in existence long before 1890.

Patents for "crying" and "singing" dolls were issued in the United States from the 1860's on. Among the most interesting were the Webber singing dolls, the patent dates for which began about 1882. It operated by means of a bellows arrangement and had only to be squeezed to emit cute little popular tunes of the day. The W. A. Harwood crying doll of 1877 operated by blowing into a reed mouthpiece inserted in the breast of the doll.

In 1893, J. P. King of Philadelphia, Pa., patented an ingenious method of producing a crying sound. Two rubber bulbs, one containing air, one water, the whole surrounded by tubes with reeds inserted therein, were placed in the body of the doll. Pressure on the bulbs caused a realistic wail. Old dolls with simple little bellows inside their bodies are legion, but the more complicated are difficult to find.

(19) Creeping doll of 1871. (20) Walking doll, circa 1869; china head. (21) Patent drawing for walking doll of 1869.

As early as 1888 a phonograph doll was invented. In that year, William W. Jacques of Newton, Mass., patented a combined doll and phonograph.

We are prone to think of the nursing doll that "drinks" from a bottle, such as the Betsy-Wetsy and Dy-Dee, as entirely modern, but the idea is not new. In 1890, Rudolph Steiner of Sonneberg, Germany, patented just such a doll in America. While the manner of elimination was a little different, the same idea was utilized. The Steiner doll siphoned the milk from a bottle, the long end of the siphon coming out from the back of the neck, down the spinal column, and ending in a pan placed under the seat.

Patents for creeping dolls were granted in March, 1871, to Robert J. Clay, and in August of the same year, to George P. Clarks, both of New York City. They were operated by clock-work mechanism. From the patent drawings, one would judge the Clay doll to be the more interesting.

The number of walking dolls of the nineteenth century is legion. Most of these acquired their accomplishment by means of mechanical equipment, and some bear the patent date. One showing the E. R. Morrison patent of 1862 has a most interesting china head with flowers molded on. It winds with a key, as so many of them did, and walks for an astonishing length of time around a wide area. Some have Parian heads.

Mrs. William Knobloch of Washington, D. C., is the proud possessor of a fascinating bisque-headed walking doll (about 20 inches in height) which not only steps along at a lively pace, but repeats in English (although she is a French doll) "Hello, hello, hello!" at the same time moving her head from side to side and bringing up her arms to an inviting outstretched position. Sketches *a* and *b* show the doll in walking and in sitting positions. Notice the symbol on the sole of the shoe with the French word for *patent* (deposé) underneath.

(22) Patent drawing for walking doll of 1873.

Two of the most interesting walkers of the nineteenth century which do not have clock-work mechanism are the A. W. Nicholson doll of 1869, and the Henry C. Work doll of 1873. Patent drawings of these two dolls are given here in order to show how they work. The heads of the actual dolls found do not look like those in the patent sketches. For instance, at least one specimen of the Nicholson doll has a beautiful china head with flowers molded on. Such dolls are apt to be found with the china legs entirely missing. This of course does not affect the forward motion. Patent for the Work doll of 1873 calls for either simple movement—pushing or pulling with the hand—or, if the manufacturer desired, clock-work mechanism. The latter was evidently not used, for those found in collections are the simple kind. The idea of the rotating wheel of legs was also used for a paper doll of the twentieth century.

Patents for automatic walking dolls were granted here in 1826, '62, '69, '73, '75, '86 and '96. Twentieth century walkers, as a rule, do not have clock-work mechanism or wheels.

In 1902, E. U. Steiner of Brooklyn, N. Y., invented the first of the walking dolls to perform by merely holding its hand and giving it a slight lateral sway as one walked with it. This was followed by the more simply constructed Schoenhut walking doll of 1913, then by the clumsy "Dolly Walker" patented in 1917 by Harry H. Coleman, a ventriloquist. In 1933, the Ee-Gee Company of New York brought out an unexceptional walker, and a few years later, the loveliest of the modern walking dolls was placed on the market by the Alexander Doll Company of New York City. It was designed by Mrs. Adel Tongren of Grand Rapids, Michigan. This doll, *Jeannie Walker*, was a well-proportioned "child" that could "sit, stand and walk like a perfect little lady."

Other dolls which performed without elaborate mechanism were the "flirting-eye" doll, used by Jumeau as early as 1895, still used in America; the clown doll (German) which clapped cymbals and squeaked at the same time by a simple pressure of his "tummy;" the recent "magic hand" doll which picks up things by means of magnetic steel hidden under the finish of the hand; the "beating-heart" doll of 1941; and "Dy-Dee and Betsy-Wetsy" of about the same time. Music boxes concealed in the bodies of dolls and stuffed animals were popular in the thirties of this century.

The art of making automata, in existence as early as the third century B. C., was revived and utilized for "play" dolls all through the nineteenth century. Attached music boxes added to the interest. An early "Jumeau" dressed as a hunter, still operating, can blow his horn and nod his head while his music box plays "Toreador," loudly and long; another, a lady, can raise a beautiful bouquet of flowers to her nose and alternately lift a fan with the other hand; ladies at a tea party pick up tiny cups and bring them to their lips; a wee woman sits at a miniature piano and plays; a bisque-headed little girl in a swing moves back and forth to bellows music; eighteenth century ladies in a "coach and two" bow their heads to the audience while an elegant coachman proudly drives his horses round and round a large table; and there are dolls galore—relatively speaking—which can curtsey and dance to music.

Creeping dolls seem to be America's specialty, although most of them are short-lived. Off and on for the last forty years street vendors in large cities have cried their wares while these little performers crawled away on the sidewalk until their clock-work mechanism slowed down and stopped. The cheap ones were soon out of order.

Movable figures and toys have always delighted grown-ups as well as children. Before the eighteenth century, they were made mostly for adults, if we except the costly affairs made for children of the rich. In Arabia and Byzantine before the year 1,000 A. D., there were artificial birds that sang and flapped their wings, dogs which could wag their tails, and dolls that could

## DOLLS OF THE NINETEENTH CENTURY

(23) German bisque-headed, kid-bodied doll, late 19th century. Courtesy Mrs. Franklin Hill Davis, Washington, D. C. (24) French doll of the 1860's with unusual joints. They are of wood, covered with kid. (25) China-headed peddler doll, circa 1840, made to represent the vendor who hawked his wares about the streets, selling everything imaginable, from hand-made lace, scarfs, ribbons, etc., to books on various subjects. (26) "The Working Doll." This was mentioned in a French book of 1864, long since out of print. (27) Jumeau doll of 1870. Courtesy Mrs. Henry A. Diamant. This doll was purchased by the owner many years ago. She has her original costume. (28) French bisque-headed doll, circa 1890. (29) Doll with bisque head, arms, and legs, circa 1880's. Her dress was removed to show her dainty bisque legs.

move. For the child of these early days, and later ones too, for that matter, there were the jumping-jack, the corn-grinder and the fist-puppet, none of which needed delicate mechanism. Today we still have the jumping-jack and the fist-puppet and many other toys moved by the simple methods employed by the Egyptians two thousand years before the birth of Christ. And the child now enjoys a greater number of more complicated mechanical toys. The nineteenth century brought a great increase in these products.

Between the years 1860 and 1900, a number of dolls with two to five faces were manufactured, and, within the last few years, Japan exported two-faced baby dolls, one with a crying, one with a sleeping face. The head revolves in a socket. The earlier multi-faced dolls were made to turn faces by means of a string attached to a revolving pin. Sketches in the chapter on *Wax Dolls* will give an idea of the method of construction. In the late sixties and early seventies of the last century a number of patents were issued for multi-faced dolls; one firm, M. Bru of France, took out three patents of this kind during those years. Germany used the idea, and one German firm took out a patent in this country (1881) for a double-faced wax doll. Domino Checkini of New Haven, Conn., patented a four-faced doll in 1866. His dolls had wax faces.

Although Germany dominated the world of dolls during the nineteenth century and earlier, each country was noted for a particular kind—England for her wax and rag dolls, Holland for her wooden ones, "Flanders' babies" as they were called; Germany for her china-heads, papier mâché and wooden dolls, and France for her bisque and papier mâché.

Before the First World War, America made few dolls. There were some of composition, rubber, cloth, wood, described in the chapters dealing with each particular type. However, as noted elsewhere, several American firms made doll bodies to be used with heads imported from Germany. One firm, Goldsmith of Covington, Ky., employed German workmen to make wax and composition heads in its own factory.

It is from the nineteenth century that collectors of antique dolls obtain most of their treasures, and every period of the century produced interesting ones. It has been said by inexperienced collectors "I do not buy any dolls marked 'Germany'—they are so common." What a mistake! There are some lovely, and also uncommon ones with this mark, specimens in flesh-colored china with beautiful coloring and well defined features. But any doll that has been loved and played with is interesting; so also are its little clothes. As Sappho said, in ancient times, when she dedicated her doll to Aphrodite: "O Aphrodite, despise not my doll's little purple neckerchief. I, Sappho, dedicate this precious gift to you!" Perhaps, in days to come, when all present collections will have passed into the hands of persons still unborn, there will be amongst them some who will despise neither these "common" dolls nor "their little purple neckerchief."

*Chapter 5*

# CHINA-HEADED DOLLS
# AND THEIR MARKS

BY the term *china* we mean that branch of ceramics which is baked and glazed. It is a far call from the common clay used by our remote ancestors, yet clay is the foundation of china.

The earliest known pottery is Egyptian and dates thousands of years earlier than the birth of Christ. The Bible speaks of potteries at the time of the building of the Tower of Babel. As civilization advanced, dolls, among other toys, were manufactured.

The term *pottery* is general; it means anything made of clay—earthenware is baked; china is baked and glazed; bisque is unglazed china, whether or not it is the late bisque with which we are most familiar, French bisque, stone-ware, sugar bisque, Parian bisque or what-have-you. Doll collectors never refer to a bisque doll as a china doll; others often do, thereby causing confusion.

There are various grades of china, as everyone knows, but of the main divisions, hard and soft paste, the collector is most concerned with the hard paste, for soft paste china doll heads are almost non-existent.

China-headed dolls come in a greater variety of make-up than is generally supposed. There are the swivel necked (turning head) as well as the more common shoulder-head (head, bust and shoulders all in one piece). Most of those we see have painted blue eyes, but a few have glass eyes, either stationary or closing, and one in about every hundred has brown. A grey-eyed china-head is still more unusual. One occasionally finds enamelled or china teeth inset; also holes for ear-rings, although these characteristics are more often found in the bisque-headed dolls. A few of the individually-made peddler dolls (representing street vendors) have china heads, and the latter were used with mechanical bodies (motion dolls) and also for music box dolls.

Of the various grades of china used for doll heads, by far the greater number are dead white; finer ones are creamy white, and the most interesting of all are flesh-colored. Collectors generally refer to all the latter as *pink lustre,* but the real pink lustre, composed of gold applied over a thin coating of

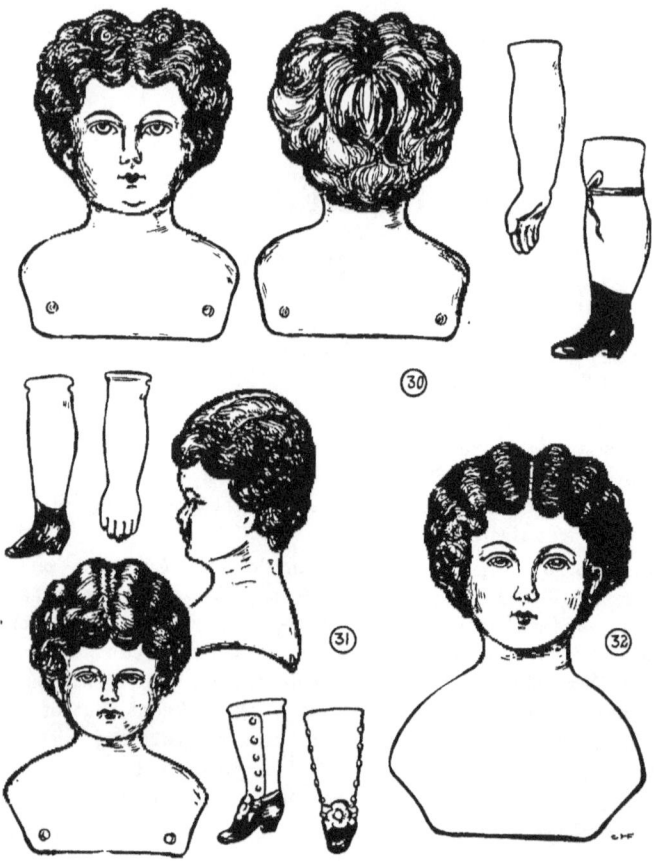

(30, 31, 32) Three common varieties of late 19th century china heads.

rose, iridescent, is not common. It was made in quantity from 1810 to 1830. Flesh-colored china dolls were made as late as the twentieth century. They all are collector's items.

With reference to china-headed dolls found today, collectors differ widely about dates and places of origin, but certain facts have been definitely established. Almost all the china heads with which we are familiar came originally from Germany. They may have been *purchased* in another country,—often were,—and the body parts may have been assembled outside their native country, but Germany manufactured by far the greater number of china parts, and for a good reason; by a clever division of work in places outside the big cities where labor was cheaper that country was able to offer lower prices than prevailed elsewhere. It was for this reason that many French doll manufactories finally went out of business.

There are a great many dolls in this country collectors proudly point to as Chelsea or Staffordshire, of which the English potteries have disclaimed any knowledge. While they admit that individual workmen might have made doll heads after hours, they state that the dolls never were made in commercial quantity. During the First World War, disabled soldiers were given work making bisque heads (often misleadingly referred to as china) at the potteries, but these are marked and are unmistakable. They were manufactured between 1918 and 1920, and are for the most part crude. By the time the soldiers had really learned the trade and were doing good work, the war was over and trade resumed with Germany, where the cost of production was lower.

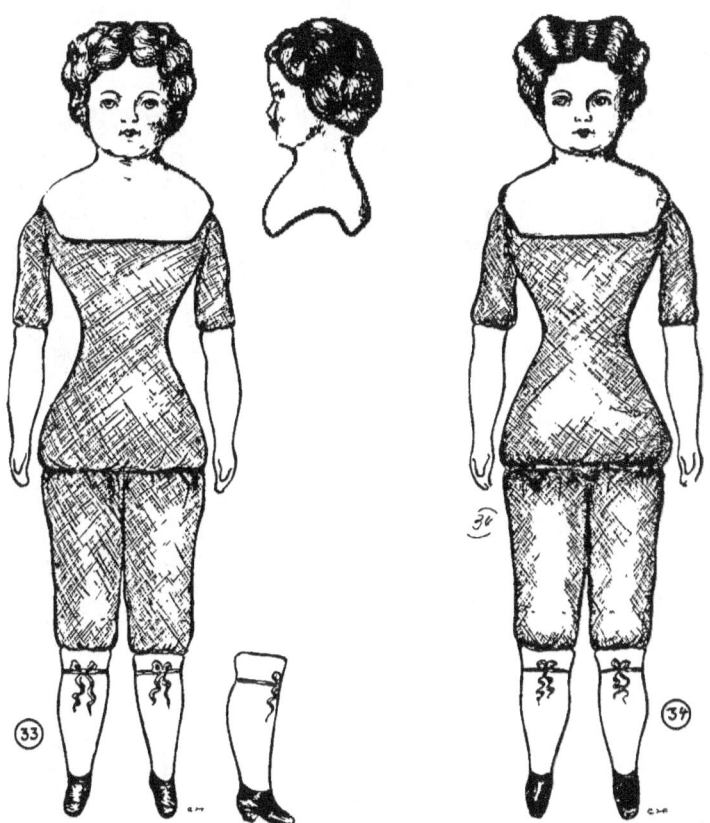

(33, 34) More common late china heads.

Earlier writers about dolls realized that Germany really was the doll country. Hope Howard, writing for *St. Nicholas* in May, 1887, has this to say on the subject:

"Now Germany is really the Doll Country. We are told of the Paris doll as the representative of 'its race.' It is true that the doll population of France and especially of Paris is very large; but it is essentially a class race in the latter place. As you pass through the streets you see them dressed in the latest mode and looking at you out of their great eyes for approval of their

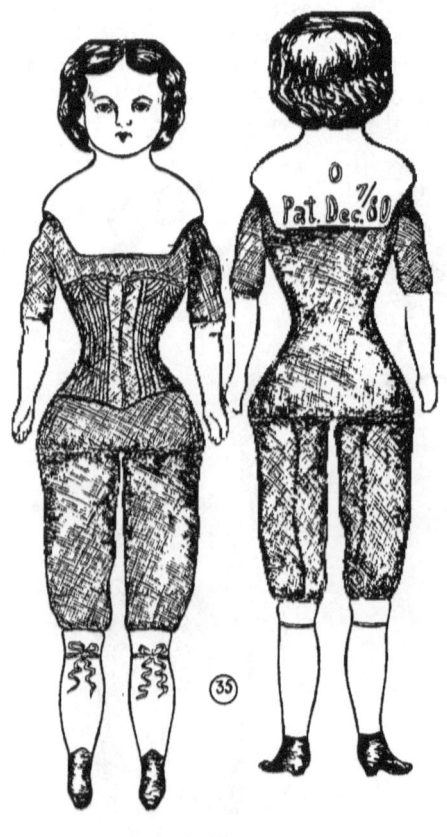
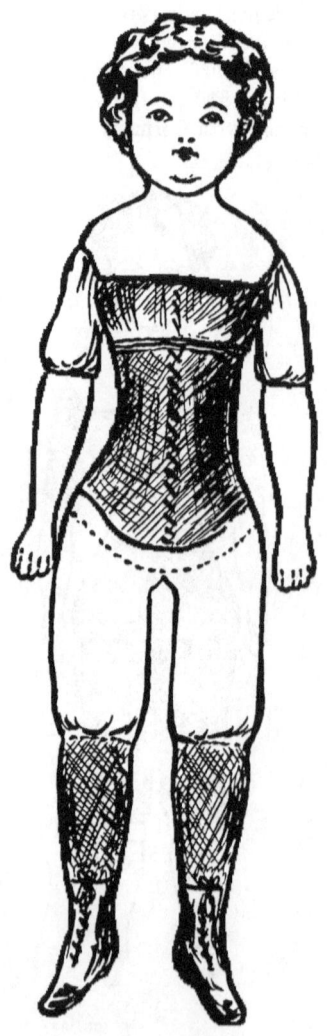

Above (35) Dotter doll with patented corsets. Body was made in U. S. A., the head imported from Germany.
Right (36) Goldsmith doll with patented corsets. Body, American-made; head, imported from Germany, 1885.

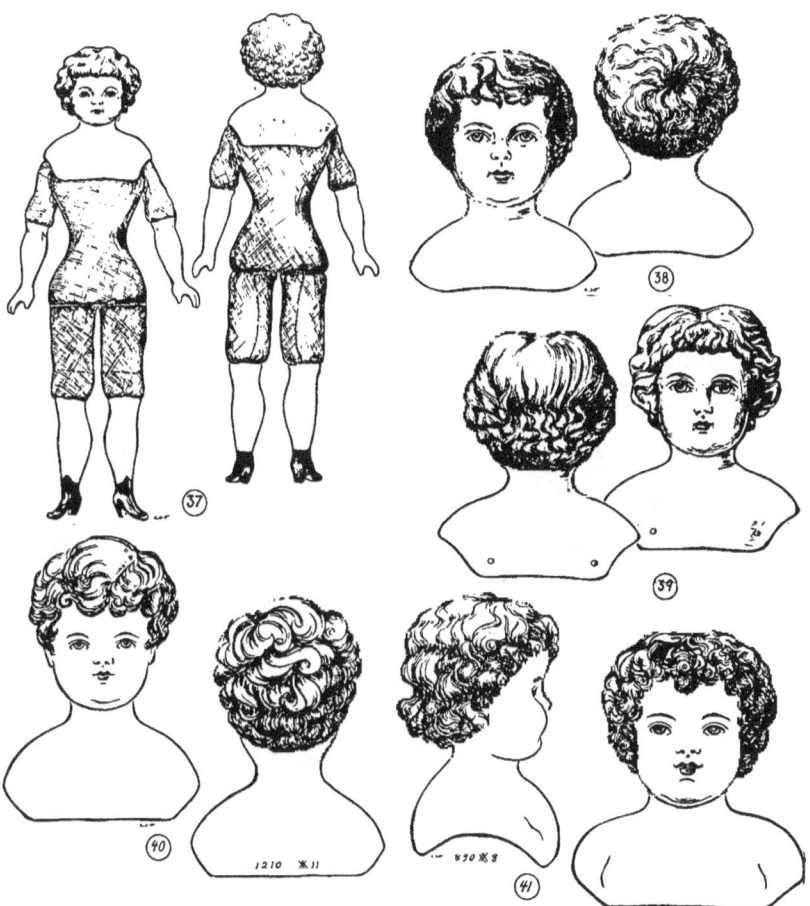

(37) China-head circa 1880. (38, 39) Brother-sister china heads circa 1880's. (40, 41) Brother-sister china heads of the late 1880's.

style. But in Dresden and other German cities, you see dolls of every rank. You see them in every style of dress and undress. You encounter them in every nationality represented by its peculiar costume, and not as in France, or Parisian. You see establishments devoted entirely to the fashioning of their clothes; you go through an adjacent town to visit some manufactory of porcelain, or historical monument, and you find wholesale makers of dolls' bonnets and you become impressed with the importance of the position the doll occupies in the community of the world.''

As before stated, most of the china heads we see today are of hard paste, and few date back as far as its discovery in Europe in 1709. (The secret of its discovery in China some 2,000 years before had been so closely guarded that the knowledge of how it was manufactured did not leak out.) Before 1709, doll heads and complete dolls had been made from the soft paste and from clay. Occasionally a soft paste china head is found; more often (but these are not common) a clay doll made by the American potteries from the 1700's to the twentieth century. These were crude. See chapter on *Hand-made Dolls*.

With reference to soft-paste china Harold Lewis Bond, in *An Encyclopedia of Antiques*, says that the most interesting pieces were made between 1744 and 1800; also, that the early Sevres porcelain was of soft paste, but its later productions are all of hard paste. "Soft-paste porcelain," says Mr.

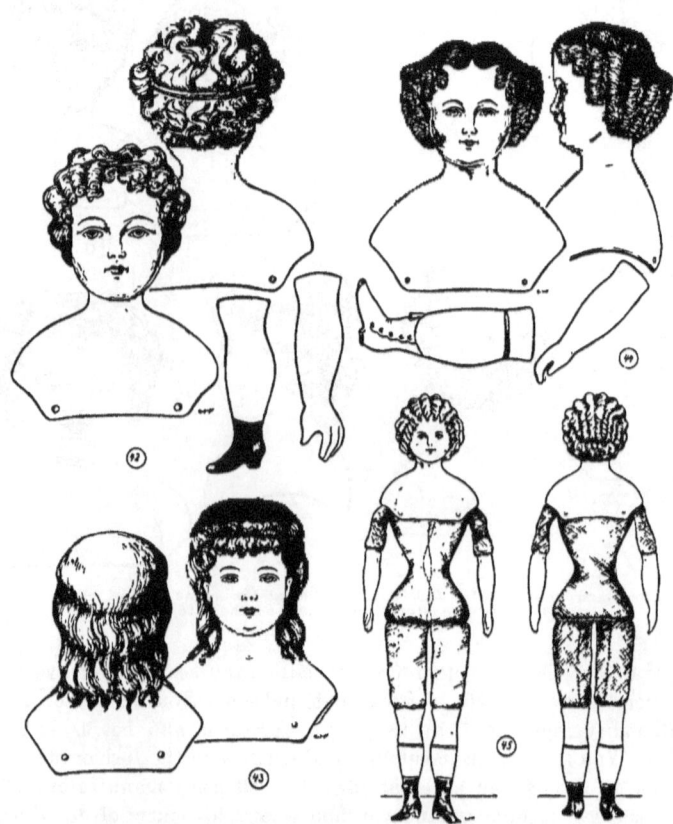

(42) China head with its foot and arm circa 1885. (43) Unusual china head of the late 1870's. (44) China head with its foot and arm common during the 1870's. (45) German blond china-head of 1868.

(46) China-headed doll of the 1850's-1860's. (47) Pink luster china-head of the 1840's-1850's. (48) China-headed doll sold during the Civil War for the benefit of the Union soldiers.

Bond, "is made by mixing white clay with 'frit,' or some other substance to get the translucency. It was first made in Florence, Italy, in 1568, but its great development came in England and France in the eighteenth century. Soft paste can be scratched, and it is warmer than hard paste to the hand, and the colors used in decoration sink in so that the effect is softer. The soft paste was the most perfect vehicle ever achieved for decorating, far more so than hard paste. Soft-paste porcelain is very fragile, liable to crack at the touch of hot liquids, and to lose shape in firing, although these obstacles were overcome to some extent by the use of soapstone."

Earthenware is opaque and coarser than china. The difference readily can be discerned when the former is chipped and one can see beneath the glaze. The chipped piece absorbs grease and becomes discolored. Porcelain or china is stronger and much finer grained. When chipped, it is difficult to tell where the glaze leaves off and the clay begins, because it is baked at such a high temperature that the glaze is absorbed into the clay. All china-ware has kaolin mixed with the clay, and this substance had to be found before hard-paste china could be made. A thin piece of the latter is so translucent that when held to the light the shadow of one's thumb is easily seen; when tapped, it rings like a bell. Kaolin is now found in many parts of the world, including America.

In 1709, when Bottger discovered the secret of making hard-paste china, the royal factory where he was employed was moved from Dresden to Meissen. Here its manufacture was continued until the Seven Years' War, when Frederick the Great confiscated the molds and took them to Berlin. Until that time,

(49) Unusual china-headed doll of the 1850's. Courtesy Mrs. Davis. (50) China head with brush marks at temple and brown eyes, circa 1865. (51) "Winnie Davis," a china-headed survival of 1870. Confederate Museum, Richmond, Va.

Meissen ware was foremost in Europe, although a little later, when France discovered kaolin, and with it, of course, hard-paste china, the Royal Factory at Sevres was a close second. Meissen never recovered its original fine ware. The modern china had its beginnings at Sevres.

It is interesting to note that porcelain decorated under the glaze is a method used only for unusual pieces. The common procedure is to decorate over the glaze, and this method has been used in all periods and countries.

The commonest of all the china-heads easily is recognized by its bushy, unnatural-looking crop of hair topping a face with small features. Its cousin, made side by side with this masterpiece (?) has a much more interesting and natural looking hair arrangement. A study of the sketches of these two dolls will give a fair idea of what they are. Notice the squat neck and short shoulders.

Short-shouldered dolls came in when the fashion for low-necked dresses was confined exclusively to evening wear. One always will find the short-shouldered china-headed and china-limbed doll with high-heeled shoes if it has its original body. High heels were re-introduced in Europe in 1860. Previously, low heels had prevailed since the First Empire period. This is a point to be remembered when trying to date a doll—the really old one with legs of the same material as the head has flat-soled shoes. A stylish doll of 1860 had small heels, becoming higher as the decade advanced. Since manufacturer's stocks had to

(52) Three rare china-headed dolls.

be used up, some dolls without heels were still sold during the 1860's, but it was not long before all the dolls with molded legs boasted the new style.

The two heads referred to in the above paragraph were made in Germany from about 1880 up to the outbreak of the Second World War; in the later period for collectors who wanted to dress dolls in Godey fashion. Those made after 1891 had the name of the country from which they came engraved on the shoulder of the doll, or, when space did not permit, on the body. There was an occasional slip-up at the factory, however, so that the rule is not infallible.

Of the thousands of late china-heads (after 1891) examined by the writer, all were marked *Germany* with the exception of a few labelled *Japan* or *Nippon* on models patterned after the German. None of the china-heads were marked *England*. Of the late bisque heads, by far the greater number were inscribed *Germany,* some *France* or *Paris,* and only a few (made in England to give help to veterans of the First World War,) *England.* England makes quantities of dolls, but she gets her china and bisque parts "on the continent." It does not pay to compete with Germany in this field of endeavor. France has come the closest with her bisque-headed dolls; America has tried to a limited extent, but

Germany has remained "tops" in this field of endeavor except during wars when trade has been interrupted. Recently Emma C. Clear of Redondo Beach, California, has made china-headed dolls for the collectors' trade, and during the period of the First World War, the Fulper Potteries of New Jersey made bisque-headed dolls, patterned from the German, the trade reverting to Germany after the war, as was the case with the English bisque-head trade.

To return to the subject of the late china-headed dolls: the two referred to are by no means the only styles prevailing during this period. There was infinite variety even among the common dolls, but the two under discussion are the commonest and should cost the least. It is unwise to turn down a doll (as some collectors do) merely because it is marked *Germany*. A study of the sketches will give an idea of some of the other late dolls.

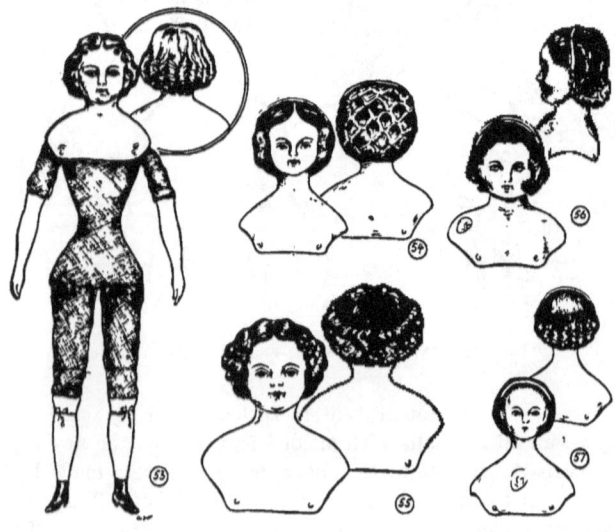

(53) China-headed doll of the 1860's. (54) China head often called Mary Todd Lincoln. (55) China head of the 1870's. (56) "Child" of the covered wagon era. (57) "Lady" of the covered wagon era.

In judging a china-headed doll, be guided by the quality, condition, the hair arrangement and general make-up. What marks are there, if any? Is the doll well proportioned? Is the neck line good? Are the features attractive and well centered? Is the coloring good? If the china is bluish or dead white, the doll is not as fine as one with creamy texture, and certainly not as desirable as one tinted flesh color unless other good points outweigh consideration for coloring and quality of china. If the doll is flesh-colored—and this is much less common than white—is the color evenly distributed? The cheaper ones are blotchy.

Hairdo is one means of identifying the old doll, but it is by no means infallible. Hair styles repeat, and the style for a *child* doll might be different from that of an *adult*. For instance, a "child" of the 1820's might have short hair similar to one of the 1880's, but the coiffure for a doll representing an adult of the 1820's would be quite different. To further confuse, a doll representing an

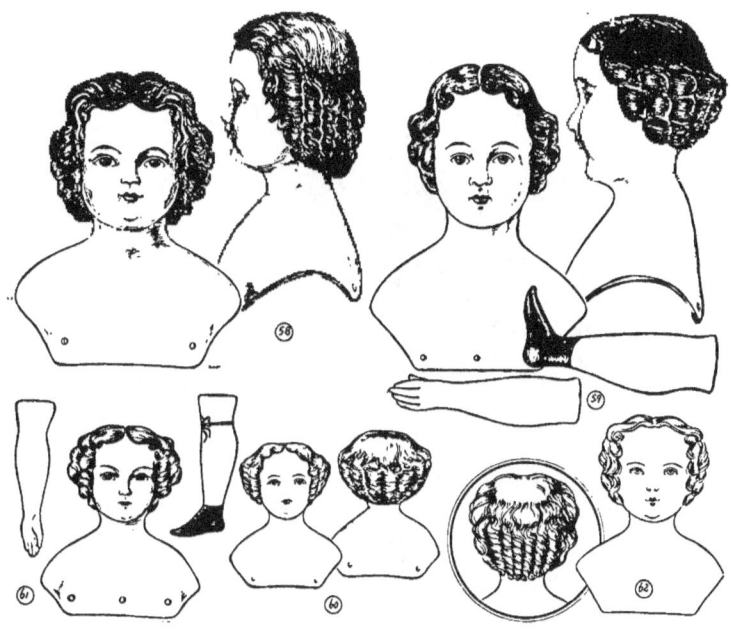

(58) Fine ringletted china head of about 1860 supposed to represent Adelini Patti. (59) China head of the late 1850's and early 1860's with its arm and leg. (60, 61) Pre-Civil War china heads with arm and leg. Notice flat-soled shoe. (62) China head of the 1850's. Courtesy Mrs. William Garrison, Washington, D. C.

adult of 1800 would be apt to have the short hair fashionable for grown-ups of that period. However, most of the short-haired dolls came late in the century, and easily can be identified by their short shoulders, squat necks, and high-heeled boots.

It must be borne in mind that popular hair styles were sometimes used for periods as long as fifty years. When the mold wore out, a new one like it was made. That is one reason why it is difficult to tell the exact age of an old doll unless it has been handed down in a family.

Few china-heads (the "Dotter" and "Goldsmith" excepted) were inscribed with the date, but some of the composition heads were so dated, and

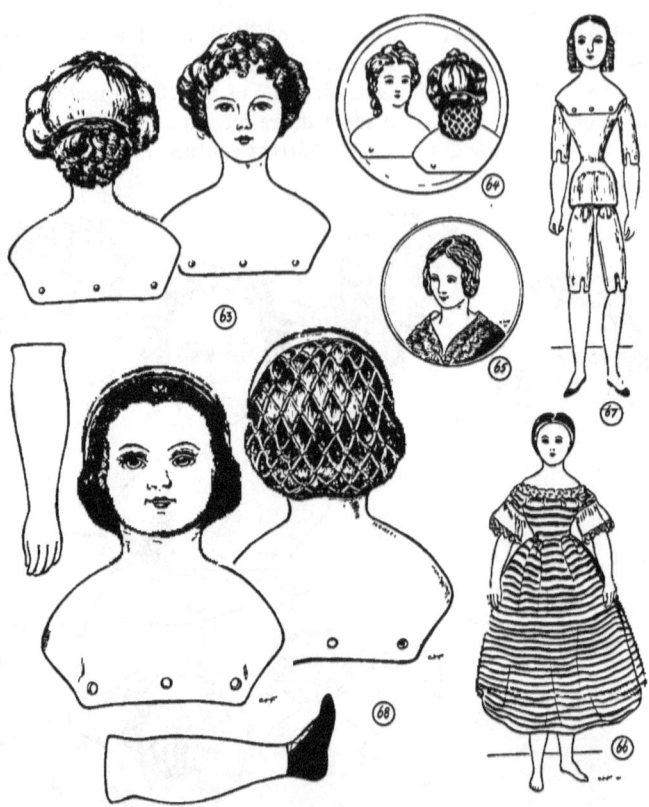

(63) China head sometimes called "Dagmar." A similar head has two puffs of hair at the back of the head. (64) Unusual china head circa 1850's from the collection of Mrs. George R. Hunt, Aux Vasse, Mo. (65) "Jenny Lind." Courtesy The Museum of the City of New York. (66) Mid-19th century bald china head with natural hair glued on (china arms and legs.) Courtesy the New York Historical Society Museum. (67) Early 19th century wooden peg-jointed doll with glazed pink luster head. (68) China head with gold luster snood. Mid-19th century.

since the latter were also made in china at the same period (and earlier) we have fairly definite dates for those with certain hair styles. For instance, the eight or more different hairdos of the dated Greiner dolls tell a story. A photograph of the original Greiner patent shown with the doll head Greiner "improved" in 1858, pictures one with corkscrew ringlets curved to the head, which proves conclusively that the first one he patented is the one the label of which reads "Improved," and that this hair style was still popular in 1858. It was copied from an earlier German model in china, made in quantity in the 40's

## CHINA-HEADED DOLLS AND THEIR MARKS

and 50's of the last century. The heads Greiner made in the late seventies copy the short-haired china variety with which collectors are most familiar, for the latter were made up until the beginning of the Second World War.

In judging the age of a doll, we must look not only at the hair arrangement and the shoes (whether or not modelled feet have flat soles) but the general contour of the face, neck and shoulders, and the expression. The meek, demure aspect of the antique doll is not there by accident. It is an indication of what was expected of women of the period. The older ones often have a rather flat face, well-proportioned nose and neck, and always long, deep shoulders. Since the "grown-up" and "half-grown-up" were more numerous than the "baby" doll in the earlier years, the eyes of the older doll are apt to be more oval, the neck and arms longer, the hands better shaped, and the whole appearance

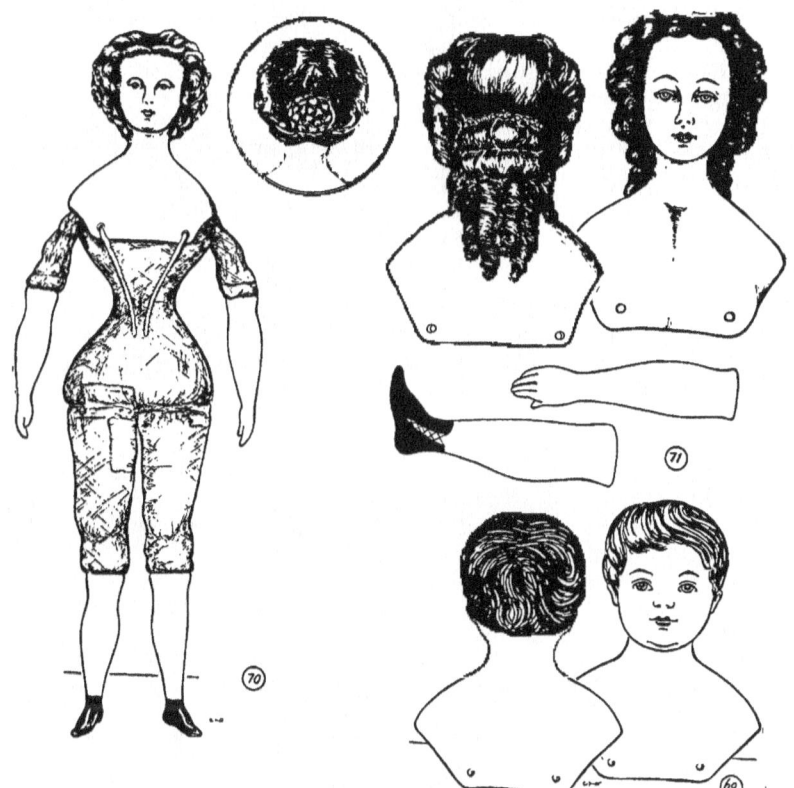

(69) Fine china head circa 1830 from the collection of Mrs. Davis. (70) "Miss Veryworn," a china-headed doll of about 1832, (bends in hairdress molded on.) (71) "Eugenie," circa 1850. Note old style arm and leg.

less child-like than later models. The *small child* doll of the late nineteenth century was represented with the rounder, more childish eyes and a figure proportionate to the child.

As stated before, it is a mistake to think that there were no early *child* dolls. There were a good many, as we know from old engravings, as well as the figures themselves, but *lady* or *teen age* dolls predominated, the "ladies" with long necks, the younger ones with necks more in keeping with the age they were expected to represent. *Baby* dolls appeared in quantity at about the middle of the century, but *ladies* were still popular. Today a representation of the child is by far the most desirable child's toy, and a representation of an adult the most popular collection doll. Since the dawn of doll history all types have been made and will continue to be made.

Among the unusual in hairdress of the china-headed dolls are:

1. A knot in back, hair rolled or plain at the sides—1820's-1850's. (The style was repeated in bisque at a later period);
2. Straight corkscrew curls at either side of the head, and a knot in back, said to represent Queen Victoria about 1840;
3. Plain corkscrew curls, sometimes ending abruptly in a kind of ledge. (Corkscrew curls curved to the head are desirable but not as rare.)—1830's-'60's;
4. A braided bun at the back in the style of Jenny Lind, 1850;
5. Hair looped at the back (waterfall hairdress) and held in place by a comb, puffed or rolled at the sides, popular in 1860;
6. Hair draped loosely and gracefully at the sides, caught in a comb at the back, underneath which is a double puff, ending in clusters of long ringlets, in the style worn by Eugenie in 1850;
7. Long curls falling loosely over the shoulders, circa 1830;
8. Long, slightly waved hair falling over the shoulders, bangs in front held down with ribbon, circa 1870's;
9. Hair with gold snood, a bow on either side of the head, called by collectors Mary Todd Lincoln (no definite proof) circa 1860;
10. Hair with roll curls completely covering head, sometimes with curls spilling over the shoulders, introduced in 1868;
11. Any hairdress with brush marks at the temples. This was done occasionally all through the 19th century;
12. Boy's hairdress with part at the side;
13. Bangs. (Some of these are late and represent the small child, more popular as the 19th century advanced);
14. "The girl with a curl in the middle of her forehead," circa 1870. Style repeated with a little different hair arrangement about 1890;
15. Page boy style, almost straight hair, circa 1860;
16. Bald-headed china dolls, some with a round black patch on crown of head. Wigs were supposed to accompany the bald-heads. This German-made head should not be confused with the Japanese-made baby bald-head. The latter has almost no shoulders, and the name of the country is underneath. The German-made have deep shoulders and are unmarked;
17. Hair with beads entwined, circa 1832, perhaps the rarest of the china-heads;

18. Back-comb dolls, hair drawn straight back from the forehead, falling either in ringlets or waved, circa 1850-70;
19. Short curly hair tied up with a ribbon bow, circa 1880's; (Similar rare doll with longer shoulders and more mature expression made about 1800.)
20. Bonnet and hat dolls of the Kate Greenaway period. (These are seen more often in stone bisque than in china). Some are earlier than the 1880's some much later.

After the discovery of Parian bisque in 1846, most of the "fancies" were made in that medium, for it was easier to get detail in Parian than in china, hence china-heads with unusual hairdo are more scarce, and are apt to be earlier,

(72) China head of about 1850 from the collection of Mrs. Virgil Wilson Hall.

although not necessarily so, for when Parian came in, the same molds were used for the Parian as had been used for the china, often with detail added.

One collector of long standing has stated that all of the "fancies" were made to represent notables. There is no definite proof of this, but we do know that many notables were made in doll form. Jenny Lind, for instance, appeared not only in china and bisque, but in the newly-invented rubber (1850), and in paper doll form.

There is a good deal of disagreement among collectors as to what doll represented what person. One way to judge is to compare the hairdress of the doll under discussion with pictures of the lady at about the time the doll was made. Certainly the hairdress of the young queen Victoria at the time the doll supposed to be Victoria was made, circa 1840, tallies with the doll. (Reference is to the one with corkscrew curls at each side of the head, a bun in the back.) The "Mary Todd Lincoln" doll appears in the style worn by Mary Todd before she became the President's wife. And the hairdress of the "Jenny Lind" doll tallies with the hairdress the sweet singer wore in private life. This method of judging, of course, is not infallible. Any popular hairdress might be copied in doll form without reference to any one person.

After the general use of the swivel neck for dolls, even a few china-heads were so made. In some cases, holes were cut out for eyes and teeth, just as in the bisque and composition, and a number of walking dolls with china heads were made. A flesh-colored china-head with swivel neck and inset glass eyes, having the earmarks of the early Jumeau, is laid up for repairs at the Cooper Union Museum, New York City.

It would be impossible to list all the hundreds of varieties of the china-headed dolls. After years of search when one thinks "now I have seen them all," another pops up and says: "How about me?" The writer has taken certain unusual dolls (sometimes not too unusual) to a collector of forty-five years'

(73) China head with gold bands in hair and guimp molded on. Courtesy Mrs. George Whichelow, Boston, Mass.

standing and said, "Have you ever seen these before?" and the answer has been, "No." The search for the rare antique doll is limitless, perhaps that is why it is so intriguing. Dealers usually find their antiques by attending auction sales and by advertising. Sometimes a dealer will "buy an attic" (contents thereof) and a few dolls may come to light in an old trunk. Often one dealer will buy from another for a special customer. Let it be known that you are interested in antique dolls and will pay a fair price; sooner or later someone will come forward with a doll you want. Remember that the dealer himself often has to pay a big price for a rare doll, even at auction, but be sure it *is* rare before you give him more than $25 for an old doll.

A collector who makes a specialty of the "frozen Charlotte"— an unjointed doll, stationary arms and legs—will find many interesting varieties in china. They were made in great, great grandmother's time as well as in our own. Here, too, watch for the unusual; they come in all grades of china in varying sizes; in pink lustre; in old-fashioned and modern hairdo; in bonnet and hat styles, and in various stages of dress and undress, all in the china mold.

## CHINA-HEADED DOLLS AND THEIR MARKS

The arms may be straight to the sides, or held out, or in an attitude of prayer. The latter is seen in what appears to be a bathrobe tied around the middle with a tasseled cord of gilt and a band of green ribbon in her curly hair. Some say she is a bathing beauty and not in a praying mood, but with arms set for a dive. It is not uncommon for one to see a *frozen Charlotte* twelve inches high and a midget scarcely more than an inch long. The average is two and a half to three and a half inches.

It is interesting to find tiny china-headed dolls with unusual hairdress. Coarse china tends to smother the lines of the little head, but it is surprising what wealth of detail is possible in a very fine china. The six-inch doll sketched is of pink lustre, perfectly modelled with fine, beautiful features, graceful "swan" neck and brush marks showing fine hairs at the temple. Such a doll is worth more than a much larger one of the same period and style in coarse china. In buying the tinies, watch for a good grade of china, well-blended coloring and features that are pleasing; the latter, off-center, can spoil a doll.

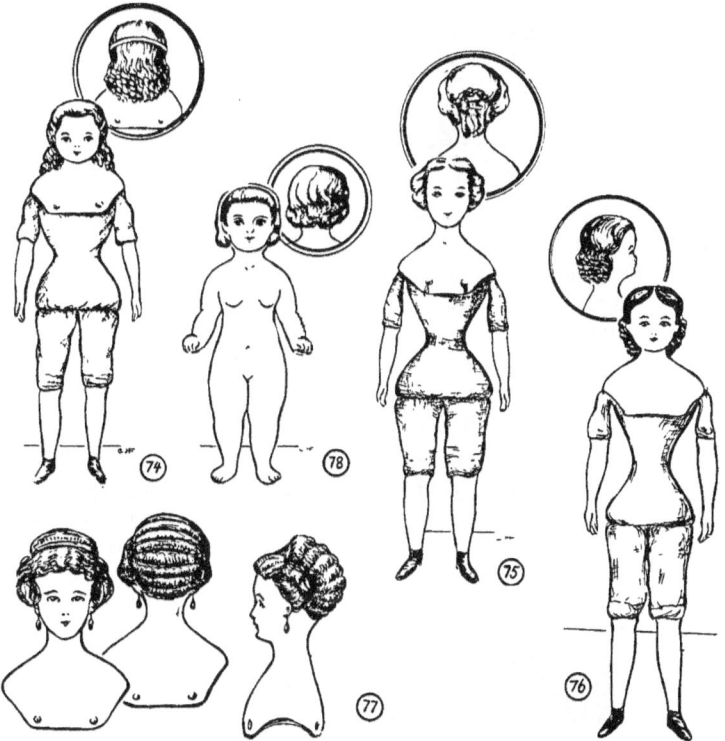

(74-78) Tiny fine china-headed dolls and a "Frozen Charlotte," (78).

(79) Old marks on china, some of which have been found on doll heads.

From the tiniest of china-heads to the largest—and some are over thirty inches tall with almost life-sized heads—the grade of china, condition and hairdress, are prime factors in judging the worth of an old doll. But study carefully all the points to be considered before paying an extravagant price, and be sure the doll is not a duplicate. Some of the duplicates are lovely and worth collecting, but the cost should be considerably less than the cost of the antique.

## Marks on China Dolls

Collectors know that almost all the early dolls have no mark whatsoever either of the date, the country where they originated, the factory, the patent, serial or size number. However, there are exceptions to this rule, and old dolls have been found with marks inside the head. Some of the marks illustrated are among those few, the most interesting being that of the King's Porcelain Manufactories—K.P.M. It was found inside a beautiful old pink luster china head with hairdress similar to that worn by Queen Victoria in 1840, when the Queen was twenty-one years old. While it was considered, at that time, beneath the dignity of the King's Porcelain Manufactories to make dolls, an exception might easily have been made if the doll actually represented so famous a person. It has been said that twelve portrait dolls of the queen were made, one given to each of her ladies-in-waiting.

In the illustrations of old marks, the three symbols on the lowest line will be interesting to those collectors who claim to own Chelsea, Staffordshire and Sevres dolls. The first on the extreme left, the encircled anchor, is the oldest mark of the Chelsea (English) factory, the date, 1747 or thereabouts. The center symbol on the same line is the oldest Staffordshire mark. This English factory was established in 1791 by Thomas Minton, and his name appears with the globe and crown symbol of his later products. The symbol at the extreme right on this line is the mark of the First Royal Epoch, (1745-1792), of the Sevres factory, which was established at Vincennes in 1740, and removed to Sevres in 1756. In 1760, King Louis XV became the sole proprietor. Soft paste was made until 1805, since then, only hard paste. For further study of this interesting subject, see Chaffer's *Marks and Monograms*.

About 1860, size numbers appeared on dolls' heads, evidently for the first time. The custom was not general until later, and few serial numbers made their appearance before 1880. A modelled head (not china) made in this country, has the date 1868, but no *china* head inscribed with the date seems to have made its appearance before 1880, at which time one imported from Germany to be used with the American-made Dotter doll body, bears the inscription *Pat. Dec. 7, 1880*. This was followed in 1885 by a china head with the date inscribed, used with the American-made Goldsmith body. Goldsmith used undated heads, too. One has a ribbon bow molded onto the head. This often is called the Dolly Madison, probably erroneously, for it is hardly likely that a head made in Germany about 1885 would represent an American lady who was famous only in her own country and in her own time,—the early part of the century. However as noted before, there was a somewhat similar head made about 1800; the latter with longer shoulders and a more mature expression than the 1880's model. As indicated before, short hair was the style for women about the beginning of the nineteenth century; whereas the same style was suitable only for the young girl at the later period. It is possible that the early doll was made to represent Dolly Madison.

China heads with shirred blouses represent an overlapping period; therefore, some are inscribed with the name of the country, where they were made, *Germany*, others have no marks. Those with the word *Patented* are fair collector's items, as they represent the first of their kind. Many are inscribed with Christian names, as stated elsewhere.

While symbols on bisque heads abound, they rarely are seen on china. A few early nineteenth century had inside marks, as stated, but only one or two have come to light on late heads. A bell with the single initial $K$ inside it appears on at least two china heads, a boy and a girl, the latter with bangs. Both are German, flesh-tinted dolls of the 1890's. Another with the same symbol appears on a bisque head of about the same period. All of them are "good" dolls. A double cross, probably a symbol for *number* is marked on other late 1880's heads. See sketch.

Reproduction dolls now are plainly marked with the date and the initial of the maker on the shoulder, but when the dolls first were introduced, there were no marks. A short time later, the letter $R$ appeared in red underneath the shoulder.

A characteristic of some of the fat-faced china heads of the late 1880's is the inscribed factory or serial number, followed by the size number of the doll. The boy and girl heads with numbers 1210 and 890, respectively, are examples. No. 890, size 8, is ten inches in circumference; No. 1210, size 11, twelve inches.

In buying a doll described as "very old" make a thorough search of the head and body before accepting it as such. Dealers usually want to be fair, but oftentimes they are misinformed.

*Chapter 6*

# BISQUE DOLLS AND THEIR MARKS

THE history of the bisque doll parallels the history of the china-head, for bisque is merely unglazed china. However. there is more variety in the kind of bisque used than in the kind of china.

How soon after the use of the glazed china for dolls, the unglazed china, or bisque. was manufactured is anybody's guess. There are some old ones which look like Parian, but which were made before the discovery of Parian bisque. and unless one is an expert in the subject of ceramics, it is difficult to tell the difference in the various grades.

Flesh-tinted bisque dolls were not in general circulation until close to the middle of the nineteenth century. We know that the Jumeau factory was turning them out in 1844, and from that time. up to the period of the First World War, 1914. bisque was used extensively for dolls' heads. Most of them were imported to this country, by far the greatest number from Germany. some from France, which made beautiful though less numerous bisque-headed dolls, a quantity from Japan, mostly the small, coarse variety, and a few from England, not because England went in for this kind of manufacture, but as stated before, they were made in order to give employment to veterans of World War I, during those years when no supplies were coming from Germany, where porcelain and bisque dolls could be manufactured more cheaply.

Our own country experimented along this line between the years 1914 and 1918. The Fulper Company of Flemington, N. J., is an example, and these have become collector's items, for they are scarce and becoming scarcer. While the bisque is coarse. the dolls are not unattractive, especially the "child" doll with closed mouth. Their "baby" doll is the next most desirable, and the open-mouthed "child" last on the list. The Fulper dolls easily are identified by the name inscribed on the back of the head. Since the factory made only the head, the complete doll varied as to body make-up; some were used with cloth bodies, others with kid, and the head with swivel neck was supplied with a composition body.

55

From 1890 to 1893 Philipp Goldsmith of Covington, Ky., who had been importing German-made doll heads, experimented with bisque, but was not altogether successful.

Our present-day "story book dolls" and Emma C. Clear's collector's items are probably the only bisque dolls now made in this country. The "story book dolls" might just as well be made of composition, for they give that appearance, the reason being that the paint is applied *over the bisque*, evidently sprayed on, so that the quality of bisque entirely is lost. Interesting costumes make this little doll attractive; it is hardly a collector's item with the possible

(80) Fulper bisque head with closed mouth. (These are more attractive than those with open mouth.) (81) Latest 20th century Jumeau French doll. (82) Early "child" Jumeau. (83) Jumeau "lady" doll of the 1860's. (84) Unusual smiling Jumeau, Courtesy Mrs. Franklin Hill Davis. (85) Jumeau circa 1860, The Maryland Historical Society. (86) M. Bru French doll patented 1868, Courtesy Mrs. Elsie Jachowski, Washington, D. C.

## BISQUE DOLLS AND THEIR MARKS

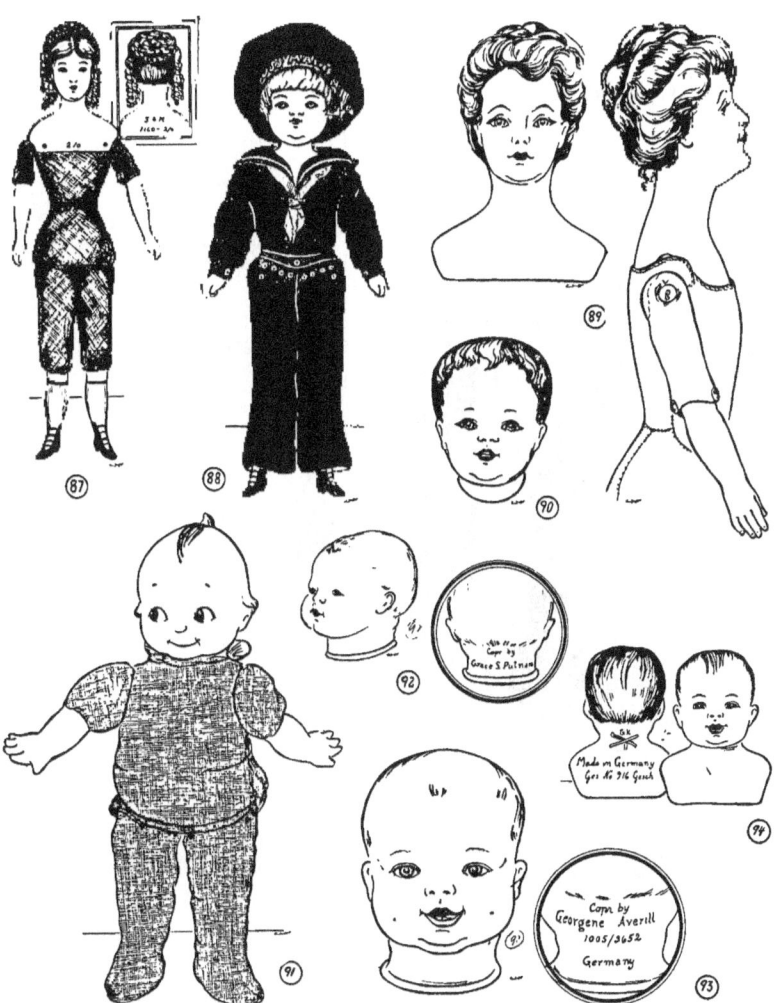

(87) Simon and Halbig German doll circa 1890. (88) Doll commemorative of Battleship Maine. Courtesy Mrs. Davis. (89) Gibson Girl. Bisque head, natural hair, Kestner German body. (90) Kestner "baby" doll head. (91) Rose O'Neill's bisque-headed Kewpie. Made in Germany. (92) Grace S. Putnam's Bye-lo, Made in Germany. (93) German bisque "baby" designed by Georgene Averill. (94) Late German all-bisque head.

exception of the luminous variety—eyes, crest of hair and trimmings on costume glow in the dark, through radium treatment.

Early bisque is identified by its delicate coloring and the absence of marks. As stated, there are many kinds of bisque, from cheap, coarse sugar bisque through the various grades of whiteware to the more delicate Parian and early French. The latter is pale flesh color, fine and desirable. By late bisque we usually mean the more highly colored.

(95) Nine German doll-house or "family" dolls, 1890-1920's.

Although some claim that the French Boltz-Massé dolls are the finest, the best early ones that we know most about are the Jumeau, and those made between 1844 and 1900 certainly are lovely. After that time, when other firms merged with the Jumeau concern, the product was not always as pleasing. A twentieth century Jumeau marked *Unis, France*, has no special claim to distinction. It is not well proportioned, in marked contrast to the earlier ones, the bisque is ordinary, and the head, while pretty, is not exceptional. Teeth are inset, it has average glass eyes (sleeping) and is highly colored. The early Jumeau has beautiful stationary blown glass eyes varying in shade from pale blue to deepest violet (also brown), and a closed, more natural looking mouth.

In the early sixties, Jumeau's son adopted the use of the swivel neck for dolls, and patented the method of joining the head to the bust. The idea evidently came from the wooden lay figure of a much earlier period. Until the late seventies, Jumeau dolls were, for the most part, ladies with slender waists

(96) 20th century Armond Marseille bisque-headed ball-jointed doll. (97) Armond Marseille "Flapper" girl of the 1920's. (98) Armond Marseille "child," bisque swivel head, composition body, painted stockings and shoes. (99) Simon & Halbig clown doll circa 1930's. (100) Earlier German bisque-headed clown doll. (101) German bisque head with modelled hair and inset glass eyes. (102) Simon & Halbig "Chinese" bisque head. (103) German bisque-headed "boy" of 1927. (104) "Willoby," German-made Gebruder Heubach bisque head with French abbreviation for patent.

(105-111) Fancy Parian bisque heads from 1875-1881.
Courtesy Mrs. George R. Hunt.

and beautiful faces of pale flesh-colored bisque, the busts exceptionally broad and deep. Sometimes the arms are of bisque. Again, they might be of kid or cloth, as are the bodies.

When child dolls became more popular, these were made at the Jumeau factory with wooden ball-jointed arms and legs and papier-mâché or composition body—papier-mâché in the early years before strong composition (necessary to stand the strain of tightly-pulled elastic used in stringing a doll of this kind) had been developed.

The early child Jumeau is in much better proportion than most ball-jointed dolls of the period. The hands are not jointed at the wrist, as is the case with many, although not all, of those of contemporary German make.

Other early French firms manufacturing dolls were the Messieurs Belton; Gautier; Mauger (who took over from Gautier—finally Jumeau bought him out); M. Brouiliet, M. Fr. Greffier, M. Voit de Hildburghausen, M. Bru, and Bru, Jeune.

## BISQUE DOLLS AND THEIR MARKS

(112, 113) Fancy Parian heads circa 1870. (114) German all-bisque head with inset glass eyes; glazed hair is like spun taffy. (115) All-bisque "boy" circa 1870. (116) Parian head with molded blouse circa 1870. Courtesy The Little Museum, Hillcrest, Washington, D. C. (117) Parian "boy" circa 1860.

We find any number of European bisque-headed dolls that are a composite in their make-up; some with French heads have German bodies, others with German heads have French bodies. The Jumeau Bebe Company was probably the only firm making entire bisque-headed dolls. Certainly the Armond Marseille Company had bisque parts made in Germany, for doll heads of this company are so marked. Some were patented in France, for the French word for patent, *deposé*, is marked on the head.

One will find a number of French heads resembling bisque, but actually made of what is known as pyro. Trade names such as La Plastolite and La Prialythe are engraved on some of the heads. They are highly colored, but one

(118) Parian with roses in hair circa 1870. (119) The "Blue Scarf Doll." Parian inset glass eyes. (120) Tiny "boy" with brush marks at temple. (121) So-called "Mme. le Bon." Parian with molded guimpe in color. (122) "Lady Valentine." Bisque, circa 1865. (123) "Freddie." Parian "boy" with hair arrangement similar to that worn by our 14th president, Franklin Pierce.

## BISQUE DOLLS AND THEIR MARKS

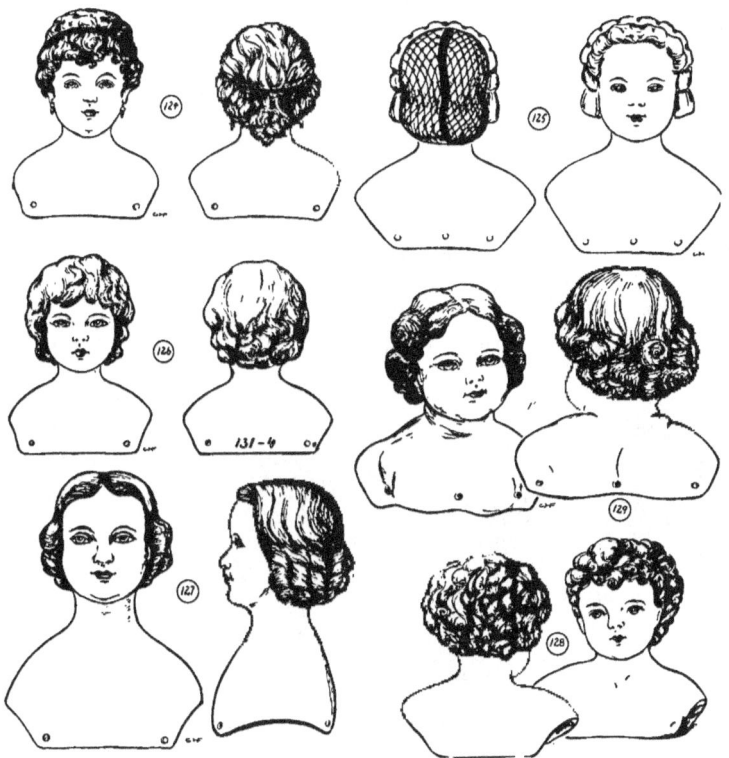

(124) All-bisque head circa 1885. Glazed ribbon band. Courtesy Mrs. Whichelow.
(125) Parian head with snood and tassled tiara, circa 1860. Courtesy Mrs. Hunt.
(126) French all-bisque head, circa 1880. (127) White bisque (unglazed china) head, Civil War period. (128) Delicately colored and fine textured all-bisque head of the 1860's and later. (129) Parian head with inset glass eyes, circa 1850's.

can see the original yellowish shade by looking inside the head. They are much lighter in weight than bisque. One marked Petite Francai, France, over an anchor with the initials $J\ V$, is much lighter in shade. All of these doll heads have beautiful blue inset glass eyes. A big one (size 11) marked La Prialythe, Paris, has the loveliest blown glass eyes imaginable, heavenly blue, full of depth and life.

In March, 1879, a beautiful bisque-headed doll with a well-shaped kid body was patented by Bru, Jeune. The striking features of this doll, aside from its fine make-up, are the artistic, life-like, well-proportioned lower arms, and hands. The face, while interesting and full of character, is not as pretty as the Jumeau. It bears a resemblance to one of German manufacture.

The twelve-inch doll illustrated, belonging to Mrs. Elsie Jachowski of Washington, D. C., is marked *deposé* and is one of the first of its kind. The label pasted just underneath the bust reads: "BEBE BREVETÉ S. G. D. G., Tout Contrefacteur sera saisi poursuivi, conformément á La Loi." Inscribed on the back of the head is a symbol showing a circle within a circle with an inverted quarter-moon above it. Lovely blown glass eyes (brown) are stationary, and tiny molded teeth are barely visible. The head has the usual large opening (stuffed with cork) of the French nineteenth century bisque doll. The body is stitched in front, as illustrated. Three rows of stitches mark the back of the body; one row down the center of the legs. Feet are well modelled, with stitched toes. The sole of the shoe bears the initial B. Clothes purchased with the doll are not original.

A thirty-inch Bru doll of the same style in the Clara Fawcett collection is evidently of a later vintage. It is marked *Bru, Jne* (junior) on the back of

(130) "Princess Parian," circa 1860. (131) Parian doll of the 1850's. Note desirable slender neck. (132) Parian aristocrat with band in hair, long ringlets. Courtesy Mrs. Frank C. Doble, Cambridge, Mass. (133) Fine French bisque-headed doll with coronet braid, circa 1880. (134) So-called "Dagmar." (Dagmar was the mother of the last czar of Russia.) Note two puffs of hair at back of head. Another similar doll has one puff and is also called "Dagmar" by many collectors.

the head with the No. 12 underneath, and the same notations are made on either side of the beautifully modelled shoulders. Instead of teeth, the tip of the tongue shows in the larger doll, and brown blown-glass eyes once had lashes. Other points of difference are the hair, which is light, rather than the chestnut brown of the smaller doll, and the sole of the shoe is marked *Bru, Jne*. Both have an extra strip of kid with fancy edge around the base of the bust, and the same label underneath. Both have swivel neck fastened to finely modelled bisque shoulders, and the quality of both throughout is of the best. Since the elder Bru took out a patent for a turning head doll in 1868, the smaller doll evidently represents the 1868 patent, the larger one with additional markings, the patent of 1879; Bru, Jeune naturally would be a generation later.

In the early days, M. Bru added an internal organ to the kid body of his doll which permitted a forward, backward and sideways movement, but this was

(135) "Lady Baltimore," a rare Dresden with inset glass eyes, original of a doll reproduced by Mrs. Emma C. Clear of California, which she calls "Elizabeth Parinn." "Lady Baltimore's" complexion is a delicate pink; she has light hair with comb and feather (brown) molded on; white molded ruff with yellow luster rose tucked in ear-rings. (136) Four small all-bisque dolls, 1850-1900. (137) Fine grade stone bisque with shirred blouse, circa 1890. Leg and arm shows the type belonging to this and other similar dolls of the period. Collection Kathryn Rodgers, Washington, D. C.

omitted in the dolls referred to above. In 1867, Bru patented a two-faced doll, and a little later, (1872), another multi-faced doll. He also experimented (1876-78) with rubber dolls.

A doll with bisque head and limbs, the top of the head bearing the Bru symbol (double circle) appeared in 1898. It is such a common-place doll that collectors are apt to get a poor impression of this famous manufacturer unless they are familiar with his earlier work. This is Mrs. Franklin Davis's little sailor lad pictured, whose uniform is his main claim to distinction. Dolls commemorating events are usually interesting.

One of the distinguishing characteristics of the earlier French-made bisque doll is the cork which fits into the opening of the head underneath the hair. In the twentieth century, the German idea, a cardboard disk, was used instead.

Collectors are apt to think that the bisque doll made in France tops anything Germany ever made along this line, but such is not the case. In Germany we find all grades and styles, from the finest delicately tinted bisque to the coarsest, the greatest variety, and by far the most numerous. French bisque does not necessarily mean that it was made in France; it is a term given a certain fine grade. J. D. Kestner and other German firms made French bisque.

It is easy to name the prominent French manufacturers of bisque dolls, but to list the numerous German firms is quite another matter. It is also difficult to say who made the best, for most of them made all grades, from the finest to the least desirable. However, the writer has never seen a J. D. Kestner or a Kestner Junior which dropped below a high standard. It was this firm which first made the American-designed Gibson Girl (circa 1900); the Kewpie, copyrighted in 1909, and the Bye-Lo of 1920. These were handled in America by George Borgfelt Corporation of New York City. The Gibson Girl referred to is the one with a head which really looks like the drawing by Charles Dana Gibson. It appears with a labelled Kestner body. The firm also made other interesting dolls, including a life-like laughing baby with painted eyes and hair— see sketches. Whether or not Kestner made the so-called Gibson family dolls is a matter for conjecture. The Gibson Girl, in this instance, does not look like the original Charles Dana Gibson Girl, but the set is unique. Grandpa, with his bald head skirted with a rim of gray locks, and Grandma with her silver-gray hair brought up to a braided top-knot, are most attractive. They are a little larger than the average doll-house doll.

Collectors scarcely know whether to call the Armond Marseille dolls French or German. Some, at least were patented in France, but the bisque parts were made in Germany and many (not all) bear the ear-marks of German design.

One of the most recent and interesting Armond Marseille is No. 323 (see sketch.) During the 1920's the firm introduced a "flapper girl" with slim waist. It represented a grown-up with beautifully modelled arms and legs, feet slanting downward, not jointed at wrists and ankles, and a lovely oval face with closed mouth, closing eyes and short, natural hair. One of medium size is No. 401—5/0. The body and limbs are of composition.

A little later, a beautiful child doll appeared with the Armond Marseille initials engraved on its swivel neck. The body and limbs are also of strong composition, such as this twentieth century is able to produce, jointed only at shoulders and hips. The modelling of the legs indicates a grown-up with high-heeled shoes painted on, but the head is definitely that of a child, a beautiful little thing with a mass of natural curling hair, closing eyes and Cupid's bow mouth. Both the afore-named dolls really look like French dolls.

In 1894, Armond Marseille made a swivel-necked, bisque-headed doll with inset "jewel" eyes. The modelling, in this case, is typically German. An in-

(138) Late stone bisque "bonnet" doll. (139) Nine bonnet heads from the late 19th to the early 20th century. (140-142) Stone bisque bonnet heads of about 1880. Courtesy Mrs. Garrison. (143) Late 19th century bonnet doll, original of one reproduced by Mrs. Clear.

teresting size is 3/0 with the abbreviation for patent given in French—DEP.

Not all the Armond Marseille dolls rank at the top. One marked *A 7/0-X-M* is not especially attractive; neither are the Floradora girls, which is a pity, for the famous musical comedy which delighted audiences at about the turn of the century deserves a better representation in doll form. The bisque head looks like a mediocre German model. It has closing eyes, swivel neck and ball-jointed body. The very large one, No. 11, is a little better than the smaller Floradora, which has cheap stick-like legs and ill-proportioned arms.

Simon & Halbig clown dolls of the 1930's are colorful and attractive. The doll has a cymbal in each hand. These come together when the clown is pressed in the middle, and a bellows sounds. They used to sell for about $3 apiece, dressed, but one would probably pay twice that much now.

An early, exceptionally lovely bisque head is marked simply with the number 13. This, with swivel neck, was used both with the ball-jointed body, and one with separate bisque shoulders mounted on a kid body. It has "sleeping" eyes, a closed mouth, and the quality and workmanship are of the best.

It is a point to be observed that the balls for all these ball-jointed dolls were of wood; the rest of the limbs might be either of papier-mâché or wood. Twentieth-century Jumeau dolls with bisque head have wooden arms and legs, earlier ones, papier-mâché. When enamelled, it is not easy to tell the difference between the strong, smooth papier mâché and the wood, unless the paint peels, which is often the case when enamel is applied over wood.

The initials K. R. (with a five-pointed star between) appear on so many German heads in conjunction with the names of firms spelled out in full, that one wonders whether K. R. refers to the designer rather than a merger firm. One of the Simon & Halbig dolls so marked, and with the numbers *117/A-50* is an unusually lovely bisque head with swivel neck and closed mouth. No. 51, without the star, marked *S & H 1249, DEP* (showing French patent) *Germany* (place of manufacture) *Santa 8*, while a good grade, has inset teeth and is not as interesting, although it has pierced ears, a good point.

Dolls marked *Handwerck-Germany-Halbig*, while pretty, are often a step below the others mentioned. The small shoulder bisque head with sleeping eyes and open mouth with the mark *K R* and the engraved star between the letters, size *0*, is one of the poorer grades of the Simon & Halbig dolls. That with the Chinese cast of countenance and yellowish coloring, swivel neck, is most interesting. The eyes are especially beautiful, the bisque a good quality.

The firm of Gebruder Heubach with the circular symbol (see illustration under *Marks On Dolls*) is one to note. The dolls are full of character and expression, made in all sizes and types, some more interesting than others. (See sketches.) The medium-sized bisque-headed dolls marked *G I 2 H* and *G 2 H*, although they are pretty, are not as interesting as others. *G 2 H* is a brown-eyed doll, *G I 2 H*, blue-eyed.

The firm of Heubach Koppelsdorf brought out one of the finest of the large open-mouth swivel-necked ball-jointed dolls with closing eyes ever produced. This is *250 S*. It should not be confused with Heubach Heppelsdorf, *250-12/0*, which is not nearly as fine.

In 1927 an especially attractive boy all-bisque head was produced by the German firm which uses a heart as a symbol. This has closing eyes and swivel neck, and is used with the ball-jointed body. Size *0* has a dot over the heart and the serial or factory number 2096. The large size (5) has the number over the heart, the letters *B S W* inside the heart, and the serial number 2096 underneath. Hair is parted on the side. A boy head quite similar, but in celluloid was evidently an earlier model, for it is unmarked.

A fairly good open-mouthed shoulder bisque doll with kid body is marked with the symbol of a horse-shoe, underneath which is the date, 1892, and the size number, followed by the phrase "Made in Germany." It should not be concluded that a doll so marked is necessarily a German model. We in America have designed and patented here, dolls "made in Germany;" likewise the French. Armond Marseille brought out two dated dolls, one 1900, the other, 1894. These are the same type as the one with the horse-shoe symbol just referred to.

It is only by seeing and handling hundreds of bisque dolls that one can realize the vast differences in coloring and quality. Cheap sugar bisque used in quantity by Japan in the manufacture of dolls belongs at the bottom of the list. Whiteware, including stone bisque, of which most of the bonnet and hat dolls are made, is often of good quality, and the fancies in stone bisque compare with late Parian, although the modelling is not as fine. Parian, as it was first discovered in 1846, and before it was mixed with too many other ingredients, is almost creamy white. It is an excellent material to use when fine detail is wanted. Unlike ordinary bisque, the slip has to be poured, not pressed into the mold, because it is full of non-plastic material. The excess water becomes absorbed by the plaster cast, and when the hardened bisque is removed, clear, cameo-like features remain. A wealth of detail can be obtained through the medium of Parian, and so we have our wonderfully modelled dolls with plumes, flowers, ribbons, ruffled snoods, etc.

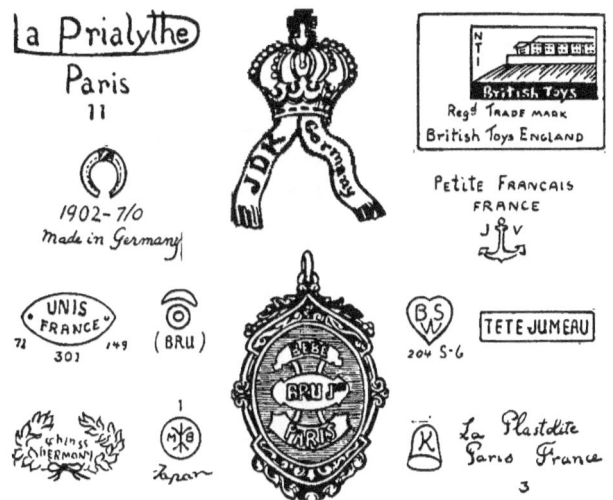

(144) Marks and names found on bisque-headed dolls. Medal (lower center) is a sketch of a bronze medal which accompanied a large Bru Junior doll.

Some of the plainer coiffures are also of Parian bisque, but the work of making these is not as great, and the price should be lower than for a fancy head. A study of the sketches of Parian heads will give something of an idea of the variety of hairdos fashioned in this material. They are expensive whimsies; some bring as high as $300. The majority were made in the 1870's and 1880's. Some are characteristically French, others German. The doll sketched with plumes and a comb in her hair, a rose in her bosom, and with inset glass eyes, is French; one with hair like spun taffy and a topknot has a German symbol (a bell with the letter K inside) inscribed on the shoulders. Parians come with either kid or cloth body, bisque or kid hands. Often a printed label on the body underneath the shoulders tells of the country from which it came.

One should not under-estimate Japan's output of small bisque dolls. While most of them were common and cheap, they often were well executed. A doll similar to our Rose O'Neill's *Scootles*, made of composition in this country, was exported in bisque form from Japan. The bisque is poor, but the modelling good. The Japanese are copyists. When a popular German or American doll appeared on the market, they promptly imitated it in cheaper form. If considered a selling point, the name of the artist who designed the doll is given. Usually just the name Japan or Nippon is printed, but one Japanese firm which imitated a German bisque-headed, ball-jointed doll, inscribed the symbol of his firm on the back of the head.

Some Japanese goods are marked *U S A*, evidently to fool the American public—*U S A* refers to a town in Japan, and not to the United States of America.

It is too bad that in the past, we have bought these cheap Japanese imitations. Japanese dolls made to represent their own people are almost invariably more interesting. Let us hope that in the future there will be less and less demand for anything cheap and shoddy. Children appreciate beautiful dolls, and we can make them of inexpensive, non-breakable material.

Collectors should guard the lovely breakable dolls of the past, among which, bisque holds a high place.

*Chapter 7*

# DOLLS OF PAPIER MÂCHÉ AND COMPOSITION

ACCORDING to the Century Dictionary, papier mâché is of two kinds: "A substance made of pulped paper or paper-pulp mixed with glue and other materials, or of layers of paper glued and pressed together, molded when moist to form various articles, and becoming hard and strong when dry." The early nineteenth century and the Greiner heads described in this chapter are of paper pulp.

The idea of making dolls from pulp in Europe goes back to the seventeenth century, as early engravings show. And they were manufactured in the same manner as those of the present time, by pressing the mixture into molds. This early pulp was dough mixed with lime water, and dolls were made from it as early as 1698. At the same time, small figures and their settings were made from edible gum tragacanth.

Europe was far behind China in the discovery of papier-mâché and its effectiveness in the manufacture of dolls. Some of the Chinese theatre dolls, still extant, are centuries old.

In the 1700's, factories in England were turning out small articles, as well as ornaments for architectural decoration, made of paper pulp, and in 1772, pressed paper articles. Probably dolls were included, although no special mention is made of them. We know that papier-mâché-headed dolls were made pre-dating the French Revolution. At first the hair, eyes, etc., were painted on; later they were given either moving or stationary eyes of glass, enamelled teeth set in, and natural hair. We judge the latter was used only for the fine trade as early as the 1820's, for in literature of the past, reference is made to the fact that England's little Princess Victoria was given "one of the new dolls with hair" at that period. However, it could not have been strictly "new" even for commercial trade, for an engraving of 1800 shows a child's play doll with natural hair. "Fashion" dolls, of course, had long since boasted real hair.

In 1800, cheap dolls with heads of a poor composition called *carlton moule* and stick-like wooden arms and legs were sold in Europe in quantity, and a few years later, dolls and heads of papier-mâché were imported into this country in large numbers. Throughout the century, papier mâché for dolls' heads was very popular. The first of their kind were mounted on extremely narrow-waisted bodies of kid or cloth stuffed with sawdust and long spindley wooden

(145) Papier-mâché head of 1810. (146) Inexpensive dolls of the First Empire period. (147) Early papier-mâché-headed dolls. (148) Blue-eyed brunette papier-mâché head circa 1830. Courtesy Mrs. Whichelow.

arms and legs. The same body style was also used for china heads before and after the introduction of papier-mâché, and enjoyed high favor until about 1840.

The accompanying sketch shows a group of these dolls. Reading from left to right, the one with the ringlets at either side of the head, and a knot in back with shorter ringlets hanging from underneath, came between the late 1820's and the 40's; the lady next to her with ringlets spilling over her shoulders originated about 1830 (an oil painting dated 1830 shows an exact likeness of the doll); the little one representing a child was born about 1840; and the one with peculiar hairdo was ultra-stylish in 1832. A variation of this hair style is shown in the sketch of a head owned by Mrs. George Whichelow of Boston, Mass.

Darky "slave dolls" of the same general type are also found. Occasionally one will find an all-kid body with a remnant of hair sticking through a hole in the top of her head. In the Clara Fawcett collection is a rare one dating from about 1800, a time when few were coming into this country.

The first doll to be patented in America—the Greiner—was of papier mâché pulp, as before mentioned. Labels read (in order of manufacture) "Greiner's Improved Patent Heads, Pat. March 30th. '58;" "Greiner's Patent Doll Heads

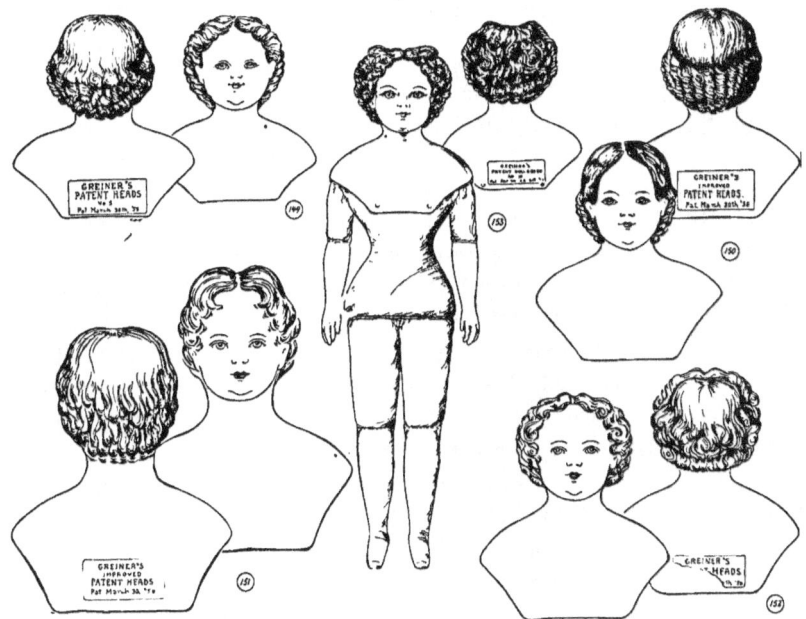

(149-153) Greiner's patent heads. Nos. 150 and 151 were the first to be patented.

(size number underneath) Pat. Mar. 30, '58;" "Greiner's Patent Doll Heads Pat. Mar. 30, '58, Ext. '72." One label omits the word Doll. Size numbers appear on all but the ones marked *Improved*. There are at least eight different hair styles (the latest like the commonest type of china-head), boy and girl dolls, blonde and brunette, in all sizes, from a tiny head no wider than the top of an ink bottle to one as big as a baby's head. Rarest of all are the tinies. Since the hair of the Greiner dolls was molded on, we know the approximate date of some of the china heads (not dated), for they followed the same general pattern. Customers usually made their own doll bodies for Greiner heads, hence they are as widely varied as people's tastes. One will find them with kid, cloth or hand-carved wooden arms.

The Greiner has been hailed as an "all-American doll," one typical of our

(154) Unusual Greiner head. Note large nose. Most Greiners had very small noses.

country. While it is true that the dolls were *made* in America, styles were copied from earlier German models, and the patent issued was merely for the method of construction. Ludwig L. Greiner was himself a German who had learned the toy trade in his native land. He established a factory for the making of toys in Philadelphia, Pa., in the early 1840's, and certainly made dolls before taking out his patent for their "improvement." His dolls are highly prized by collectors because they were the first to be patented in America. Labels in the sketches are enlarged to facilitate reading. They are usually placed in the center between the shoulder blades underneath the finish. So many similar dolls were made in that period that unless the label is there, it is impossible to say whether or not it is a Greiner. One almost exactly like an "Improved" but earlier, and not labelled, is in the Clara Fawcett collection. It has corkscrew curls typical of the 1840's, and may have been one of Greiner's early products. If not, it was the model from which he made the "Improved" girl head of 1858. The boy head is also an "Improved."

It has been stated that one way to tell a Greiner is by the patented reinforcement inside the head. This is not a reliable way to judge, because after the patent expired, many papier-mâché dolls were made with this reinforcement. As stated, the only proof of a Greiner is the label.

The place of origin of a composition doll marked "GL 2015 Superior (or Excellent) Perfectly Harmless" is not known, but the hairdo is copied from a German model, so that if made in the United States, it is certainly German in spirit. German immigrants to this country in the nineteenth century were often connected with firms which made dolls; some were even brought over for that purpose. The coiffure of the *Superior* is similar to other German-designed dolls of the period from the fifties to the seventies.

New doll manufactories came into existence in America during the post Civil War period, and some of these firms made composition dolls. One such was labelled "Lerch and Klagg, Philadelphia." Phillip Lerch was a toy maker in business between 1866 and 1870.

A few years later, 1875, another firm (before referred to) making composition dolls sprang up in Covington, Ky., headed by Philipp Goldsmith. While the material for his doll heads was not confined to composition (there were wax and porcelain) and most of them were imported, some designed by German workmen were made at the American factory. The panic of 1893 slowed down the doll business, and after Philipp Goldsmith was drowned in 1894, his son abandoned it in favor of the manufacture of sports equipment. As such, it still exists.

## DOLLS OF PAPIER MACHE AND COMPOSITION

In 1877, a new composition, the forerunner of our present-day manufacture, was invented by Lazarus Reichmann of New York City. It consisted of sawdust mixed with dough and glue and was meant to be used under wax because (so it was claimed) wax would adhere to it more satisfactorily than was the case with ordinary paper pulp. Our modern composition has added ingredients, including resin, and is stronger than the pulp of 1877, but the basic substance is the same.

Collectors are apt to speak of the "bisque-headed *composition*-bodied jointed dolls" of the late nineteenth century, but if one examines the body of the doll referred to, it almost invariably turns out to be heavy pressed papier-mâché so beautifully enamelled that unless one looks underneath the finish, it would not be possible to detect the make-up. However, the hands of these ball-jointed

Unnumbered doll (top left) "Nina," papier mâché composition. A doll which played a part in the Civil War. Confederate Museum, Richmond, Va. (155) Dewees Cochran child portrait doll, 1937. (156) Shirley Temple doll sans hair. (157) Mme. Alexander modern composition doll sans hair. (158) Peggy, the McCall fashion model. Modern composition.

dolls are almost always of composition, although some are of wood, enamelled of course.

After the Reichmann composition was invented, others followed suit. In 1887, Joseph Schon of Germany obtained a patent in this country for doll heads manufactured of infrangible. A Russian, Solomon E. Hoffman, was issued a patent for "composition for and method of making heads and limbs of dolls" in 1892, and three years later, George Doebrich of Philadelphia, Pa., obtained

(159-162) 20th century German composition "flirting eye" dolls.

a patent for composition for hands and feet of dolls. Since then, there has been constant improvement in the manufacture of this material.

One of the finest English composition doll heads is the Pomona. The body, arms and legs of this doll are of cloth. German character dolls of this substance are also interesting, as are those of China and Japan, and the Canadian firm of Lines Bros. Ltd.

America has advanced rapidly in the making of durable composition, and it is now the principal material for doll manufacture. It is inexpensive and will stand a great deal of punishment at the unmerciful hands of children. Some of the stronger modern rubber dolls have composition in their make-up, and when the new plastic again takes its place in the world of dolls, it is likely that bodies will still be made of composition. From the collector's viewpoint, it is not ideal; the material fades and cracks with the passage of time. Despite this fact, there are so many beautiful examples of modern composition that they are worth adding to collections. Among the best are the Dewees Cochran child portrait dolls. These (durably made and well-proportioned), are modelled from American children. The earlier ones, with hand-painted eyes, are the best collector's items. They were discontinued because the cost of hiring artists to paint the eyes was greater than the expense of inserting glass eyes. These lovely portrait dolls and similar "costume" dolls were on the market in the thirties of this twentieth century. Since the price was higher (and rightly so) than for an ordinary doll of the same size, they were not sold in great numbers. A fair-sized doll undressed cost $8; dressed, the price varied according to costume. Outfits included little kid gloves perfectly tailored. In the present Post-War period, the price seems little enough—far inferior dolls bring more money—but in the thirties, $8 was considered a big price for a child's doll. As with other interesting dolls, there were plenty of imitators. The Dewees Cochran doll helped bring into vogue beautifully modelled hands and slimmer waists for the "child" doll. Her commercial portrait dolls were the outgrowth of Miss Cochran's made-to-order portrait dolls. One such was an order from the Irving Berlin family in 1935 for their two children. She designed four basic head types, painted the face and coiffured the doll to look like the child it was intended to resemble. Dolls made to order were, of course, much more costly than those manufactured commercially, but all of them are good collector's items, and we have reason to be proud of these truly American dolls. We hope that soon they will again be easily available. Fleischaker & Baum of New York City (trade name, Effanbee), who made them, deserve credit for discriminating taste.

The custom, centuries old, of making dolls from living models has been popularized in modern times by representing stars of the screen, especially child stars. The Shirley Temple doll of a decade ago was a tremendous seller, due more to the popularity of the child than the doll itself. The doll is far less attractive than Shirley was, except for its redeeming feature, a mass of curls. Small ones are the best collector's items, for at present the doll is not important enough to afford it much space in a group. Then, too, the smaller ones are often more attractive than the large sizes. Most of the Shirley Temple dolls which find their way into Thrift Shops are either wigless or with hair so matted that it has to be discarded, in which case, it is well to have your local Dolls' Hospital write to the manufacturer for a new wig—the Ideal Novelty and Toy Co., New York City. This company also introduced the Deanna Durban and Judy Garland dolls, pretty toys, but not as well proportioned as some. Another attractive doll was the model of Carol Anne Beery, the adopted child of Wallace Beery. Hosts of other celebrities were also made in doll form —Charlie McCarthy and Lew Fields (the originals were good, the imitations poor); story book characters like Snow White, the Seven Dwarfs, Prince Charming, the Blue Fairy and Pinnochio, all in composition.

Another firm specializing in composition characters from books and from the screen is the Mme. Alexander Doll Company of New York. They have introduced Scarlett O'Hara of "Gone With The Wind" fame, the charming McGuffey Anna and her baby sister (the latter two at the centenary of the famous Reader, 1938); Flora McFlimsey, Madeleine De Baine, and Sonja Henie. They also offered "Butch," an interesting boy doll; Pinky and Little Genius baby dolls, and Jeannie Walker, one of the most attractive walking dolls that ever has been placed on the market. The Alexander doll which bends at the waist as well as at the neck, shoulders and hips, is considered by many a collector's item. So also the Dionne quintuplet babies, products of the same company.

The Patsy all-composition dolls which made their appearance in the 1920's and were said to be modelled from an American child are holding their own. A 1941 edition claps its hands and "cries" when pressed on the chest. It is called Pat-a-Pat, and is an Effanbee product.

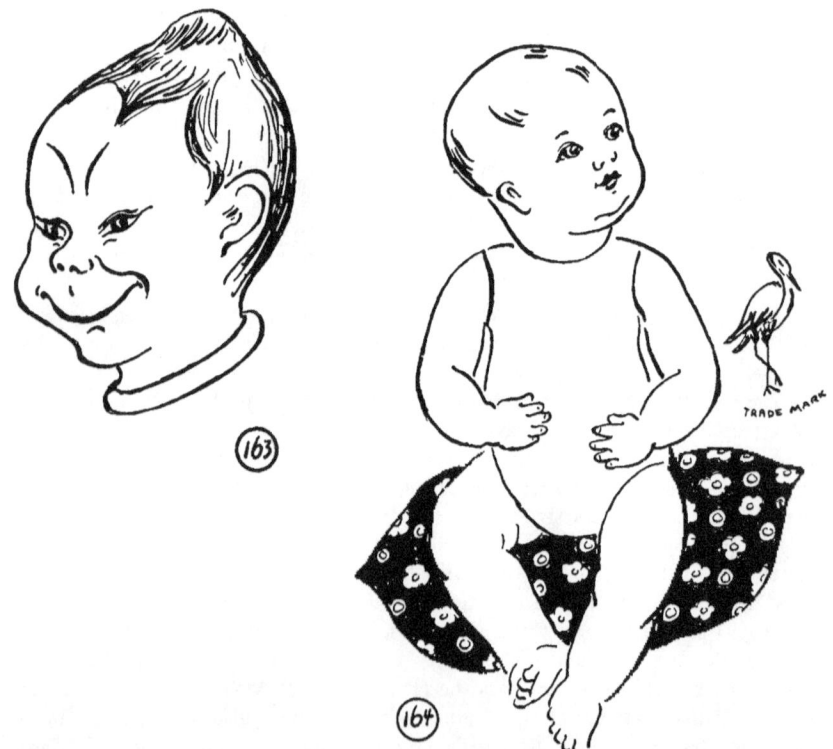

(163) Billiken, 1909.   (164) Parsons-Jackson "baby," 1914.

Just before the Second World War, composition dolls with mechanical mechanism began to make their appearance in America. These are referred to in the chapter on *Dolls of the Nineteenth Century*.

Fashion dolls appeal to old and young alike, and it is no wonder that the Deb-U dolls (*Deb-U*, 22" and *Little Sister*, 16") of the Margit Nilsen Studios are appreciated by those who like good-looking and well-proportioned dolls. They were made of lasticoid, and for that reason, were off the market during World War II. See chapter on *Rubber Dolls*.

But the Deb-U are not the only dolls designed by Miss Nilsen. Since 1939 "fashion" dolls of her creation fifteen to thirty inches tall have been seen in many a store window, modelling the latest garments for sale. Doll enthusiasts made inquiries as to whether or not the small sizes might be purchased, and the result is a whole series of such dolls, including "Glitter Girl" with complete wardrobe, "The White House Ladies" and other outstanding American ladies, and dolls showing fashions from early Grecian days to the present time. Miss Nilsen's English Queens are especially attractive.

Costume dolls of World War II have no rubber in their content; they are made of sturdy composition. In their wake have come doll heads of light-weight all-composition accompanied by squares of material with instructions for draping around the head. They are not as popular as complete figures, and for that reason many of the stores have sold them recently at half-price—$1.

Within the past year or so an attempt has been made to revive the Bye-Lo baby doll, using composition for the head instead of the original bisque. They are not to be compared with the bisque heads made in Germany.

An especially fine composition doll of about three years back, still on the market, is the Monica with hair embedded in the scalp after the style of the wax Montanari of 1849. There are fifteen dolls, varying in size, costume and price. Since the average sized Monica is over $20, it is a collector's item rather than a child's plaything. Large department stores carry them, or one may write direct to the Monica Studios, Hollywood, California. An advertisement reads: "Craftsmanship and artistic ingenuity combined have created a doll so lifelike, so beautiful, so different, that every little girl will love to include the 'Monica Doll' in her family. It's real human hair, and . . . . . yes, it's grown on the head!"

Novelty dolls of foreign composition are common, but our American-designed Billiken of 1909-10 tops them all. For two years the popularity of Billiken knew no bounds, but it suddenly ceased, and now he is a rarity. This laughing little elf with his composition painted hair rising to a point on the top of his head, came in two styles, one representing a child, with cloth body; the other with the same head, but an animal body—"Plushie" as he was called.

Among other interesting dolls made of composition and designed in this country are the Uneeda Biscuit doll, the Campbell Kid, and Rose O'Neill's Kewpie and Scootles. While the composition Kewpie made here cannot compare with the earlier German-made bisque, it is still an interesting doll. On the other hand, the composition Scootles made by the Cameo Doll Co. of Port

Allegany, Pa., is more attractive than Japan's bisque variety, for the bisque, in this instance, is of poor quality.

France, as well as Germany and other European countries, was making good composition dolls prior to World War II. The latest to come from France was given by the children of Brittany to General Eisenhower in tribute to his part in the liberation of France. One may see it at the Smithsonian Institution, a fine big doll beautifully dressed in the elaborate traditional costume of the peasant of Brittany.

A study of the sketches will show some of the German-made composition dolls in which the flirting-eye is a principal attraction. We also produce flirting-eye dolls with composition heads and bodies. America has as great variety and as interesting dolls of this sort as are found anywhere else in the world. Collectors should look to the ones which represent those in the Service—the WAC, the WAVE, etc. These are part of the annals of our own times, and as such, will become more and more valuable as collector's items. A fine doll of any period is a treasure, but a fine doll which also tells a story is doubly interesting. We are making history in a big way, and generations yet unborn will feel for the dolls of our time, just as we feel about those of the romantic past.

*Chapter 8*

# HAND-MADE DOLLS

Hand-made dolls are of every description and material—pottery, wood, papier-mâché, cloth, shingles, pine-cones, corncobs, nuts, nursing nipples, soap, coal, sea-shells, lobsters, sponge, clothespins, electric light bulbs, even mummified dried apples—anything that can be made into a semblance of a human being. A great deal of it is junk, made to satisfy a craving for the sensational or curious without regard to line, form or feeling. An artist bent on serious work will choose a lasting material, one that will show his talents to best advantage; he will not waste his precious time on anything else.

In ordering a hand-made doll, it is advisable to ask the weight, especially if one wishes to exhibit from time to time. An average-sized suitcase filled with small dolls made of heavy clay or composition will prove too weighty for comfort. Composition mixed with paste rather than water makes a light yet tough pulp; if mixed with water, it is apt to be heavy. Powdered stone or marble sometimes added to a pulp mixture, will add considerably to the weight. This is a point not to be regarded lightly.

For a really fine doll, one should expect to pay a sum commensurate with the amount of work and skill involved. It is strange how many persons do not realize this fact. Recently a Washington man called upon an artist to make him a doll for his daughter's collection. He described elaborately just what was wanted. The doll would have taken at least twenty-five hours of working time to complete, to say nothing of the materials required for its construction. When asked how much he expected to pay for such a doll the reply was, "Oh, about $5!"

The sketch "From Rags to Riches" in the chapter on cloth dolls illustrates the vast differences between hand-made dolls. The one by Dorothy Heizer must have taken months of labor. Pictures and costumes of Eugenie had to be studied and careful plans laid before the work was even started. To make a twelve-inch, three-dimensional portrait accurately scaled to size and worthy the best efforts of a skilled artist, is no small matter. Of course such a doll is out of the price range for the average collector. It might cost as much as

$300. But there are beautiful dolls by fine artists which take considerably less time, and consequently, less money.

Beware of anyone making extravagant claims for hand-made dolls to be sent through the mails without first producing photographs of the dolls in question, and without a money-back guarantee. A Washington woman recently "fell" for a magazine advertisement of two dolls costing ten dollars each, which were supposed to be beautiful beyond description and made by an artist at the top of his profession. The lady, a trusting soul, was fired with enthusiasm; she immediately mailed a hard-earned check for $20, and awaited eagerly the result. Finally, when the package arrived containing, as she confidently believed, two heavenly little figures, she could hardly wait to unwrap it. Imagine her disappointment when she found under the wrappings two ugly dolls, poorly painted, gaudily dressed to be sure, but of the cheapest material and make. Tears were very near the surface, for the lady in question could ill afford the loss. The figures were candidates for a waste-basket.

An artist well known for the quality and workmanship of her dolls, which are also reasonably priced, is Mrs. Muriel Atkins Bruyere of 36 Barrow St., New York City. She makes no extravagant claims, but photographs of her creations speak for themselves. One may have a fine portrait doll for $25 and up, according to size and materials used, and the amount of time spent upon it. A few in stock are less costly. Nine-inch charming little "Vie" modelled by Mrs. Bruyere from an 1860 daguerreotype of four-year-old Viola Vernon, (who became the mother of Mrs. McKim of Kimport) sells for $10.

Dolls by Gertrude Florian, a sculptor of Detroit, Michigan, are among the best of the hand-mades. Those sketched here (through the courtesy of Mrs. William Knobloch of Washington, D. C.) represent some of the characters she has translated into doll form. While they seem high in price, the labor alone is worth the cost, $50.

Miss Grace Stanley Miller of Long Beach, California, a water-color artist, has displayed some of her work with dolls at the Los Angeles Museum. They represent characters from books and foreign folk children, and are especially attractive to the younger generation.

On the other side of the continent, Evelyn Durnbaugh and Mrs. Kathryn Rodgers have created beautiful crèche figures with composition heads, hands and feet; Mrs. D. L. Boyer, charming heads of papier-mâché; and Claire Fawcett has whittled so many jointed wooden dolls that it would take a whole room to display them to advantage. These four persons all are from the Washington, D. C. area.

Across the Atlantic, Violet M. Powell of Dublin, Ireland, has brought to life through her dolls a fascinating acquaintance with the Irish peasant, with special reference to dwellers on the Island of Aran. Mrs. Elsie Clark Krug of Baltimore, Md.; Kimport, and, on occasion, various department stores throughout the country, have displayed these, together with other hand-made dolls from all parts of the world, including those from our own United States.

# HAND-MADE DOLLS

Mrs. Aileen Harris, one of Kimport's best artists, has made portrait dolls of Louisa M. Alcott, the famous characters in her classic "Little Women,"— Meg, Jo, Beth and Amy,—Florence Nightingale, Betsy Ross, Elizabeth Browning and others. All the dolls are good collector's items, and reasonably priced. Eight-inch Betsy Ross, including flag and chair, is $10; "Little Women" in eight-and-a-half and nine-and-a-half-inch sizes are $7.50 each; Florence Nightingale and Elizabeth Browning, both ten inches tall, $5.95 and $10, respectively.

Another Kimport artist of merit is Erma Fiske Austin, who has immortalized, in doll form, Charlie Chaplin and Marie Dressler, the latter as Tug-Boat Annie. These dolls are $15 each.

At the same establishment, individual dolls of distinction from Persia and Syria are $15. An artist creates the figure and native girls do the costuming.

(165) "Alice in Wonderland." Hand-made doll by Muriel Atkins Bruyere. (166, 167) Sketches from dolls sculptured by Gertrude Florian, Detroit, Mich. Courtesy Mrs. Wm. Knobloch. (168) Hand-made doll head of papier-mâché by Mrs. D. L. Boyer, Takoma Park, Md. (169) Hand-carved wooden doll by Claire Hallard Fawcett, Washington, D. C. (170) "Jo" of Little Women, an Aileen Harris doll.

Other dolls from the Far East, imported before the War, may be obtained for less than American-made ones of the same quality, due to cheaper labor conditions abroad.

The lifelike old peasant dolls by Bernard Ravca are so well known that a description is hardly necessary. The majority are done in cloth, but his breadcrumb dolls, which look like wax, are more finely modelled. Mr. Ravca reports it is unlikely that any more of the latter will be made in the near future, as he cannot get the right kind of bread in America. Peasant dolls are not the only ones that Mr. Ravca now creates. The sketches of Pocahontas and John Smith were made from Ravca dolls in the collection of Mrs. Knoblock.

Colorful hand-made Katchina Ceremonial dolls by our North American Indians tell a story of Indian customs. The larger doll pictured shows, on the head, the Indian symbol for clouds and rain, and was probably meant to propitiate the rain god; the little one is a Hopi goat doll. The superstition surrounding these dolls has largely faded, but the Indian is quick to take advantage of the interest in them shown by the white man, and the sale is fairly large.

Pomono hand-made dolls from London, England, are intriguing to both child and adult. Those shown here are hand-made and hand-colored. A few made their way to this country fifteen or twenty years ago and sold for $10 apiece, about twice the price they brought in their native country.

Dolls made by workmen in the American potteries from the 1700's through the nineteenth century are crude but interesting. Most of them have the initials of the maker and the date inscribed underneath the shoulder. Pictured is a family of red pottery heads made in the Pennsylvania potteries in 1840.

Those interested in hand-made dolls should get in touch with Kimport. While foreign dolls are limited at present to dwindling supplies on hand, good hand-made dolls from sections of our own country find their way to Independence, Mo., and to the McKim establishment. Twelve issues of a spicy and instructive leaflet called "Doll Talk" are sent for 50 cents. This is well illustrated. Periodically, a Kimport "show" is staged (in normal times) in leading department stores through the States.

Hundreds of dolls, some good, some bad, some indifferent, have been made to help in the War effort and for charitable purposes. This idea goes back into past history and other wars. The number of Civil War benefit dolls still extant is surprising. Those best remembered from the period of the First World War are mentioned, and illustrated, in the chapter on Cloth Dolls. Although colorful, the dolls themselves are crude, but precious in their associations and should be welcome additions to any collection.

The organization of a nation-wide club to make dolls for benefit purposes, supervised by the best doll portrait artists available, would be interesting not only to members, but the public at large. Help can be gleaned from such books as Edith Flack Ackley's "Dolls to Make for Fun and Profit," and "Marion-

HAND-MADE DOLLS 85

ettes,'' the patterns for which, contained in a pocket at the back of the book, readily can be adapted for the cloth doll.

Most persons prefer a doll with modelled features. The chapter on Puppets tells how to make a light-weight tough composition, which could be tried out with small dolls, as the author suggested in an article for "The Guardian," a Camp Fire Girls' publication. The illustration accompanying the text is reproduced here.

Many attempts to make dolls from clothespins have been made with poor results, because the head of a clothespin is too small and ill-proportioned. If one builds up the head with a screw-eye covered with strips of Scott towelling soaked in paste, the result is a firm foundation for a modelled head which can be really interesting. Or the head can be made of cotton batting covered with cloth.

(171, 172) Cloth dolls with embroidered features by Bernard Raven. Courtesy Mrs. Wm. Knobloch. (173) Pomona (English) hand-painted dolls, circa 1928. (174) Katchina American Indian dolls. (175) American redware dolls from the Pennsylvania potteries, 1840.

Use long, small-eyed screw eyes, and do not screw them in all the way, because you will want to leave as much room as possible for the head of the doll.

If one has difficulty in finding the powdered papier-mâché in local craft supply shops, a good quality of finely powdered asbestos from the hardware store will do, provided it is free from lint and hair. Powdered papier-mâché may be secured in quantity from The Papier-Mâché Novelties Co., Reading, Mich.

In the use of muslin over cotton batting, be sure the muslin is long enough to come down over the neck, and tie it securely with carpet thread. Arms are made of dressmaker's wire or pipe cleaners looped in and around the screw eye. Turn up the ends just a little for the hands, and wind a thin strip of adhesive tape over the wire. White Cross adhesive tape is better for this purpose than Red Cross, because it will take paint; the latter is water-resistant.

Devoe's is a good American oil paint. Make flesh color by mixing a tiny speck of red and a still smaller amount of yellow with a tablespoonful of white paint. Paint cheeks before the basic flesh color dries to facilitate blending, but the paint must be perfectly dry before outlining features. India ink is splendid for this purpose.

Your doll can be made to stand alone if you will fill the points of the clothespin with the plastic and shape it to resemble feet; or dress with a full skirt long enough so that the figure will stand alone. To make your dolls of special interest, look up costumes of early America or other countries and dress in authentic style.

As one becomes more proficient in the art of modelling, larger and more finished dolls may be attempted. A head with an elongated neck may be pushed down into a sawdust-stuffed body until it attains the proper length above the shoulders. Carved wooden arms and legs are suitable for the larger doll, but commercial doll limbs may be purchased at almost any large dolls' hospital or supply company.

A course in doll making may not make a finished portrait artist, but it will give an understanding of the time and effort required for such things, and will enable one to arrive at a better understanding of the worth of a hand-made doll; and it *may* result in the discovery of hidden talent.

*Chapter 9*

# THE CHRISTMAS CRIB

A collector's opportunity to acquire really old dolls is represented in the Christmas crib or crèche figure, for so many thousands were made, especially during the eighteenth century, when the figure was at its height, that a number still remain. Since they were shown only at the time of the Christmas festival, and often hundreds of figures used in a single set to tell the story of the birth of Christ, many beautiful examples have come down to us well preserved through the years. Two illustrations are given here, one of a modern, another of an old figure. The Madonna, as recent as 1925, nevertheless gives an idea of how the old ones were made. At least two centuries have rolled over the head of the peasant boy. Notice the characteristic hands.

Clothing helps to identify these figures. Modern ones usually have machine-stitched garments, whereas the old ones are completely hand-made. The material of which the doll is made also differs; the antiques are mainly of terra-cotta, wood or wax, the later ones of clay or composition. One sometimes may tell the exact age of a crèche figure by examining the lining of the gown. When newspapers became available to all, this was a favorite material for lining the cloth, and often the date is given.

We are indebted to Pope Liberius for introducing the Christmas crib. Established in the year 354, the custom finally spread from Italy to other European countries. It is probable that at first only the principal characters were used, Mary and Joseph and the infant Jesus. Later, the animals of the stall were added, then the angels, the shepherds with their sheep, the wise men, the three oriental kings in their rich raiment, etc. The idea grew so popular as time advanced that models of the inhabitants of whole villages with their horses, cattle and sheep, were added to the crib as representing the people going to the fair supposed to be in progress at the time of the birth of our Lord. They remain now as a valuable record of the life of the times.

Family chapels of the wealthy were richly endowed with these crib figures. The best artists of the age were employed, and special emphasis was given to character and expression. As stated above, hands were made large in proportion to the figure (the same is true in paintings of the period) and that is one means of identification. Early painters and sculptors realized the importance of the hand as an indication of character.

The work of the Christmas crib was not confined to the artist alone. The peasant in his field and the king upon his throne took equal pleasure in creating personally these symbols of religious thought and feeling. The crib seldom was completed in one season, but was added to year by year.

There was keen competition, rich and poor vied with one another. When the Nativity group which the King of Naples made at his own work-bench about

Crèche figures. (176) Madonna, Italian, 1925. Terra-cotta head, hands and feet. (177) 18th century village boy, terra-cotta head, hands and legs, inset glass, eyes. (178) Modern crèche figure. Head designed by Evelyn Durnbaugh; doll completed by Kathryn Rodgers.

the year 1760, was placed on exhibition, the crowds coming to see it were so great that it necessitated a double guard. The figures, five hundred of them, a magnificent spectacle, were of wood and wax, clothed in materials cut from the Queen's own wardrobe. There were also two hundred animals. Figures of peasants of the preceding century were used as models for the shepherds. It was the artist's custom to pose real persons, and perhaps that is why these dolls are so life-like.

An added touch of realism was given when automata was introduced into the German Christmas crib. Animated figures presented a fascinating story of the Nativity. The Church was quick to use the opportunity it afforded to draw the people into the Fold. It was a good substitute for the old miracle plays until the time when representation of every day activities became more popular than the sacred story. It was natural to enjoy seeing a miniature carpenter, or tailor, or thresher at work, but these earthy touches spoiled the religious sentiment for which the crib was originally made. For this reason, at about the end of the eighteenth and the beginning of the nineteenth century exhibition of the crib in some places at first was limited to religious figures, then banned altogether. The ban was not universal, however, and artists continue to make beautiful crèche figures even to this day. In Germany there were, at least until recently, schools for instruction in making the Christmas crib, notably at Oberammergau, home of the famous Passion Play.

Elsewhere in the 19th century, with a decreasing of religious feeling for the crib, the figures began to decline. In the Alpine Tyrol, where wood-carving has always been at its best, the artistic crib remained longest, and Johann Kleninger, until he died in 1899, kept up the tradition. In Engelberg, Josef Partsch retained the religious feeling and made many beautiful figures tinted with water color. The work of his hand, stilled in 1886, gives mute testimony to this fact. An abundance of figures characterizes the crib of the Tyrol.

Max von Boehn says in "Dolls and Puppets" (1932) that in Italy only one crib maker remains who still retains the old high standard of artistry and feeling in his work. World War II may have eliminated some fine examples of this art in Europe. We in America are fortunate to have the Thayer collection at the University of Kansas, the Antonio Rossellino groups at the New York City Metropolitan Museum of Art, and many fine individual pieces salvaged by doll collectors throughout the country.

*Chapter 10*

# THE CLOTH DOLL

"FROM Rags to Riches"—such is the story of the evolution of the rag doll. The sketch of the crude Roman rag doll (from the Royal Ontario Museum) found in Egypt represents centuries of existence; that of Eugenie, accompanying it, was made only a few years ago by a skillful artist, Dorothy Heizer of Essex Falls. N. J., for the late Mrs. Frank B. Noyes of Washington, D. C. The doll is not only perfectly proportioned from head to toe, but the materials of the costume represent the greatest care in selection, and the most minute attention to the tiniest detail,—a far cry from the doll played with by a little Roman child more than sixteen hundred years ago. Even the jewels are scaled to size, and the stitches in the hand-made clothes are so tiny that it is almost impossible to see them.

It may not be fair to present such a contrast, for in the long ago dolls made for royal families by artists of the time were little marvels of workmanship, but they were not made of rag, except for the average child.

The rag doll has always been a favorite, ever since the earliest history of the toy doll. Note sketches of an old French rag doll, and a "Queen Anne" (about 1700) with embroidered features and dress of brocade. Cloth dolls were beginning to come up in the world.

Early rag dolls were made by hand, and it was not until the latter half of the nineteenth century, or after the sewing machine was invented, that they were manufactured in quantity. England was doing beautifully in this direction as early as 1850, and ever since has been noted for this particular type of doll.

Four "collector's items" (of secondary importance for the most part) of American manufacture are the Hawkins doll of 1868; the Isannah F. Walker stockinet, patented in 1873; the Columbian (same general kind, 1893-1908), and the Chase Stockinet of about the same period as the Columbian, and so similar that they are often confused. There are differences, however, not only in facial expression, but in construction, judging from the examples in the Claire Fawcett collection. (See sketches.) The body of the Columbian is covered with a tan colored sateen-like cloth, square at the neck and terminating just past the shoulder and hip joints, whereas the body of the Chase doll is all stockinet. Other points of difference are that the Columbian has elbow and knee joints, where the Chase is not so jointed. The latter also has a slightly longer neck. Both have raised features reinforced from underneath; (in fact, all four dolls have this characteristic); both are painted in oils; both have interesting shell-like ears, except in one or two varieties of the Chase, where the ears are covered, or partly covered, by modeled hair. The features

(179) From rags to riches. a. Roman rag doll, 3rd century A. D. Royal Ontario Museum. b. Modern cloth doll by Dorothy Heizer of Essex Falls, N. J. Courtesy the late Mr. Frank B. Noyes, Washington, D. C.

of the Chase doll are more definitely modelled. Columbian dolls as well as the Chase Stockinet still may be found occasionally in antique shops. The latter are now being made for demonstration use in hospitals.

Early Columbian dolls, (those made between 1891 and 1900) painted by their originator, Miss Emma E. Adams, an artist of merit, are worth collecting. Those painted by other persons after her death in 1900 are not as well done. The year 1893 saw the beginning of their popularity. Examples exhibited at the

Chicago World's Fair received a diploma of merit from the Columbian Exposition Commission. They were made of muslin, sized and hand painted. Costumes were by Miss Emma's sister Marietta. Mother and Father Adams helped with the business until their death at the beginning of the twentieth century. Boy and girl dolls and negroes were represented as in the case of the Chase doll. They were not patented, but rubber-stamped "Columbian Doll, Emma E. Adams, Oswego Centre, N. Y." until 1900; after that period, "The Columbian Doll Manufactured by Marietta Adams Ruttan, Oswego, N. Y." If the doll has been used a great deal, this lettering in nine cases out of ten, has been rubbed out. In the Doll Museum at Wenham, Mass., there is an early Columbian doll which has traveled around the world.

In the "gay nineties" and on into the twentieth century all sorts of rag dolls were produced. Many persons will remember those put on the market by various manufacturers of food and clothing, such as the "Aunt Jemima Pancake Flour" darky dolls; the "Cream of Wheat Rastus," "Buster Brown," and "Puffy" (Quaker Puffed Rice.) Dolls of this kind are seldom worth collecting, but the "Brownies" (made by the Arnold Print Works of North Adams, Mass., to advertise "Dry Goods,") patented in January, 1892, are interesting. They were designed by Palmer Cox and included various nationalities—the German, the Highlander, the Canadian, John Bull and a Sailor. "Other Household Pets" by the same company, released during the following October, included, besides animals, "Pitti-Sing," "Our Soldier Boys," "Topsy," "Pickanny," "Little Red Riding Hood," and a jointed cloth doll.

So many rag dolls were made during the late nineteenth century and in recent times that it would be infeasible to list them all. Dolls sketched are representative examples. The late American dolls sketched belong to a series representing different nationalities.

Among the earlier less commonly found American rag dolls are the Martha L. Wellington stockinet doll of 1883 (this has a wire frame outlining the head, neck and features); the E. S. Peck "Santa," patented in 1886; the B. Wilmsen dressed "raggie," patented in 1895, and the caricature of "Teddy" Roosevelt, 1917.

Modern rag dolls are more interesting. Raggedy Ann and Raggedy Andy have delighted children since 1919. They are made by the Georgene Novelty Co., of New York City; their inspiration, the late Johnny Gruelle and his famous books for children.

Another attractive American rag doll is Rose O'Neill's Kewpie of stockinet. However, collectors would rather have this in bisque form.

Hand made rag dolls for children by Edith Flack Ackley are so intriguing that they have become collector's items. A daughter, Telca, makes water-color portrait sketches to accompany her mother's dolls.

No discussion of cloth dolls would be complete without special mention of the Kathe Kruse creations. Her dolls, modelled from her own children, were first noticed at an exhibition in Berlin in 1912, and attracted immediate attention. They are so like real little children at their adorable best, that one feels actual love for these symbols of babyhood. Besides being beautifully painted and of good proportion, the dolls are well made. Notice from the sketch with what care the seams are cut and fitted to make the body natural looking. Metal reinforcement under the cloth features assures a lasting shape. The dolls sold in this country in 1914 for $8; now one in good condition should bring $15. Look for the name, Kathe Kruse, on the sole of the foot.

(180) a. Old French rag doll. b. Queen Anne cloth doll with embroidered features. (181) A group of American rag dolls. (182) The Bernhard Wilmsen dressed rag doll of 1895. (183) The Palmer Cox "Brownies," 1892. (184) Raggedy Andy and Raggedy Ann. (185) American-made cloth doll, modern; "A Blossom Creation." (186) Modern American-made cloth doll. Georgene Novelties Inc.

Other well-made German dolls—felt comics for the most part (identified by a metal tag on the ear)—are those of Margaret Steiff.

Rag dolls with hard, raised features reinforced from underneath, have become popular in almost every country in the world. Most collectors are familiar with the beautiful, extensively advertised Lenci (Italian) dolls. Lenci is the trade name of Di E Scavini, taken from a pet name given her. The earlier ones of felt (see sketch) were made much better than the later dolls of pressed cloth, but the latter are made attractively, with elaborate clothing. They were patented in Turin, Italy, Sept. 8, 1921.

Lenci is not the only name to look for in fine Italian dolls. There are many others just as desirable. The doll sketched with thick, curly natural hair marked *Bambola Regina—FIRENZE—made in Italy* on the underwear, dressed in felt with a pretty little muslin apron, is made better than the late cloth Lenci, although the clothes may not be as flamboyant.

The cloth dolls of France and England reached a high stage of perfection at the beginning of the First World War, when the allies were cut off from their supplies from Germany. England has her Royal Family and others in the limelight represented in the world of rag or felt dolls, as well as fascinating child dolls, sailors, soldiers, etc.

Norah Wellings' English cloth dolls are among the best known, for they have come to this country in quantity, and have been sold to tourists on shipboard. The cloth baby sold through I. Magnin & Co., California and Seattle (see sketch) is most desirable.

The faces of Dean's Rag Book Co. (London) dolls are worthy of special note. The eyes are evidently hand-painted; the body, a floppy little cloth affair, makes the doll especially suitable for the young child. Nora Wellings' soldier and sailor lads have the same type of body. Labels give the maker's name.

A medium-priced felt doll, nicely dressed, and with glass eyes set into the felt, is manufactured by the Chad Valley Company.

Pomona (London) dolls are the most artistic of all, but the majority have modelled heads, which puts them out of the class of the all-cloth doll.

Of the two Russian dolls sketched, the "child" with the basket is by far the most interesting. Many of Russia's tiny dolls were sold through our Five-and-Ten-Cent Stores for 15 cents each, before World War II.

A few years ago Greece made beautiful 9-inch felt dolls, distributed through the Near East Relief Fund. The one sketched ($4) is worthy a place in any collection. The hand-painted face was done by an artist.

France has gone far in this field. Quoting from extracts of the article by Jeanne Doin in the *Gazette des beaux Arts*, December, 1916, translated by Esther Singleton:

"To-day the French doll is triumphant. Let us salute it with joy.

"The situation before the war can be summarized very briefly. The German doll reigned everywhere. This was the result of a methodical and patient contest. The Germans acted regarding the doll-industry as they acted in so many matters, offering articles at a reduced price, producing with rapidity of execution and with easy payments and exemption of duties. In Paris the examples in the shops continued to multiply; and, moreover, the incessant activity of the Germans always responded to the needs of the moment. . . .

"In a few years Germany had completely ruined our doll-industry. Several houses (Rabery, Bru, Pintel and Eden-Bébé) gave up the struggle and about 1900 became absorbed in the Bébé Jumeau, the one house that manufactured entire dolls. All the other houses had bought porcelain heads and glass eyes from Germany. After 1900 Fleischmann & Bloedel, Gutmann & Schiffnie, and Margarete Steiff continued, and with great energy, their pacific conquest. At Sonneberg, the great center for the manufacture of dolls, a number of houses concerned themselves especially with exports to France under the protection of

(187) Kathe Kruse doll, 1912, German. (188) Margaret Steiff felt clown doll, 1908. (189) Italian Lenci doll, 1921. (190) Bambolo Regina, an Italian felt doll of the 1930's. (191) English rag "baby" with painted hair; artist, Norah Wellings. Modern. (192) Typical Norah Wellings doll. (193) Two English cloth dolls.

the Imperial Government and the Chamber of Commerce. Nuremberg, Eisfeld, Georgenthal, Ilemenau, Neustadt and Walterhausen also sent dolls across the frontiers by the thousands.

"The factories beyond the Rhine produced very finished dolls. Thanks to their perfected material, the regularity of the manufacture was such that no other country could show any equivalents. At the beginning of the war the situation had become critical.

"Creators now arose. In August, 1914, Mme. la Baronne de Laumont made her first doll. In the following month *l'Association des Petits Fabricants* engaged certain master porcelain-makers to undertake as quickly as possible the manufacture of biscuit heads. Six months later the Maison Damerval et Liffranchy formed its collection. Limoges and Boulogne-sur-Mer followed the example. Soon in a Polish *atelier* the rag-doll appeared.

"Thus out of individual and collective efforts came the movement of which we are now speaking.

"The first rag-doll was created by Mme. Lazarski in December, 1914. Like the others made by Mme. Lazarski the year before in her native country this doll wore a Polish costume. Mme. Lazarski visualized a rational simplification in feature and form, partaking of that childish intelligence which is struck first of all by the elemental aspect of things. In the same *atelier* Mlle. Fiszerowna showed her originality in applying to the face of her first creation some rings of pink or blue stuff to give colour to the cheeks and clarity to the eye.

"To fix the date of their history it should be noted that these Polish dolls were exhibited for the first time at *la Vie Féminine* in May, 1915, when they were neighbors with the dolls of Mme. de Laumont.

"The dolls of Mme. Lazarski and Mlle. Fiszerowna were the vanguard of a multitude of rag-dolls, a brilliantly coloured medley by other hands, which were made known in the recent expositions of Decorative Art. It was after the one organized by M. Metman (May-June, 1916) that the rag-doll was propagated. While in some workshops the Polish doll persisted, in others it died out and dolls of true French character began to appear. It owed nothing to the current exotic dolls. In fact every *atelier* expressed its own particular style and details varied infinitely. The body, the hair and the method of assembling the parts led to notable differences. Imitations were rare; original models were many. The form of the hands and feet were similar in a general sense; but in some cases they were elongated and in other cases they were contracted. As for the 'hair,' we saw all kinds of material: tow, cotton, wool, fur and silk. Sometimes this hair was sewn on, sometimes it was quilted and sometimes it was embroidered.

"Certain types were à la mode. The yellow and black races, which were easily represented without contempt, enjoyed particular favour. At 14 *concours Lépine* you could buy a Japanese for 16 *francs* and a Negro for 10 *francs*, which was not dear. Perhaps one would prefer to the dolls by Mme. Daffonds the little Negro by Mme. Alexandrowicz, which was very well done and had the advantage of being a mascot.

"We must make two distinct groups of the rag-doll; the first with the face made by sewing; and the one without the sewing. Each doll without a sewn face has a nose and those with a sewn face have no nose. Question of material? Doubtless; and the reason is also because of the cut and of the model.

"Finally in the result obtained the will of the artist asserts itself as the preponderating fact. Nevertheless, the numerous and difficult materials worked with account for many of the suppressions. Certain dolls have no necks. That is because the work was easier without necks. Others have two pink dots in the place of a nose. This is sufficient for the drawing, so to speak, and we must be contented. Moreover, and in the interest of simplification which always guides the creators, the body and limbs become rigorously linear and often hard because so solidly stuffed. It is curious to note in this connection that the old wooden doll of our grandmothers with its excessive rigidity and rudimentary articulations is much copied today. The costumes, however, take us away from all likeness to those archaic models and bring us back quickly into the present time.

"Mlle. Swiecka has brought to her task the charm of a great tenderness. We regret she forsook her first manner to produce those Zobeides and Haroun-al-Raschids. Mme. Alexandrowicz, who before the World War possessed the very rare gift of amusing children, has made some dolls with the most stupid expression; and, oh, my goodness! the world was astonished that it liked them!

"With regard to colour and general effect the dolls by Mlle. Desaubliaux are very French. We must congratulate her. The model of the Bébé Gallia is due to Mme. Roig, who has treated the childish features with amenity. Mme. d'Eichthal has given to the Bébé Yves and to the doll Cita exact proportions and, something that does not spoil it in the least, the colours of health. The 'cabriolet hat' of the little Cita recalls the illustrations of Little Ann expressing that flowing and pure style of Kate Greenaway, whose influence lives with us today.

"Mme. Manson is inspired first of all by the fairy tales of Perrault and Mme. d'Aulnoy. Then she has made a Sophie and a Cadet Roussel, which have been unreservedly praised by artists. Now she has given us a belligerent *Marlborough s'en va t'en guerre*. These creations, most happy in their power to amuse children, will give them other ideas. The Gavroche and the Charlot of Mme. Vera Ouvré lead to more modern types: they are very personal and very popular. The wide-awake and awkward children of Mlle. Verita, made in such great numbers, are scattered throughout the world: tottering babies, overgrown girls and blustering boys amuse many children in many well-appointed nurseries. As for the dolls of Mlle. Duvall, they please because of their smiling expression so rarely found among rag-dolls. With her lovely dress, her childish chin and her pretty cheeks Clarabel made many converts.

"In the Théâtre Italien of M. Bricon there is a Polichinelle; and it is a pleasure to see a Punch, whose ancestors have been so numerous and so humble, attired in superb and sparkling clothes. Also I admire the ease with which the clowns of Mme. Dhomont fall into all kinds of attitudes.

"Among the rag-dolls we must also note the Bretonnes of *La Francia*. The natural and artless faces of Mlle. Lloyd are extremely sweet. Parmentier and his sister by Mlle. Rozmann are so real that they awaken the sentiment of protection which little children always draw forth.

"The wooden doll is related to the rag-doll because its body is so often stuffed with flock. Among this kind are the Gilles and Marion of M. Georges Lepape; but the Mimi by Mme. Alexandrowicz is made entirely of wood.

"Mme. de Laumont's peasant dolls represent France and her dolls dressed in historical and modern costumes are valuable. For twenty years Mlle. Koenig has been making dolls of this kind, but they were destined for museums. Mme. de Laumont's dolls, on the other hand, have carried into many countries our national costumes, which tend more and more to disappear.

"Mme. Pierre Goujon renovates the costumes of old dolls, replacing the old silks and satins with simpler materials. Mme. Berthe Noufflard, Mlles. Lloyd and Duvall of *L'Adelphie* are also engaged in the transformation of dolls' wardrobes. The dolls of *La Francia* are very charming on account of their elegance and general aloofness."

The Polish dolls of 1915, originated by Jedrek, a sculptor, and Michele, an artist who painted the faces, were sponsored by Madame Paderewski. A great many came to New York to be sold through the National American Committee of the Polish Victims' Relief Fund, and it is not unusual to find some of these dolls in antique shops. They represented every section of Poland, children and adults, bride and groom, etc. Jan and Hanska, the "Waifs of Cracow," were the most popular. A medal accompanying each doll reads, on one side: "Health and happiness to you, kind doll lover who by taking into your heart and home one of my little doll waifs of Poland have fed a starving mother or child in that saddest land. (signed) Helena Paderewski. Copyright 1915." On the reverse side of the medal is engraved the symbol of a spread eagle with the words "Polish Victims Relief Fund."

Foreign cloth dolls in native costumes made especially for collectors and distributed through such places as Elsie Clark Krug's establishment in Baltimore, Md., and Kimport, Independence, Mo., are a convenient size (about 9 inches) to place on display shelves. They are made with skill and care, but of course, are not play dolls—merely statuettes in cloth.

Colorful cloth dolls seem to be the favorite with the child up to the age of about six years. Experiments with a healthy, normal five-months-old infant, housed with hundreds of rare and beautiful old and modern dolls, clearly demonstrated her preference above all others for an attractively made rag doll. The most gorgeously dressed and lovely "lady" French bisque met with only mild approval.

## The Cloth Doll

Centuries come and go, man makes progress, but a child is always a child; so it is that rag dolls, as old as woven cloth, as new as today, will continue to be made as long as a little child loves to cradle in her arms a beloved "baby."

(194) Russian cloth doll—Ukrainian woman. (195) Russian "child" in cloth. (196) Russian "village boy." (197) Greek felt doll—Sophocles of Skyros. (198) French felt doll. (199) Polish Victims Relief Fund doll of 1915. (note medal.)

*Chapter 11*

# WOODEN DOLLS

THERE is something fascinating about a carved wooden doll, whether fashioned by the hand of an artist for the pride of a princess, or a peasant in the field for his humble little daughter. The feeling for wood is understandable; for countless centuries we have depended upon it for shelter, protection from the cold of winter and the heat of summer, and for thousands of things which advancing civilization has demanded. Our very existence has depended upon it.

The art of carving the human figure from the limb of a tree was practised by our primitive ancestor worshippers. The early stages of this cult traces back to prehistoric times. Later, kings and queens had their portraits carved from wood. It always has been used for the play doll, even up to the present era, and when beautiful wax, papier-mâché and china dolls came into their own, wood still was used for parts of the doll's make-up.

Wooden dolls were among the first to be manufactured in quantity. Early ones were hand-carved, then painted. Egyptian graves of the sixth and seventh centuries A. D., yield wooden dolls, and evidences of toy factories, including toys of this substance, have been unearthed from the dry soil of Egypt, where civilization came early. These ancient dolls and toys find their way into museums, but seldom into the collector's hands.

We can get an idea of the first wooden doll to be brought to this country from a detail of an old engraving in the Library of Congress. (See sketch.) Only the back of the doll is pictured, but from it we know the general style of the figure, which has the Elizabethan costume of the period. Settlers who came to this country with the Sir Walter Raleigh Expedition (1607) commanded by Captain John Smith, brought such dolls for native children. In the Imogene Anderson collection at Greenwich, Conn., is a wooden doll said to have been brought over by William Penn in 1699. The latter is known as a *Queen Anne*. It has a stiff, angular body with an egg-shaped head, sometimes overlaid with plaster, and comes with either painted or glass eyes inset. Hands are often of bamboo, with ugly fork-like fingers. The figures are by no means attractive, but because of their age and rarity, bring high prices.

## WOODEN DOLLS

(200) "Lady Raleigh," back view of first known European doll to arrive in America. Detail from rare print. (201) "Miss Knot," an early 19th century wooden peg-jointed doll. (202) "Vickie," wooden doll purchased in England in 1935. (203) "Heil," wooden doll from Europe, 1925. (204) "Miss Old," a wooden doll of uncertain age. (205) East Indian wooden play doll of 1874. (206) Modern wooden peg-jointed doll from Switzerland.

In 1413 there were craftsmen in Nuremberg who made the carving of wooden dolls their principal business, and old woodcuts show these doll makers at their work. By the seventeenth century toy factories in Europe were thriving, but in the next century, because of guild restrictions, they could not be produced in the enormous mass quantity reached in the nineteenth century. The guild divided workers into groups, and no trade was allowed to infringe upon another. Wood-carvers must stick to carving wood, joiners to their trade, tinsmiths to theirs, etc. Early in the nineteenth century, these restrictions were lifted, and the trade in dolls flourished as never before, for now complete dolls came from one factory. However, long before the nineteenth century, hand-carved dolls were produced in surprising quantity in the richly wooded sections of Germany. Peasants worked during the long winter months, then brought their wares to big cities to be distributed by agents over the whole world. Nuremberg was a great toy center. At first the wood-carvers peddled their toys in the country surrounding their homes, and guilds did not interfere so long as the making of toys was only a side line, but demand for them increased to such an extent that their manufacture became a main business. Then the guilds stepped in and the work was divided. By the middle of the eighteenth century, the painting of the wood or "tubbing" of the toys was done largely in Oberammergau, another great center for the toy industry. The earlier carvers of Sonneberg stained toys with blackberry juice before the so-called bismuth coloring process was discovered.

Despite trade restrictions, the wooden toy industry alone brought as much as 150,000 gulden in a single year; in 1729, six hundred tons of toys were exported. Sonneberg agents reached the whole of Europe. During the nineteenth century, with wholesale manufacture at top speed, the wealth of the toy industry was immense. After 1900, export duties decreased profits.

As with the china and bisque-headed doll, Germany remained tops in the production of wooden toys up to the Second World War. The Dutch, with their "Flanders' babies," wooden dolls exported in large numbers to England, have made a great many dolls, but often dolls in museums and in private collections supposed to be made in other European countries have proven on closer examination to be of German origin.

Wood was used, at least in part, in the making of all kinds of dolls, trick dolls, musical dolls, etc. Thousands of them with bisque or wax or papier mâché heads had arms and legs and sometimes whole bodies of wood. Even the ball-jointed type were at first made with wooden bodies, and as late as the beginning of the Second World War, one of the child Jumeau dolls has ball-jointed limbs of wood. There is hardly a more interesting material to use. Wood can be polished to a smoothness resembling bisque, and, in the hands of an artist, may become a thing of beauty which will last indefinitely. See sketch of a hand-made wooden doll by Claire Fawcett in the chapter on *Hand-Made Dolls*. Those fashioned on a lathe never are as attractive. The nearest approach perhaps, is the twentieth-century Schoenhut, but these, especially the later ones, have typical doll faces, and at a short distance away, often are mistaken for average bisque-headed jointed dolls.

Most collectors are familiar with the Peggity doll-house wooden peg-jointed doll originated in 1935 by Marion I. Perkins of Providence, Rhode Island, from an old doll found in an attic. It is well worth the price formerly asked for it—$2.

(207) Chinese doll with wooden head and hands purchased in 1930. (208) Wooden dolls from the collection of Queen Victoria. (209) a. Joel Ellis wooden doll of 1873. b. George W. Sanders wooden doll of 1880. (210) Harry E. Schoenhut all-wooden doll of 1912.

Caution should be used in buying the wooden peg-jointed doll familiar in Victoria's time, but of modern manufacture. Collectors, mistaking the newer ones for the early, have sometimes paid big prices without justification. As recently as 1935, the old-style doll marked Vickie in the illustration, sold in a tiny shop on Oxford St., London, for two shillings and sixpence. Heil, another old-style, was purchased in Europe about 1925. Miss Old is what her name implies, but only an expert in dating wood could tell her exact age. Before the nineteenth century, dolls usually were not made with ball joints, if we except the artist's lay figure. Miss Knott (see illustration) represents the typical early peg-jointed doll. These peg joints do not belong only to the past.

Notice the East Indian wooden play doll of 1874. This was typical of its time in that country. Now the tourist trade has demanded all types of dolls from India, dressed in native costume. Most of the dolls imported from that country just before the Second World War were of cloth. Kimport has this to say of them: "From India, flamboyant in our imagination with the wealth of the Rajahs and mystery of the soothsayers come humble figures that portray life there as it really is. The lowly sweeper, or 'Mathier,' is the poorest of all, the yogi in prescribed habit of henaed yellow must beg his sustenance. Castes range from beggared 'untouchables' to bejeweled Brahmins. Indian dolls are more toy-like than most native costume dolls, perhaps because the makers, girls in a widows' home school, are little more than children themselves Soft and lovable, the dolls are of warm brown cloth, firmly stuffed into plump figures. Features are rather sketchily embroidered but the impression of India and her peoples is correct." The dolls, including a Chaprassee (British government aid), a village girl bearing two children in her arms (tiny dolls), an Orderly, Bombay lady, Sweeper, and a Mother, sell for about $4 apiece. These cloth dolls are secondary collector's items. The brightly colored wooden play doll of India is more representative of its kind.

Modern wooden dolls from Switzerland (see sketch), Ceylon, China, and from British South Africa are well made, but the primitives we carve in the Ozarks and the mountains of Tennessee are for the most part second-rate.

During the early years of the nineteenth century the wooden peg-jointed doll was a pet plaything. It was inexpensive, could sit and bend, and the small ones fitted admirably into doll houses. Princess Victoria of England owned 132 small ones, which she and her governess took delight in dressing. A book about them, published in 1894 by Frances H. Low "with the gracious permission and approval of Her Majesty the Queen" is beautifully illustrated in color by Alan Wright.

Nearer our own time is the Joel Ellis (Springfield, Vt.) jointed wooden doll patented in 1873. Heads were of hard wood steamed and pressed into shape, the bodies turned on a lathe, joints of the slot and tendon variety. The latter were not over-strong, and a year later, Ellis gave up manufacturing dolls. In the meantime, F. D. Martin, also of Springfield, produced a similar doll but with more durable ball joints. His patent was granted in 1879. A year later, George W. Sanders of the same city obtained a patent for a similar type of doll with "a new and improved shoulder, elbow and knee joint." A typical Sanders doll has the common hairdress of the late German china-headed doll, whereas the Ellis doll has the earlier popular ringlet style.

In 1881, Henry H. Mason and Luke W. Taylor brought out another doll of the same general style, but with still further improvements in the matter of joining. The revolving head was of composition.

Another doll first patented in 1879, followed by improved patent joints in 1880 and again in 1882, was manufactured by C. C. Johnson. The head was of composition over a wooden base, and the neck longer than the other wooden dolls of the decade. Another distinguishing mark is a black waist band with patent dates printed thereon.

During this nine-year period of wooden doll manufacture in Vermont, "baby" as well as "child" dolls were made. Some of the "babies" had composition hands, but most of the "child" dolls had pewter or wooden hands, and pewter feet.

While the Vermont dolls were being made, another toy manufacturer, a German by the name of Albert Schoenhut, had set up a toy factory (1872) in Philadelphia, Pa., which was destined to specialize in the making of wooden dolls in the early years of the nineteenth century. The dolls were introduced about 1911 and sold for $5 to $25 at that time. A 1912 copyright reads "Schoenhut all wood perfection art doll."

Heads were at first sculptured by Italian artists, later by Albert's fifth son, Harry E. Schoenhut, who had studied under Charles Grafley. Dolls made after the patent was granted are easily told by the patent mark as well as by their steel spring hinges. The earlier ones usually have modelled hair of self material, the later ones natural hair. Schoenhut dolls represent the infant, the baby and the child; some are jointed only at neck, shoulder and hip, others are fully jointed. There are walking dolls, and those with sleeping eyes of wood. Sizes vary from eleven to twenty-one inches. Among the most interesting are those made to accompany a wooden circus. The Schoenhut family were all toy makers, specializing at first in toy pianos, later in dolls. Foreign competition after World War I ended manufacture of these famous wooden dolls.

A wooden doll which in all probability always will be available is the artist's lay figure, beautifully proportioned and capable of being placed in any desired position. This has been with us through the centuries from the Middle Ages to the present time, and it was evidently this figure which served as a model for various improvements in doll joints. "There is nothing new under the sun." But we must give credit to those who had the foresight to apply the principle of the lay figure to the manufacture of dolls.

Independent artists find pleasure in carving dolls from wood, but their manufacture in large quantities is not a simple matter. We probably always will have doll parts made of wood, although it remains to be seen what the new plastic materials in doll manufacture will bring in years to come.

*Chapter 12*

# THE WAX DOLL

AMONG the oldest dolls available are those made of wax. Records show that they were made in commercial quantity from the 16th to the 20th centuries. Christoph Weigel, writing in 1698, speaks of the manufacture of wax dolls in Germany, and we know that the early Greeks gave their children dolls of wax to play with. In the 17th century Paris was making wax fashion dolls. European museums abound in examples dating back more than two hundred years, a considerable time, because wax is frail and not many in comparison with the number manufactured have survived. Our present-day wax pieces are more durable than the older ones, and even these are subject to deterioration due to climate and lack of knowledge as to their care.

The Encyclopaedia Britannica has this to say on the subject of wax: "The facilities which wax offers for modelling have been taken advantage of from the remotest times. Figures in wax of their deities were used in the funeral rites of the ancient Egyptians, and deposited among their offerings in their graves; many of these are now preserved in museums. That the Egyptians also modelled fruits can be learned from numerous allusions in early literature. Among the Greeks during their best art period, *wax figures were largely used as dolls for children;* statuettes of deities were modelled for votive offerings and for religious ceremonies, and wax images to which magical properties were attributed were treasured by the people. Wax figures and models held a still more important place among the ancient Romans. The masks (effigies or images) of ancestors, modelled in wax, were preserved by patrician families, this *jus imaginum* being one of the privileges of the nobles, and these masks were exposed to view on ceremonial occasions, and carried in their funeral processions. The closing days of the Saturnalia were known as *Sigillaria*, on account of the custom of making, toward the end of the festival, presents of wax models of fruits and waxen statuettes which were fashioned by the *Sigillarii* or manufacturers of small figures in wax and other media. The practice of wax modelling can be traced through the middle ages, when votive offerings of wax figures were made to churches, and the memory and lineaments of monarchs and great personages were preserved by means of wax masks as in the days of the Roman patricians.

"In these ages malice and superstition found expression in the formation of wax images of hated persons, into the bodies of which long pins were thrust, in the confident expectation that thereby deadly injury would be induced to the person represented; and this belief and practice continued until the 17th century. Indeed the superstition still survives in the Highlands of Scotland, where as recently as 1885 a clay model of an enemy was found in a stream, having been placed there in the belief that, as the clay was washed away, so would the health of the hated one decline.

"With the renaissance of art in Italy, modelling in wax took a position of high importance, and it was practised by some of the greatest of the early masters. The bronze medallions of Pisano and the other famous medalists owe their value to the art qualities of wax models from which they were cast by the *cire perdue* process; and indeed all early bronzes and metal work were cast from wax models. The *tete de cire* in the Wicar collection at Lille is one of the most lovely examples of artistic work in this medium in existence. Wicar, one of Napoleon's commissaries, brought this figure from Italy. It represents the head and shoulders of a young girl. It has been claimed as a work of Greek or Roman art, and has been assigned to Leonardo da Vinci and to Raphael, but all that can be said is that it probably dates from the Italian Renaissance. In 1909 Dr. Bode, the director of the Kaiser Freidrich Museum at Berlin, purchased in England, for (it was stated) £8000, a life-sized half-length female figure in wax, which he attributed to Leonardo da Vinci or his school. The figure was shown to have once been in the possession of Richard Cockle Lucas (1800-1883), a sculptor and worker in ivory, wax, etc. It was claimed that the figure was really Lucas's work and was a reproduction in wax of a picture of "Flora" attributed to Leonardo da Vinci, now in the possession of the Morrison family at Basildon Park, near Pangbourne; this view was repudiated by Dr. Bode, but was generally accepted in England (see *The Times*, Oct.-Dec., 1909; and particularly the *Burlington Magazine*, May, June, August, 1910.) Till toward the close of the 18th century modelling of medallion portraits and relief groups, the latter frequently polychromatic, was in considerable vogue throughout Europe. About the end of the 18th century Flaxman executed in wax many portraits and other relief figures which Josiah Wedgwood translated into pottery for his jasper ware. The modelling of the soft parts of dissections, etc., for teaching illustrations of anatomy was first practised at Florence, and is now very common. Such preparations formed part of a show at Hamburg in 1721, and from that time wax-works, on a plane lower than art, have been popular attractions. These exhibitions consist principally of images of historical or notorious personages, made up of waxen masks on lay figures in which sometimes mechanism is fitted to give motion to the figure. Such an exhibition of *wax-works* with mechanical motions was shown in Germany early in the 18th century, and is described by Steele in the *Tatler*. The most famous modern wax-work exhibition is that of Madame Tussaud in London."

John Flaxman's work in sculpture and bas-relief is found throughout all England. His "Apollo and Marpessa," bas-relief, in the Royal Academy of Arts, is one of the most beautiful things of its kind ever made.

Few of us can hope to obtain famous examples of wax dolls, but those made in the 19th century in commercial quantity are possible to find. Topping the list of such is the Montanari, made of poured wax with hair embedded into the scalp, first exhibited in 1849. Although not produced in great quantity, for the dolls were difficult and expensive to make, we still have some fine examples, despite their frailty and the care which must be exercised to keep them in condition.

Some collectors have fine examples of hand-made wax dolls brought from Europe and from Mexico, and a few found in our own United States. Commercially made wax dolls of course cannot compare with those fashioned by artists.

One of the most unusual of the early wax dolls still in existence was evidently made from the same mold as the papier-mâché head with the peculiar hairdo ultra fashionable in the early 1830's—curls bunched at either side of the head, and draped over a high comb on top. The body is the same as the papier-mâché-headed model.

It is easier to tell the age of a wax doll when shoes are painted on, for those made before 1860 have flat soles. It is not easy to tell the age by the condition of the wax, for a doll packed carefully for generations and not exposed to light or to great variations in temperature, will be a lot more new looking than one not so protected.

By far the greater number of old wax dolls have been found in such deplorable condition that it is best to have them re-waxed. It is not too difficult a task for the amateur. (See chapter on Reconstructing the Old Doll.)

One type of rare wax doll is that with the hat or bonnet molded on, popular in the 1860's. In the next decade, another wax doll had roll curls modelled onto the front part of the head immediately above the forehead, much like a modern style. The arms and legs of the latter (in the Clara Fawcett collection) are of cheap composition, the legs terminating in heeled boots.

Many "pompadour" dolls of the 1850's made of wax over papier mâché, with wooden arms and legs, flat-soled shoes, are still extant. The example sketched is from the collection of Mrs. William Garrison. Most dolls of the type had straw-filled cloth bodies supplied with squeakers.

Geraldine (see sketch) is a typical wax doll of the next two decades—1860-1880. The complete figure is sketched in order to show her original costume. Although the dress looks quite "grown-up" to our modern eyes, it was a style for young girls in those days. Note length; an adult in 1870 would be considered indecent in such a short skirt. Geraldine has sleeping glass eyes of blue and natural blonde hair. The head is wax over papier mâché composition; arms and legs of composition; heeled boots.

# THE WAX DOLL

(211, 212) Wax "hatted" dolls, circa 1860. Courtesy Mrs. Garrison. (213) Wax-headed peddler doll of the 19th century. (214, 215) Two-faced wax dolls. (216) D. Checkeni's four-faced wax doll head, 1866. (217) Mme. Montanari wax doll head with hair strands imbedded in wax. (218) Wax over papier-mâché, wooden arms and legs, circa 1850's. Courtesy Mrs. Garrison. (219) Wax over papier-mâché composition. Limbs of same material. Late 1860's. (220) "Geraldine," typical wax-over-papier-mâché of the 1870's-1880's. (221) Wax Civil War benefit doll. Red Cross Museum, Washington, D. C.

A wax "benefit" doll exhibited in New York City at a Sanitary Fair during the Civil War to raise funds for the wounded, was given the Red Cross Museum in Washington, D. C., twenty-eight years ago by the erstwhile little girl who won it—Mrs. Horace Chittenden. It has the complete original wardrobe (made by young society women of the day), dresses, bonnets, etc., and all sorts of accessories—jewels, furs, calling cards, etc., furnished by leading merchants of the time.

Many of the early dolls were of wax poured into a mold, forming a shell like the bisque and china heads. These were so fragile that it was thought better to make them over a base. Metal, as well as papier mâché and composition was used for this purpose A study of the base of the wax doll head will give a clue as to its age. The earliest is usually of poured wax, the next earliest has a metal or papier mâché base (more often the latter), and the latest is wax over composition. There are exceptions to the rule. Individual artists use their own preferred methods.

One way to tell a poured wax doll is to hold it up to the light. Light is seen through unless the shell is very thick or the head is solid. If lips and cheeks are painted *over* the wax, it is likely to be either of poured or solid wax, for the head of wax over papier-mâché or composition is painted before the wax is applied. This permits a more life-like appearance. Fine, early wax dolls are well proportioned. One with wax feet has toes curling under in a most natural way. Thousands of cheap ones flooded the market in the late nineteenth century, and on into the twentieth, such dolls as are described in the chapter *On Collecting Dolls*.

A discussion of wax figures hardly would be adequate without reference to Madame Tussaud's famous wax works. As Marie Gresholtz (afterwards Madame Tussaud), a promising pupil under the tutelage of her uncle, John Christopher Curtius, she was soon able to take her place at the top of the profession, which, by the way, was a thriving one in the eighteenth century, patronized by royalty. Nine years of Mademoiselle Gresholtz's life was spent in giving lessons to the ladies of the French Court. Uncle Curtius had two places in Paris, one in the Palais Royal, where he exhibited portraits of illustrious personages, another on the Boulevard du Temple, filled with portraits of criminals.

Little did they dream of the agonies of mind and spirit that this gift of modelling would bring them, or, on the other hand, the pleasure that it would bring for generations yet to come. Uncle and niece were caught in the bloody revolution of 1789. In July of that year they were faced with an angry mob demanding effigies of their heroes to carry in triumph through the streets of Paris. This was only the beginning. When the Reign of Terror started, Mademoiselle Gresholtz was forced to model from the dead faces of her old friends. When the mangled head of a dear friend, Princesse de Lamball, was brought before her, it was almost more than she could bear. She begged and pleaded in vain, and finally was forced to comply, the tears dimming her eyes as she worked at the grievous, torturous task. Then came the heads of Corday, Marat, Robespierre and others from which she was obliged to model. Finally, she herself was thrown into prison and knew not from day to day whether the next would be her last. (She lived to be ninety.) It was in prison that she met Josephine de Beauharnais, who became Napoleon's Empress. Afterward, when peace was restored, Josephine asked Marie, who was then Madam Tussaud, to make a likeness of the Emperor. But Madame Tussaud had experienced enough on French soil; from thenceforward, England was to become her home. In 1802 she packed up effigies and molds which she had inherited from her uncle, and had exhibitions in almost every large town in the United Kingdom. In 1833 her permanent Exhibition was established in London. In 1925, fire destroyed nearly all but "the Chamber of Horrors" which was in the relatively secure basement, but the molds were saved, and from it, like the phoenix, arose from the ashes a new Madame Tussaud's Exhibition, the history of a people in wax, more popular than ever before.

The famous Wax Works might have had something to do with the immense popularity of the wax doll in England. Certainly England's wax dolls were known all over the world for their beauty and worth.

Many collectors specialize in the wax doll. Care should be used in selecting such a doll if one is putting real money into it, for a great many cheap ones were put on the market in the late nineteenth and early twentieth centuries. Examine the body as well as the wax parts. The best are well made. It should be remembered that not all dolls with hair embedded into the wax are Montanaris, for that method was used for many years after its introduction by other manufacturers. In fact, the idea is still used for modern dolls. As explained in the chapter on Composition Dolls, hair is embedded into the head of the Monica, a modern doll.

Top prices are paid for the rare ones of poured wax, but there are many wax dolls made over a papier mâché or composition base which are beautiful and well proportioned and worthy a place in any collection.

The era of the wax doll for the child is over, but for the collector it has scarcely begun. We have learned to make wax that is more enduring than of old; artists are re-discovering the possibilities of the substance, and in years to come collectors undoubtedly will have undreamed of treasures in wax.

*Chapter 13*

# METAL DOLLS

METAL-HEADED dolls most familiar to collectors are the Juno and Minerva heads illustrated. They were first made in Germany about fifty years ago, and attached to cloth or kid sawdust-stuffed bodies, with eyes inset or painted and either natural or modelled and painted hair. Heads of metal other than the two mentioned were quite diversified. At the time fancies in Parian were delighting children and grown-ups alike, the metal head with fancy hairdo made its appearance. It was never as popular with the fine trade as the bisque, for enamel peels off metal fairly easily, with unbeautiful results.

Precious metals, gold and silver, were used centuries ago for wealthy European families, and occasionally one finds a really old "charm" doll of precious metal. The tiny doll illustrated of gold and white metal (1⅛th inches long, came from an antique store in Paris. Although so tiny, it is perfectly jointed at elbows, hips and knees.

The most interesting modern doll with an all-metal body is the Swiss doll illustrated. The metal joints come apart and are brought together by suction. It is of adult proportion, and the series represent a fireman, policeman, clown, etc. Head, hands and feet are of composition. The dolls sold in this country about six years ago for a few dollars apiece. They could be used as artist's lay figures, but were sold as toys.

About the middle of the nineteenth century, metal was used under wax. Two such dolls, belonging to Mrs. Franklin Hill Davis, are illustrated here. The one with teeth inserted is far less attractive than the smaller doll, but the wax is in a better state of preservation. The little one is full of yellow spots, possibly caused by climatic conditions and its contact with the metal. The bodies of both dolls are sawdust-stuffed and equipped with jointed wooden arms and hands. The smaller one has flat-soled wooden shoes painted on; the other has lost both legs in the struggle to exist, but still retains the front and back portions of its wooden squeaker.

How early metal was used for the toy doll is not recorded, but we know that the tin soldier made its debut in Europe in the Middle Ages. Those we find today were probably not made before the 1850's, if we except the antique "charm" dolls.

## METAL DOLLS

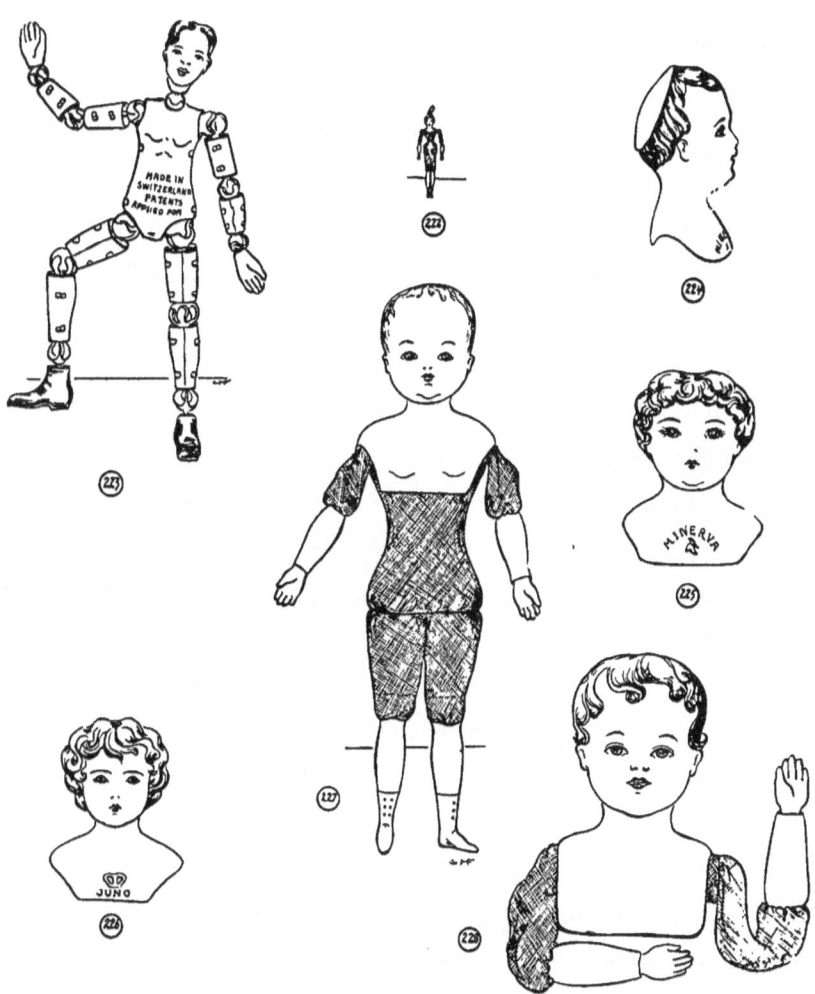

(222) 1⅛" charm doll of white and gold metal, perfectly jointed. (223) Swiss metal ball-jointed doll. (224) Minerva metal head meant to have natural wig. (225) Typical Minerva metal head. (These come with either glass or painted eyes.) (226) Typical Juno metal head with hair of self material. (Juno and Minerva metal heads were first used about 1894.) (227, 228) Metal-headed dolls circa 1850. (Wax has been poured over the metal.) Wooden arms and legs, cloth body. Courtesy Mrs. Davis.

Until recently, tin or like metal has been used to strengthen parts in a doll's make-up. For instance, the lovely Kathe Kruse baby doll is reinforced with metal under the cloth to preserve intact the features, and the large Bru, French kid-bodied doll, has metal at the elbow joint for added strength. While metal has never been as popular for the complete doll as other substances, all varieties have been made, from the bow-legged "baby" to the sedate "lady" doll. The beauty of the metal figure depends upon proportions, style and coloring, as is the case with any other doll. Most of the late common tin-heads are secondary collector's items, but interesting as part of the record of doll history.

*Chapter 14*

# LEATHER DOLLS

LEATHER in its various forms—rawhide, tanned leather, kid— is a material used for dolls both in this country and abroad. Although kid was utilized for doll bodies well over a hundred years ago, it was not until 1865, in this country, that patented heads were made of it. In that year, Lucretia E. Sallee of Decatur, Ill., obtained a patent for a doll head of pressed leather reinforced (inside) with plaster.

The following year, 1866, Frank E. Darrow of Bristol, Conn., manufactured dolls' heads of rawhide. The process described in patent papers issued to him is as follows: "The rawhide is first cured in the usual way. It is then cut into blanks of suitable size for the purpose desired. Then take a box of concentrated lye, (about one pound, usually found in stores for sale), put it into about two gallons of water, then place said blanks in a suitable apparatus into which steam made from said composition or liquid may enter, and thereby saturate or steam said blanks, when they may be taken therefrom, one at a time, and introduced to the die and press, and pressed into the desired form or shape. There may be other liquids by means of which this effect may be produced.

"The particular object of saturating or steaming is to produce an elastic or flexible state of the rawhide during only the time occupied in pressing it into its mold or die.

"I have found by the use of alcohol the same result may be produced; but it will be seen that it is too expensive. I therefore believe that the process particularly described will be found to be the best and cheapest."

The patent was granted for the process of saturating rawhide for the purpose of making doll heads.

Few Darrow dolls remain, as their manufacture was short-lived. Rodents enjoyed the rawhide, and after repeated damage from these pests, the factory was abandoned in 1877.

Portrait dolls of leather or kid made in the South, with hand-painted features and hair, and representing those who have helped make Southern history, are worth collecting. A label on the doll reads: "This doll is hand-painted

(229-230) Moroccan dolls: Fisherman and Housewife. From the collection of Mrs. Wm. Knobloch.

and copied from an authentic portrait of the subject in New Orleans. It is one of a series of twelve characters who have helped make Southern history." Among the dolls are Audubon (a good likeness), Baroness Pontalba and Bienville. The labor and material represented in the doll would today bring about $8, yet it sold a few years ago for as little as $2.75. The face is flat, and not as good-looking as one steamed and pressed into a mold might be, but it is ingenious and well made, and of historic value.

The finest leather dolls still on the American market (in diminishing quantity) seem to be those from Morocco. One (see sketch) is a baby doll with rather a mature expression and beautiful hand-painted features. The head has either been steamed and pressed into shape, or modelled over a plastic base, for the result is as perfect as any of bisque or china. The doll was purchased through Kimport, Independence, Mo., for only $5. An explanatory leaflet (a feature with Kimport dolls) reads: "A Moroccan Baby. Not so many years ago Morocco was the haunt of pirates and the hideout of desert chieftains, but today under French rule, it is as safe for tourists as their own home. At least, almost as safe!

"Little Ameera will have no doll of her own to play with other than some crude makeshift, for the Mohammedans believe that if you make a human image you must provide a soul for it. Her education will consist mainly in learning the Koran; and in that she will be taught that man is her master, and she will believe it right. When she is older, like Moslem women the world over, Ameera may go unveiled only in the privacy of the women's quarters;

(231) Leather Baby Doll from Morocco.

whenever she goes out, she must be shrouded in a thick impenetrable cloak or 'bhurka.'

"Though fierce riots sometimes break out between the Mohammedans and other religious sects, still the centuries of being neighbors has given them a superficial friendliness.

"This doll was made in one of the great leather bazaars of Tangiers. Morocco—a thriving metropolis on the African coast."

Collectors who want only small dolls will be interested in other Moroccan figures from the same establishment. The nine-inch fisherman and housewife, sketched from the collection of Mrs. William Knobloch of Washington, D. C., are only a small part of the offerings from Morocco.

Morocco, according to the Century Dictionary, is "a fine leather made from goatskins tanned with sumac, orig. in Morocco; hence, any leather made in imitation of this."

Among other leather dolls of interest in the Kimport "family album" are "Koko" ($7.50) from Alaska, whose face is of home-tanned reindeer hide, and "Becky Blue Cloud," ($3.95) a Winnebago squaw.

Persons interested in giving talks about their dolls will find the descriptive leaflets which come with Kimport dolls especially helpful.

*Chapter 15*

# RUBBER DOLLS

WHILE modern rubber dolls do not usually excite much interest—with the exception of the model or fashion dolls—there are a few (not typical rubber babies) which may be classed as collector's items. The little Dutch girl illustrated, purchased in Amsterdam, Holland, has a sweet, child-like expression, and better coloring than most.

Rubber seems best adapted to represent the baby, but after hard rubber was introduced by Charles Goodyear in 1844, the first ones made were supposed to typify the lady or the half-grown girl. One was a portrait doll of Jenny Lind, the "Swedish nightingale;" another wore her hair in loose ringlets falling over the shoulder; others wore the typical hairdo of the period.

Note sketch of rubber fashion doll modelled by Margit Nilsen, 1941, and Goodyear's rubber-head of 1851. The hair of the Goodyear doll is modelled; the modern one has natural hair.

It was not long after Goodyear's discovery that Europe began the manufacture of hard rubber dolls. One Mlle. Calixto Huret of France made gutta percha bodies to be used with turning porcelain heads, in the 1850's, and some years later, the French manufacturer M. Bru patented a rubber baby doll (1878) and rubber statuettes.

Attempts have been made to insert glass eyes into the rubber. Isaac A. Ronmer of Brooklyn, N. Y., was issued a patent for this in 1927.

Of the three early American rubber doll heads sketched—*a, b* and *c*—the two end ones represent ladies and are marked I. R. C. Co. The center head, a girl, is marked "Goodyear Pat. March 28, 1854-1868." The sketch showing a complete Goodyear doll reads, on the shoulders: "Goodyear Pat. May 6, 1851 —Ext. 1865."

Dolls *d* and *e* are, respectively, the Wesley Miller hollow rubber doll of 1875, which was made to stay bent in any desired position by means of a wire armature, and the Ansil W. Monroe hard rubber head with swivel neck patented the same year. Both of these dolls wore wigs of natural hair.

Typical rubber babies are also sketched. The doll standing, made by the Sun Rubber Co., Barberton, Ohio, of soft yellowish rubber, is not a collector's item, but the unmarked baby in a sitting position, of pink better quality rubber, is attractive enough to be treasured. A metal tube from the mouth ends just under the neck at the back of the head, showing that it was meant to be a "bottle baby." Rubber dolls lend themselves nicely to this idea.

The manufacture of rubber toys began here in 1837 with Benjamin F. Lee of New York City. It is doubtful that any of these early toys remain, for they were of soft rubber. After the now well-known Charles Goodyear patented hard rubber in 1850, the manufacture of dolls began on a large scale, and some of these, patterned after typical china and papier-mâché-headed dolls of

(232) Rubber-headed doll with painted eyes purchased in Holland in 1935. (233) "Jenny Lind" all-rubber doll. (234, 235) Rubber dolls old and new: 234. Goodyear, 1851; 235. Nilsen, 1941. (236) Three Goodyear rubber-headed dolls. (237) The Wesley Miller hollow rubber doll of 1875. (238) The A. W. Monroe hard rubber head of 1875. (239) Typical small rubber "baby." (240) Unmarked rubber doll of good quality.

the time, still exist, as before stated. These old ones are worth restoring. Emma C. Clear of Redondo Beach, California, is an expert along this line.

Europe, America and Japan have each contributed its share in the making of rubber dolls. The all-rubber baby doll makes an excellent plaything for the small child. It can be bounced, bitten and thrown about with impunity. And, best of all, it can be washed. In fact, rubber babies *must* be bathed (and powdered) regularly to keep in condition.

Many dolls have been made from time to time with parts, but not the whole figure, of rubber; some have rubber hands only, others are made with just the body or head of rubber, the rest of the doll of some other material such as composition or cloth.

Just before World War II, a new and altogether delightful rubber-bodied doll called the "magic-skin baby" made its appearance. The hollow body of the doll is filled with specially treated air-blown kapok, and the limbs are so flexible that they can be pinched and wrinkled like a human being. It looks and feels like skin, so much so that its use has been considered for the making of artificial limbs. The head of the doll is of the new plastic material which looks like celluloid. Legs and body are all in one piece, yet the legs can swing naturally.

A few years ago *model* dolls used by department stores to display in miniature, garments for sale, were made of rubber. Now they are made of a more durable composition with rubber content.

Among the most interesting modern rubber dolls are tiny doll-house or "family" dolls. Unadulterated rubber is not the ideal material for collector's dolls because of the care it needs.

*Chapter 16*

# CELLULOID DOLLS

JUST how early celluloid dolls were made is a matter for conjecture; it was probably soon after its successful use for billiard balls in 1869, but there is no patent in America for a doll of this kind until 1881, when M. C. Lefferts & W. B. Carpenter (assigned to the Celluloid Manufacturing Co. of New York City), obtained one. However, reference is made to earlier celluloid dolls made by the same company.

According to Walter Ross, writing for the March, 1945, number of *Mademoiselle*, the first commercial plastics, or celluloid, was invented in 1869 for a billiard ball company who offered a prize of $10,000 to anyone discovering a material which could be substituted for ivory. John Wesley Hyatt, working with collodion (a glue-like substance used to form a coating or film on wounds, photographic plates, etc.) then invented celluloid. A patent for cellulose nitrate had previously been granted to Christian Frederick Schonbein (1846.)

The word *celluloid* is a trade name, derived from cellulose contained in cotton or raw cotton. The cotton is treated to a weak solution of nitric acid, the effect of which is to transform it into a pulp similar to paper pulp. Then, after it has been thoroughly cleansed of the acid, it goes through a partial drying process, mixed with camphor-gum, rolled into sheets, and dried on hot cylinders. It can be softened by steam, but hardens when dry again.

The older celluloid dolls in the sketches are marked alphabetically *a* to *f*— *a*, the first to be patented in this country. Dotted lines indicate method of articulation. Some of our present-day model dolls are similarly jointed.

*b* has all the ear-marks of a doll of the 1880's, but her head was meant to be screwed onto the body after a patent issued to D. Wiener in 1921. All the coloring has gone from her head, and it has reverted to its original shade, ivory. The cap, molded on, shows the Kate Greenaway influence, and there are no marks such as one finds on dolls later than 1890. It may be that this particular doll was patented in Europe, for there is no record of it in the patent office here. And it is entirely possible that no patent for it was granted.

*d* and *e* are also unmarked and have reverted to their original ivory shade.

*c* is one of the earliest of the marked celluloid variety. It came from the factory of Schultz Brothers, Germany, the largest manufacturer of celluloid dolls before World War II.

*f* (early 20th century) shows an advance in celluloid doll making. Glass eyes are inserted, and the head is made to receive a wig. (*h* also has glass eyes, but the hair is molded on.)

*k* marks a still further advance,—sleeping eyes, the head strengthened by a wooden bar to prevent sagging with the weight of the lead attached to wire from the eyes.

Doll-house dolls were also made of celluloid. Notice the tiny one with natural hair.

The French celluloid doll was sketched from one in the little museum of Hillcrest Village, Washington, D. C. The Village was started by Dolly Madison and a friend in the early part of the nineteenth century to care for children of soldiers killed in the War of 1812. It is under the jurisdiction of the District of Columbia. The Museum, founded by Miss Portia M. Oberly a few years ago, has other celluloid dolls, including a dapper diminutive gentleman.

The all-celluloid doll marked *l* was very common in Germany in 1935, and many found their way to this country. It is made in small and medium sizes.

(241) a. Lefferts & Carpenter celluloid doll of 1881. b. Bonneted celluloid doll of the 1880's. (242) Unmarked German celluloid "boy." (243) Unmarked celluloid head, painted eyes. (244) 20th century celluloid head with glass eyes inset. (245) Schultz Bros. German celluloid "baby." This doll resembles a Bye-Lo. (246) Schultz Bros. German celluloid "boy" of 1927. (247) French celluloid doll from the Hillcrest Museum, Washington, D. C. (248) Unmarked all-celluloid doll circa 1890. (249) Celluloid doll with natural hair wig. (250) German celluloid doll head with sleeping glass eyes and teeth inset. (251) a. All-celluloid doll of 1935. b. Doll with celluloid head and hands circa 1930.

America made a number of celluloid dolls during the period of the First World War. One will sometimes find in dolls' hospitals and antique shops, celluloid heads labelled Marks Bros., Boston. They are unexceptional copies of a German model. Ball-jointed bodies came with the large swivel-necked Marks Bros. heads. They are interesting only as part of the record of doll history.

Immediately after World War I, Germany produced vast numbers of ball-jointed, cloth and kid-bodied dolls with celluloid heads, as well as smaller ones made entirely of celluloid. Among the most attractive is the boy's head sketched. A similar one in bisque is dated 1927. These were evidently copied from the earlier model *d*. Eyes were either painted on or of glass inset, or sleeping, with and without lashes. Sometimes teeth, too, are inserted, and both the rotating and the stationery or shoulder heads are used.

Old and unusual celluloid dolls are worth collecting, but for the most part, they are secondary collector's items. The new plastics heads made prior to World War II are the latest derived from cellulose. They look like the old celluloid, and fade in the same way, but are stronger. It would be interesting to know their future history.

Kimport of Independence, Mo., has handled gaily-attired peasant costume dolls with celluloid heads, and good examples of the old type are often picked up in Thrift Shops and Dolls' Hospitals.

*Chapter 17*

# OLD PAPER DOLLS

JUST as in the case of the real doll, unusual paper dolls have been unearthed after a long rest in dusty attics, and are becoming more and more appreciated, both for their beauty and their wealth of information about costumes and customs of the past. Whole villages are sometimes represented, including not only private homes with furnishings, and public buildings, churches, theatres, museums, picture galleries, etc., but trees, flowers, animals, pets and toys the children played with. During the 1880's the House of Hapsburg was pictured in a set of paper dolls consisting of more than sixty sheets. These included not only the Royal Family with their elaborate costumes and accessories, but houses, furniture and towns.

A drawer full of paper dolls with dresses, etc., can give us a century of costumes for which the plastic doll requires a queen's ball room. They wouldn't show the back of the costume you say? Ah, but many of them did just that, for in earlier days it was the custom to paint the back of the doll and dress as well as the front. With the wider edges (except top and bottom) pasted together, they were drawn over the head of the figure. In this way, a complete record of costume and hair style is left to us. What a boon to the playwright as well as to the student of costume! It is too bad that present-day artists who create paper dolls seldom paint the back of the doll's wardrobe.

Museums have recognized the interest and value of the paper doll as an authentic record of past styles, and many have fine collections. Among the sketches here is a paper lady of 1822. This was brought from Paris by Mrs. Benjamin Welles, grandmother of Miss Georgiana A. Sargent, who presented it to the Museum of the City of New York, where the doll stands before a tiny mirror so that the back as well as the front of her charming costume may be seen. At either side are seven dresses and six hats.

Another doll from the same museum is the hand-painted, nine-inch paper ballet dancer of 1830 (also with seven dresses and six hats), painted by the great, great grandmother of the donor, Miss Constance Kilbourn.

We are indebted to Mrs. Jennie Calvert of Washington, D. C., for making possible copies of the boy and girl of the 1850's sketched here. These two dolls are part of a set which is destined to go to the Smithsonian Museum in the near future.

Jenny Lind is another paper doll of about the same period. At the Essex Institute, Salem, Mass., one will find a complete set including ten dresses with separate headgear worn by the singer in her various operatic roles. Notice how the hair of the doll is slicked down so that a separate wig might be added.

(252) Paper doll and costume of 1822. Courtesy Museum of the City of New York. (253) Hand-painted ballet dancer, 1830. Courtesy Museum of the City of New York. (254, 255) Girl and boy paper dolls of the 1850's. Courtesy Mrs. Jenny Calvert, Washington, D. C. (256) "Jenny Lind." Separate wig folds at top and slips over head of doll as shown in inset. (257) Jenny Lind costume. This is folded double at top and slips over head of doll.

A coating of egg-white, applied nearly a hundred years ago, has helped preserve these old treasures.

A few years later (about 1860) appeared another celebrity in paper doll form,—little Mrs. Tom Thumb, copied through the courtesy of Miss Lenore de Grange of the District of Columbia. This is one of a long line of paper dolls issued by McLoughlin Brothers since they started in the publishing business in New York City in 1828. Mrs. Thumb's "thirty-two inches of feminine charm" attracted almost as much attention as her famous husband, the General. As Miss Lavinia Warren she closed her 10 A. M. to 10 P. M. exhibition at Barnum's American Museum because, it was stated, "the little queen of beauty will positively be married to General Tom Thumb on Tuesday, Feb. 10th," etc., etc. Other paper dolls in the set with General and Mrs. Tom Thumb included Commodore Nutt and Minnie Warren, sister to Lavinia, and bridesmaid at her wedding.

Typical McLoughlin Brothers dolls are seen in the accompanying sketches of a girl with flowers in her hand, and Topsy and Eva, the last two issued in tribute to Harriet Beecher Stowe's "Uncle Tom's Cabin," a book as popular in its time as "Gone With The Wind" in our own, and in recognition of which we also have paper dolls.

It was in this period that Raphael Tuck and Sons Company, Ltd., of London, Paris and New York, former "publishers to Her Majesty, the Queen," (Victoria) brought out one of their most interesting series of paper dolls entitled "Six Famous Queens and Martha Washington." Illustrated here is one of the dolls—Queen Isabella of Spain, with three costumes (A, walking; B, court; C, reception gown.) The original set, in full color, from which this was copied, belongs to Miss Lydia Hurd of Belmont, Massachusetts. It was passed down in the family. Inquiry about the "queens" brought the information from Raphael Tuck and Sons Company that none of their paper dolls are now available since the German blitz of a few years back destroyed all the plates.

Throughout the nineteenth century many paper doll firms printed the back of the doll as well as the front as before noted. The gentleman of the 1870's pictured has this characteristic. The original doll is accompanied by a clean-shaven young man, on the back of which is written in a childish hand, "26 years. Charles Allen." Four costumes, one of which is a military uniform, accompany each doll.

A series of paper dolls representing famous actresses and singers of the day, was patented in 1880. Arms and legs were attached by paper fasteners, so that the limbs could be placed in any desired position. These were supposed to be costumed by the purchaser, who generally used crepe paper for the purpose. Some time ago a New York dealer acquired a quantity at auction and resold a number of them to Kimport, where they may be purchased for $2 apiece.

(258) Mrs. Tom Thumb and costume. Courtesy Miss Lenora de Grange, Washington, D. C. (259) Typical McLoughlin Bros. paper doll of the 1860's. (260) Topsy and Eva paper dolls. (261) Queen Isabella of Spain and three costumes, a Raphael Tuck & Sons paper doll of the 1860's. Courtesy Miss Lydia Hurd, Belmont, Mass. Costumes—A, walking; B. Court; C. Reception gown. (262) A gentleman paper doll of the 1870's.

By this time there were so many improvements in paper making machinery that the business increased tremendously. Paper dolls in the nineteenth century reached the height of their production in the 1890's. In 1894, Raphael Tuck and Sons Company again came to the fore in the making of paper dolls. The sample of "Artistic Series III" illustrated does not show the beautiful coloring, but it gives an idea of what the doll looked like. One set represented fairy tale characters—Red Riding Hood, Mother Goose, etc., another the Cinderella story, but most of them were clothed in contemporary fashion.

These Raphael Tuck dolls of 1894 are quite different from those of 1860 or thereabouts. Heads of the later dolls were made separately and pasted onto an elongated neck to allow space under the chin so that the costume, also supplied with a long neck, might slide into place underneath. The set is dainty and colorful.

The custom of printing paper dolls in magazines and newspapers goes back at least as far as the 1850's, at which time Godey's Lady's Book featured both boy and girl dolls. Recently, although a quantity have been sold in booklet form through the five-and-ten-cent stores, not so many as formerly have been issued in magazines and newspapers. During the years 1895-96, the Boston Sunday Herald printed as a supplement one adult costume and hat in color each week with the information that the model figure for the outfit would be sent to subscribers upon receipt of two two-cent stamps. The "model figure" shown here was sketched from the original doll in the Museum of the City of New York. Many of us remember the Letty Lane and Betty Bonnet Series in the *Ladies' Home Journal* of about 1908, and those in *John Martin's Book*.

During the 1890's, "advertising" dolls appeared by the thousands, and are still fairly easy to acquire, for those treasures of childhood which do not require much space are often kept as fond mementos. Some, notably the Barbour's Irish Flax Thread and the New England Mincemeat Company dolls, consisted of head and arms only. The head was pushed through a slot cut at the neckline of the double-folded gown, and the arms slipped around in front of the dress, making a complete doll.

Those advertising Clark's O. N. T. Spool Cotton were complete, both front and back of doll and costume in color. Part of the advertising on the under side of the dress reads: "If the little girl who gets this doll is sent to the store for thread she should ask for Clark's O. N. T. Spool Cotton."

Among other products advertised through the medium of the paper doll were Diamond Dyes, Dennison's Crepe Paper, and the Cordova, Lion and McLaughlin's Coffees. The dolls (an extensive series) advertising McLaughlin's Coffee should not be confused with those of the publishing house *McLoughlin Brothers*, who sold paper dolls independently for over seventy-five years. In each bag of coffee was a doll, with extra costume, and with those figures representing queens, a piece of cardboard furniture with instructions for folding into position. Although women and girls in paper form were by far the most popular, men and boys shared the honor. Included in one set (eight men and eight women in the lot) were two dapper gentlemen, one with "sideboards" and moustache, the other smiling and elegant in a simple moustache engagingly curled up at the ends. Lines on the reverse side of the woman and girl doll indicated where the figure was to be folded in order to sit or stand. (Men were "stander-uppers.") Some of the ladies had separate waists and skirts. The "gentlemen" were equipped with extra coats and pants, which fitted through slots. Most of the sets consisted of sixteen figures.

How far back in the annals of human history the paper doll goes can be judged from the description by Marco Polo of paper funeral images seen by him in China about the year 1280; also by the fact that they were used in ancient purification ceremonies, the doll rubbed on the body of the person wishing to be cleansed of sin, the paper effigy then thrown into the river.

OLD PAPER DOLLS 129

Much later, in Europe, we had the pantin of 1662, an outgrowth of an early Egyptian toy doll which was activated by means of a thread attached to the loose limbs of the figure. The idea achieved the height of its popularity in Paris (1746-1756) when famous artists devoted themselves to its perfection. Women took such delight in the toy that finally it was prohibited by law "because" as the authorities said, "women, under the lively influence of this continual jumping, were in danger of bringing children into the world with twisted limbs like the *pantins*."

Paper figures and paper toys were used in Europe as early as the fifteenth century. But the eighteenth century saw a tremendous increase in toys of

(263) Paper doll and costume from Artistic Series III, Raphael Tuck & Sons, Ltd., 1894. (264) Paper doll of 1894 with yachting costume. Courtesy The Museum of the City of New York. (265, 266) Four paper dolls used for advertising purposes during the 1890's. (267) Four German paper dolls with costumes circa 1900. (268) Swinging-limbed paper doll patented in 1880. (269) An 18th century pantin.

this sort,—paper soldiers, animals, castles, houses, street scenes, the opera, the picture gallery, etc. Then came the peep-show, the first model for which was the Christmas crib, followed shortly by secular subjects. German artists made such elaborate and interesting peep-shows that no public fair or festival was complete without one. It consisted of a box inside of which pictures and cardboard figures cut out in several planes were arranged vertically, one row behind another, so that they formed an attractive and realistic whole. Colored mica or oiled paper covering the opening and properly lighted, produced a beautiful effect as seen through a lens set in front of the box.

Paper dolls to dress and undress, such as we know today, made their appearance in Europe rather late. In the *Journal der Moden* for 1791 they were advertised for the first time:—"A new and very pretty invention is the so-called English doll which we have lately received from London. It is properly a toy for little girls, but is so pleasing and tasteful that mothers and grown women will likely also want to play with it, the more since good and bad taste in dress or coiffure can be observed and, so to speak, studied. The doll is a young female figure cut out of stout cardboard. It is about eight inches high, has simply curled hair, and is dressed in underclothing and corset. With it go six complete sets of tastefully designed dresses and head-dresses which are cut out of paper . . . . . The whole thing comes in a neat paper envelope which can be easily carried in a hand-bag or work-box to give amusement at parties or to children."

Not only flat figures were made at this time, but three-dimensional ones were pinched into shape by enterprising persons. Today we have "round-about" dolls and think they are a new invention; the idea was figured out a hundred and fifty years ago. Many of the paper toy inventions of that period are still used. The present-day "pop-up" books, for instance, were popular in 1840, but were then known as *the surprise books*. When a page in such a book is opened, a little scene, built up in sections, one figure or row of figures behind the other, "pops up," the figures being pasted only at the base.

Early in the nineteenth century England introduced one of the most interesting ideas for paper dolls. They were used to illustrate characters in books for children and placed in a pocket at the back of the volume. American publishers copied the idea, but until 1840, issued the dolls in sheet form bound into the book, as they did not have the facilities for die-cutting the figures until that date. Herbert H. Hosmer, Jr., of South Lancaster, Massachusetts, has a fascinating collection of toy book dolls. He comes of a paper-doll-minded family, for his great, great uncle, John Greene Chandler, a wood-engraver and lithographer, published in Boston, Massachusetts, in 1857, a series of paper dolls which he designed. "These dolls and their outfits," says Mr. Hosmer, "were printed in black and white and then delicately tinted with water colors by hand." Some of the proof sets which Mr. Hosmer has formerly belonged to the originator's two little girls and to his small nieces and nephews. "Jack" and "Little Fairy Lightfoot" with costumes (1857) have been reprinted by Mr.

Hosmer. Unpainted, the leaflet sells for 50 cents a copy, $1 if it is hand-tinted.

Mrs. Earle E. Andrews, president of The Doll Collectors of America, Inc., is especially interested in antique paper dolls. One of her prize items is a hand-painted copy of the Jenny Lind paper doll. Mr. Hosmer has a companion box to the Jenny Lind set entitled "The Dancer of Paris," which illustrates the famous ballerina of the 1840's—Fanny Elssler. Some of Mr. Hosmer's English Toy Book paper dolls go back as far as 1800. Mrs. Frank C. Doble of Cambridge, Massachusetts, and Mrs. Louis F. Wood of Clinton, Massachusetts, also have fine collections.

In 1874 William H. Hart, Jr., of Philadelphia, Pa., patented a "walking" paper doll. The figure was put together in sections. When held by the finger piece at the waistline and moved forward on a flat surface, the head and legs oscillated in imitation of a person walking. This was followed by other "walking" paper dolls. Fastened to the body of the more recent, is a rotating wheel of legs (five legs), one pair visible at a time from underneath the skirt. The doll is propelled by hand. One copyrighted in 1920 by Daddy Long Legs, U. S. Toy Corp., N. Y., has a detachable stick to facilitate handling.

The rotating wheel of legs was used for a real doll about 1870. See chapter on *Dolls of the Nineteenth Century*.

Paper dolls have always been interesting to children, but, as is the case with other wares, they were at first costly. The earliest "fashion" paper dolls were printed on hand-made paper. It was not until 1798 that a paper-making machine was invented, and not until 1880 that improvements in the machine reached a high state of perfection, although improvements had been made from time to time as the years advanced. The price of paper dolls diminished as the cost of making them decreased. In 1791, a set of the new paper dolls were priced at about $1.25; today a slim dime will pay for a beautiful booklet of dolls in full color, a considerable difference when one remembers that the value of money today is much less than it was in earlier times. The popularity of the paper doll has never decreased; children's literature of the past is full of references to them, and they are as eagerly sought today as in the time of great great grandmother.

We hope that before long, the beautiful toy cardboard theatres with their many scenes lighted from behind colored celophane surfaces will re-appear. We also hope that some enterprising firm will bring back the pasteboard toy book which opened out into four rooms with doors leading from one to the other, and with pictures and shelves of books, and fireplaces neatly painted on the walls, such as appeared during the 1890's, and, in a simpler form, in 1868, when it was patented by G. W. Cottrell of Boston; and the instructive picture gallery of a still earlier date. How beautifully the latter could set off the colored miniature reproductions of famous paintings which have been on the market for some time, especially if it were so arranged that the pictures, from time to time, could be replaced with others. As visitors to the gallery, dolls representing the artists who painted the pictures, or those showing costumes of various periods in history, would add to the interest and instructive value of the toy.

With an eye to the future, modern paper dolls should be included in every museum interested in such things. There has been a wealth of paper dolls representing the Second World War—the WAC, the WAVE, the Army, Navy, etc., not to mention actresses, singers and others in the public eye. New sets are constantly appearing on store counters. These sell out quickly, and unless a record is kept, many interesting types will soon be lost to the general public. If every worth-while set were saved, dress designers as well as students of history and the theatre, in years to come, would be grateful.

*Chapter 18*

# PUPPETS AND HOW THEY ARE MADE

TEACHING the ancient art of puppetry for at least a decade in a camp for girls, entertaining children and parents each summer, has brought home to the author not only the kind of plays most suitable for the wee actors, but also the need for simplicity in the matter of making and operating the dolls—not too great simplicity, however, for that would defeat its own purpose, but a happy medium. The tedious method (employed by many puppeteers) of building up a papier-mâché head layer upon layer after a mold laboriously has been made for the purpose, then making a dozen or more heads all much alike from the same mold, is not nearly as interesting as direct modelling, each head different from the last. It may take more practise at first, but will save time in the long run.

Many persons have a poor impression of puppet plays through seeing only poorly operated, poorly constructed dolls. To quote from the author's own articles in the Camp Fire Girls' paper *The Guardian* for April, May and June, 1939:

If you have ever seen a *good* marionette performance, you will want to know the keen joy of having a little, inanimate body come to life in your own hands and at your own command. And should you have any aspirations to become an actress, the puppet is an inspiration and a real help.

In a class of this sort, each of you will find an attractive role to play suitable to your own individual talent. You who like mechanics will revel in the things you can do to make the doll walk, dance, gesture with hands and feet, back-bend, twirl, juggle balls, and do all the various tricks that seem so difficult to the uninitiate, but so simple to the puppeteer, and you will be surprised to find how easy it is to learn to handle the controller. For instance, take the trick of the juggler. I have been asked, "However do you make the balls pass from one hand to the other?" The answer is "By a simple turn of the controller to the left or right." All you need to accomplish this miracle is a bit of wood, some wire and screw eyes, paint, cloth, and string, and a large wooden bead for the juggler's ball.

Those of you who like to model will find plenty of opportunity in molding the head of your doll. In my case, the difficulty was not so much in modeling as in finding the right kind of material. I realized, of course, that a light weight, easily carved wood like white wood or sweet gum made the ideal head, but this was out of the question, for I wanted to teach an easier method to my girls, to whom the time element is important.

After years of experimenting, I found that papier-mâché in powder form mixed with paste makes a light weight but exceedingly tough product. It can be modeled like clay, and when dry will take screw eyes, can be sandpapered, and beautifully finished with either water or oil color.

A puppet's wardrobe presents no great difficulties. Many of you like to sew, and scraps of material are usually available in every household. Painted paper beads and cardboard make a jeweled necklace and crown for "royalty," and the kid of old gloves will handsomely shoe a lilliputian king.

Stage sets offer quite a field for creative activity. Painting scenery will prove fascinating to the artists among you. For quickly-made outdoor scenery, trees cut from green cardboard pinned to a sky background serve the purpose. Plywood and dowel sticks and boxes covered with cloth are a help in making furniture. A cylindrical salt box with a velvet throw makes a throne fit for a queen. Last summer one of my puppeteers needed a spinning wheel in a hurry. She made it in five minutes with old spools, a stick and a scrap of plywood weighted with lead.

All of you will want to make the tiny characters come to life on the stage: at least, that is my experience at camp. Even those who do not themselves make marionettes, want to operate them. For each play there are two or three girls back stage: two to handle the puppets, the third to manage curtains, scenery, music, and sound effects. It is well to have a phonograph, and you will find records especially suitable for marionettes, some actually made for them, for many of our famous musicians have been keenly interested in puppets. Music means a great deal in the production of any play. The gay minuet enlivens a tiny dancer; a dramatic moment is enhanced a thousand times by such music as Elgar's "Pomp and Circumstance."

We usually have a puppet announce the act. He may be a wee fellow in "tails" who bows and struts and calls to the audience: "Ladies and gentlemen, you are about to behold the matchless performance of one who has come to us all the way from Russia," etc., etc. "Ladies—gentlemen—let me present Madame Petruska Ballerina." (Much handclapping.) If the announcer is a clown, he stands on his hands, back-bends, gestures clownishly, and tries to make his exit by climbing over the screen.

Our campers have a great time choosing a play. Sometimes they write it themselves around favorite characters. I will never forget how well a trio of ten-year-olds produced an original show, nor how excited they were when the moment came to open the curtains. Unable to contain themselves, they squealed and bounced up and down on the bridge back stage. A mechanical imperfection suggested a play for one of our marionettes. He walked like a frog, so he took a lead in "The Frog Prince."

Make your first play short with plenty of action and not much talk, something which brings out the special talents of marionettes, like fairy tales. "Rumplestiltskin" is excellent for beginners. Don't try to stick too closely to the text. The puppets themselves will show you what is best to do as you rehearse. Always have a variety of specialty acts to give at a moment's notice, which take not more than five minutes to perform, something simple and amusing like the old English folk songs and ballads; excerpts from *Alice in Wonderland*, Mother Goose rhymes, etc. Our dancer is most popular, and the juggler a prime favorite. These two have entranced many an audience while waiting for the play to begin. And don't think that you cannot make a marionette. The first may not be a marvel of ingenuity, but keep at it, and you will find that your skill as artist and puppeteer grows with practice.

MATERIALS: *For head*, Prepared papier-mâché (arts and crafts shop or papier-mâché company*), wall paper paste, paint, floss for hair.

*For body*, Whitewood or white pine blocks and dowel sticks.

*For joints and hands*, Thin and medium-heavy wire, adhesive tape, screw eyes (⅜-in. wide at the eye for knee and ankle joints, smallest size for remainder of joints).

*For weights*, Sheet lead (medium thickness which may be easily cut with scissors).

TOOLS: Coping saw, drill, vise, pliers, pen-knife, auger (convenient but not imperative).

At Puck's Workshop, the marionette center of Camp Kiwanis, we always begin a puppet by making the head (a), and while that is drying (it takes a few days) we work on the body.

Mix three handfuls of prepared papier-mâché with about a cup of wall paper paste, and knead thoroughly until it is of a consistency to model easily. Mold into an egg-shaped mass over a dowel stick, leaving about half an inch of the stick showing below the small end of the "egg" to form the neck. Now model the papier-mâché gently but firmly over the neck. The eyes are made by pressing your thumbs into the dough about half-way between the top of the head and the end of the chin. Add a piece for the nose and chin, and perhaps a little for the cheeks, and mold carefully and as simply as possible. Tiresome attention to detail will make your puppet face uninteresting, for it leaves nothing to the imagination. Remember that a child's head is rounder than an adult's. While modeling, wash your hands frequently, and use paste on the tips of your fingers to smooth the surface of the papier-mâché. The ears should be about the size of the nose and at the same distance from the top of the head.

Good proportions for marionettes are seven heads tall for an adult character, six heads for a ten-year-old.

If your puppet head has cracked a bit in the process of drying (don't dry it too fast) it can be filled in with fresh papier-mâché. When thoroughly dry, sandpaper and paint.

---

* Papier-Mâché Novelties Co., Reading, Mich.

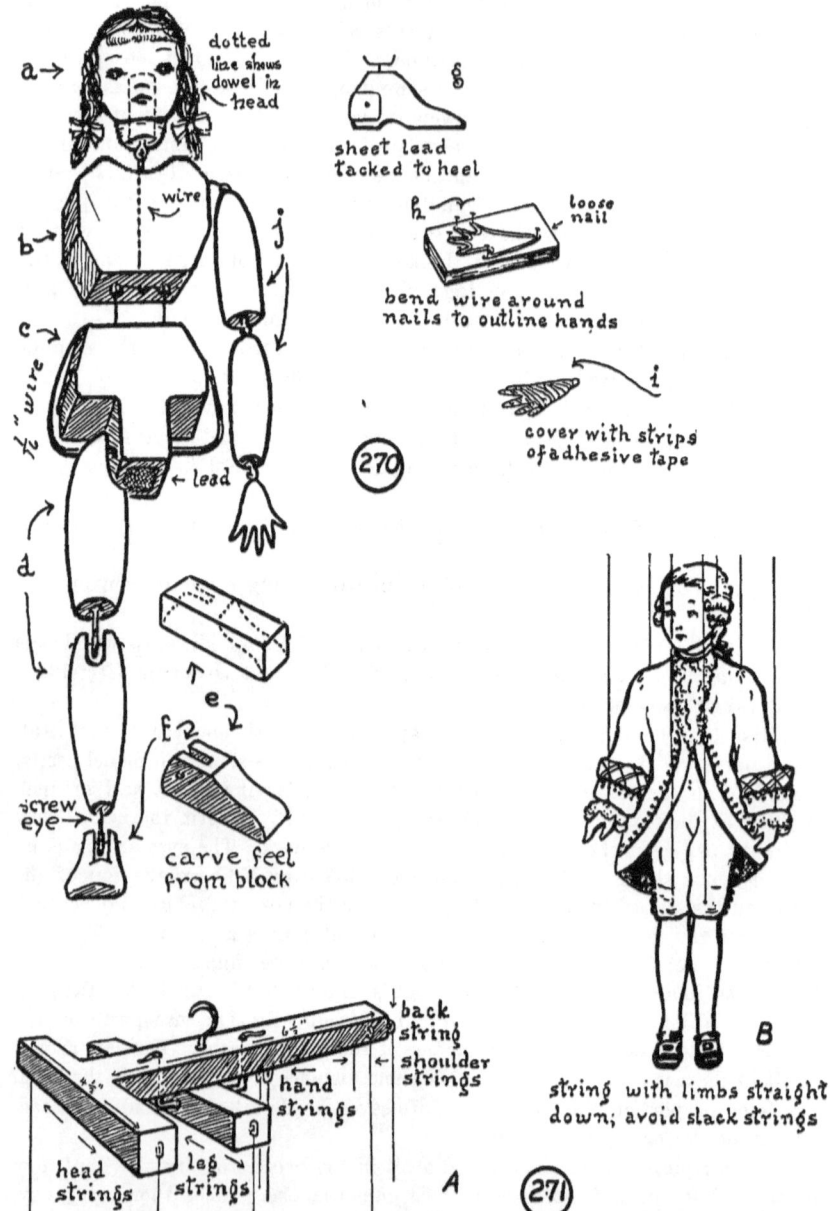

(270) Diagram showing how to make a marionette. (271) A. Controller for marionette. B. Marionette dressed with strings in place.

The trunk of the body is made in two parts, torso and hips (b and c), joined with plenty of space at the middle so that the character can bow low and back-bend. Use two blocks of wood about two inches by two inches by one and one-fourth inch, and carve as in the diagram, using saw for the "v" of the neck and the part where the legs are joined to the hips. It is better to have the lower block a little longer than the upper, for we must have plenty of room for the legs to swing. Join upper and lower body with wire fastened to screw eyes. A small square of sheet lead tacked to the lower part of the hip piece will make your character sit more readily.

To fasten the head to the torso, put a screw eye into the lower part of the neck. Then drill a hole through the length of the torso. Run a thin wire through the screw eye in the neck, and pass the wire, doubled, down the hole in the torso, and fasten to screw eye at base of torso.

Inch-wide dowel sticks are used for the leg (d), five-eighths-inch dowels for the arm. For a fifteen-inch marionette (a good size for a camp puppet), make the upper leg three inches long, the lower one three-fourths of an inch longer, and shave off a little of the dowel where it joins the hips. Taper a little at ankle, knee, and hip joints. (See diagram)

Carve the foot (e) from a block of wood two inches by seven-eighths by five-eighths inches, using your own as a model. Now saw a slit lengthwise in the ankle of the foot wide enough and deep enough to hold the eye of the screw eye (f). The latter is fastened at the bottom of the leg, so that it will fit into the ankle of the foot. Drill a hole through the ankle, and put the leg in place with the screw eye in the slit of the ankle, pass thin wire through the hole and through the screw eye, twisting the wire at each end to secure the foot to the leg. For balance and extra weight wrap a strip of sheet lead around the ankle (g). If you will drill a hole in each end of the strip of sheet lead, it can be fastened to the heel with the same wire that holds the foot in place.

Use the same joining method for upper and lower leg. The heavier (one-sixteenth inch) wire is used to swing the upper legs to the hips, as in diagram. Hold it in place with adhesive tape or two-pronged tacks.

Hands are made by outlining with thin wire and wrapping fingers and palms with narrow strips of adhesive tape (h and i). Do not get the waterproof adhesive tape as it will not take paint readily. Leave a loop of wire protruding at the wrist so that it may be fastened to the arm. A thin leaden bracelet makes the hand fall naturally.

For each arm (j) use two dowel sticks an inch and a quarter long, and fasten with wire and screw eyes, or a strip of cloth glued on. Three-fourths of an inch between sticks at the joints makes the extra arm length, and provides freedom of action.

Wires protruding at joints should be bent flat and covered with adhesive tape, and any sharp edges in the wood whittled off and sandpapered. It is a good idea also to put a band of cloth around the waist of your doll. When the puppet is complete, it should swing loosely at all joints.

We use floss for hair rather than wool. The latter, although effective, invites moths and soils easily. Make a "part" on the sewing machine with a strip of paper above and below the floss so as to avoid tangling, then strip the paper from the floss.

Now your puppet is ready to dress.

Costuming a marionette requires careful thought and the best material available, because if a puppet is worth making, it is worth the best you can give it in the way of apparel. If you are not sure of the style of costume which belongs to the period you wish to represent, consult your nearest librarian. I have often purchased in a five-and-ten-cent store books showing costumes of many lands and different periods.

If you wish to design your own puppet clothes, first make a rough sketch in colors, always keeping in mind the color scheme of your stage background. Now take the measurements of your puppet's neck, shoulders, waist, arm length, and skirt length, and make a paper pattern.

Since the strings of the doll prohibit a change of costume, you can sew the garment right on the puppet. Clothes should be loose to allow freedom of motion. A graceful, flowing sleeve is made with a piece of cloth doubled, cut off diagonally, and the small end tacked on at the shoulder. The edge at this point does not need to be turned in, for when the waist goes on, the latter is turned in where it joins the sleeve. A straight piece of goods folded flat makes collar and cuffs. Many of our dolls have ruffles or lace at neck and wrists.

A coat is made in the same manner as a plain waist except that it is longer, the front is cut at the center all the way up, and the top ends turned over to form lapels. Colored thumb tacks make buttons which do not have to be sewn on, but if you need tiny buttons, felt is a good material to use. There are also on the market pins with round enameled tops. A straight piece of goods shirred at the top may be used for the skirt.

Heavy material is out of place on a marionette, and underwear isn't necessary except under very thin material, or for a dancer who must do some high stepping, back-bends, and twirls. Ruffles or contrasting bands on a skirt are effective, and we have transformed many a plain costume by a pretty little lace-edged apron.

Make pants by cutting a slit through the middle of a scant petticoat (not too scant), sew on wrong side, turn. For stockings, make a tube of stockinette, turn it inside out, and put it on over the foot and leg so that the sole of the foot is exposed. Tack it on with a strip of adhesive tape. Two pieces of thin glove leather glued onto the foot form the shoe. Make the sole of the shoe with adhesive tape cut larger than the outline of the foot, so that it overlaps the leather and makes a neat finish. Avoid stiff, heavy headgear. Dutch caps, peasant shawls, and lightweight crowns are all right.

The controller consists of two sticks of wood, one about six and a half inches long, the other four and a half inches, both about five-eighths inch wide and thick, which are nailed or screwed together to form a "T." To this main controller, a stick of wood is added which swings from the under side of the controller about an inch and a half from the cross of the "T." This swinging bar is about four inches long and three-fourths of an inch wide and thick. It eliminates the necessity for a separate controller for the legs, which is of immense value in handling a marionette. When the controller is held in a horizontal position, the bar swings from the under side by means of wire drawn through holes (an inch and a half apart) in the control stick, and the middle of the bar. Bend your wire with pliers so that between the main controller and the bar there is a space of about one-fourth inch to allow free swinging back and forth with thumb and forefinger. A twist at either end of the wire holds it in place. Be sure that you nail or screw on your cross piece very firmly. If you nail it, put in two or three nails at least an inch long. For stringing we use black and white fish line, eighteen-pound pull. It takes about eleven yards for one puppet.

To fasten the head strings, there should be a hole or screw eye at either end of the cross of the "T"; for leg strings, at either end of the swinging bar; for hands, two directly at the back of the swinging bar on the main controller; for the bow string, a screw eye at the very end (small end) of the controller; and for the shoulder strings, two opposite each other about a half-inch from the end screw eye.

When the doll is fully dressed, fasten tiny screw eyes to either side of the head, shoulders, upper part of knees, and the small of the puppet's back. (The hand will not need screw eyes, for the string is fastened to the wrist.) Care should be taken to put the screw eyes in the right place on either side of the head. Hold up your marionette by the head with your thumb and forefinger, to insure correct position, and place the screw eyes at the point held by thumb and forefinger.

Set the controller horizontally in a vise a little above elbow height from the ground. Your puppet should be strung so that the controller may be held elbow height from the ground while the doll is in action. Begin with the head. Fasten one end of each "head" string to the screw eye in either side of the head, the other end to the corresponding hole in either end of the cross piece of the "T." Next, fasten the shoulder strings between the screw eyes in the shoulder and the corresponding screw eyes at the back of the controller. Now the puppet is balanced directly under the center of the controller, and can stand erect.

So that he may walk, fasten the "knee" strings between the screw eyes in the knees, and the corresponding holes at either end of the swinging bar. Be sure that the legs hang straight, but don't have your thread slack. By holding the controller steady in a horizontal position and swinging this bar back and forth with thumb and forefinger, at the same time bringing the controller slowly forward with the feet barely touching the floor, your marionette can walk in a very realistic manner.

The hand strings are attached between the wrists and the screw eyes at the back of the swinging bar, within easy reach of your middle finger. A pull at the strings brings his hands into action. The bow string attached between the small of the back and the screw eye at the end of the controller, when given an upward pull, makes your puppet bow low or merely nod his head, depending upon the force of your movement.

To make the puppet shake his head, turn the controller left and right. If you wish him to back-bend, two extra screw eyes will be necessary, one at the base of the torso, the other at the center of the cross piece of the controller. Never fasten your string to the clothing, because that will pull it out of shape.

(272) Fist puppet head and body.   (273) Fist puppet with hand in place.

Use a bodkin to pass the string through the cloth. When completely finished, insert a cup hook in the controller, so that you can hang up the puppet when not in use. Practice before a mirror. To pack, bunch the strings in your hand and wrap around center of the controller, tie with tape and place in cloth bag.

With this simple controller, you will be able in half an hour to handle the marionette, but you will need careful practice to make every action count in giving a play. The greater your love for these little people, and the more time you are willing to devote to them, the greater your proficiency as a puppeteer.

In making dolls and puppets, each individual will want to work out his own method. For that reason, it is well to consult your public library for books on the subject. A series of four well-illustrated booklets on Hobby-Craft by Treasure Chest Publications, Inc., New York, N. Y., will give other methods in the construction of the puppet. Book I illustrates clearly how a doll's head is made from a plaster mold.

A special booklet on how to make animal marionettes was written by Paul McPharlin, who issues *Puppetry*, a yearly bulletin. A simpler method than his, one best for the inexperienced, is to de-stuff a suitable cloth animal (Thrift Shops often have good ones, slightly used), place wood inside the head and body (not only to fill out, but to fasten screw-eyes for the purpose of stringing) leaving plenty of room at joints for action, and weight the feet and the end of the tail with sheet lead, easily cut with scissors. Never try this method with an ordinary commercial doll unless it is of cloth and happens to have good proportions. Cloth dolls may be destuffed and adjusted for action, but manufactured composition play dolls are not properly weighted for the balance necessary for motion, and weights cannot be screwed into the plastic successfully. It is easy enough to slip lead weights into cloth feet and hands.

Many persons have asked: "Is a marionette a puppet?" The answer is *yes*. The word *puppet* is a general term. Those operated by strings from above are marionettes; those activated by a hand placed inside the body of the puppet are *hand* or *fist* puppets; the flat figures operated by rods from below and at the rear of a curtain in such a way as to cast their shadow on the screen are shadow puppets. Shadow and fist puppets are as old as the pyramids. Marionettes are a later development, but were used in the Middle Ages, the first ones much simpler in construction and operation.

Fist puppets were used to entertain the workmen who built the pyramids, and reference to them runs through ancient literature.

The Far East excels in intricately patterned shadow puppets of tanned and brilliantly colored hides. Punch and Judy and their equivalent in other European countries have taught religion and ridiculed political intrigue. They were banned by the Church when they became solely an entertainment feature instead of a medium for lessons in religion, and in England Punch was banned for a hundred years after he was ordered "executed" by Henry VIII,—how dare he ridicule the monarch's eight wives! Early French settlers in Louisiana brought puppets with them, but this form of entertainment was not general in America until about thirty years ago, when Tony Sarg stimulated enthusiasm. Now professionals in the entertainment field have taken up the art, and it is possible to see really fine performances. To become a good all-around puppeteer takes time and talent, but a group of persons, one gifted in the art of modelling, one scenery painting, one writing, one mechanical skill, others with acting ability. etc., can accomplish wonders. Amateurs have, in the past, put on remarkable performances, and the future shows still more promise. America, slow to take up the profession, is rising so rapidly in its perfection that one dares to predict that we will soon take our place at the top.

Members of doll clubs wishing to have periodic money-raising exhibitions would do well to take up the subject of puppetry. A good puppet show is always an attractive feature and will draw enthusiastic crowds. With the simple controller described, it is easy enough to operate the dolls, and experience will show the kind of plays best adapted to the little theatre. As before stated, a short play, one that brings into action not more than two or three puppets at a time, is best.

## Directions For Making a Hand Puppet

Follow directions given in chapter on *Marionettes* for making a doll head, or use "clay" that will not break by mixing powdered asbestos (free from hair and lint) with wallpaper paste, about three-fourths asbestos to one part of paste. Knead it together until it is like dough. Experiment, adding one ingredient or the other, until it is of the right consistency to model, frequently washing hands so that the plastic will not stick to them. Roll dough between the palms of your hands into an egg-shaped mass, and at the narrow end of the "egg," press a hollow cardboard tube up into the middle of the mass, so that some of the tube will stick out to form the neck of the doll. With the blade of a flexible knife or orange stick, smooth and model. Study your own face in a mirror to get an idea of proportions. Make places for eyes by pressing your thumbs about halfway between the top and bottom of the head, add a little piece for the nose, and dry over a warm radiator for two or three days. If you wish a very smooth surface sandpaper well when the head is dry. Paint with oil colors or ordinary water colors. This will not only preserve the paint, but will help to keep it clean.

To make the tube, roll a piece of cardboard around your forefinger, and tie together with string.

The body is little more than a bag (see sketch) with an opening at the neckline and places for fingers to stick through. The neck line should be just large enough to fit into the neck of the doll. Glue in place, then bind with adhesive tape. If the hollow tube is lined with cloth, it will be easier to fasten onto the body. Make a simple dress. One may add hands and legs if desired. The legs can be sewn to the bag underneath the dress. Yarn makes attractive hair, but a modelled coiffure is more easy to take care of.

To operate, put your hand into the bag so that your forefinger sticks up into the head of the puppet, the middle finger through one sleeve of the dress, and your thumb through the other sleeve. If you do not want the bother of making hands, the end of your middle finger and thumb make easy substitutes. To make the doll nod his head "yes," bend your forefinger down, to make him say "no," shake right and left. Practice before a mirror, and while you are wiggling your forefinger, try to keep the rest of your hand still. With practice, you can really amuse.

*Chapter 19*

# EXHIBITING DOLLS FOR FUN AND PROFIT

IN staging a successful doll show, the first thing to remember is that advertising pays. Your show may be the best thing of its kind ever produced; if it is not properly advertised, it will fall flat. This fact was brought home forcibly to a puppeteer in the suburbs of Boston; one excellent show was given but since the advertising was casual, only a few persons came. Shortly after, a second performance was given, this time well advertised; it wasn't as good as the first, but the place was packed.

Get the cooperation of your local newspapers and shops. Conspicuous posters in store windows are bound to attract attention. Advertise to the limit of your ability, making sure, of course, that you really have something to advertise. In designing posters, consult the art teacher in your public schools; have a poster contest and reward the winner.

Choose a hall for display purposes as nearly centralized as possible; appoint committees on arrangements, publicity, etc. Determine the number of tables available, and the number and character of dolls to be exhibited. A hodge-podge of dolls on one table might be interesting, but the effect will be more pleasing if dolls of a kind are grouped together—antiques on one table, foreign costume dolls on another; dolls representing persons or events on another; dolls made of peculiar materials (such as cornhusks, shells, nuts, etc.) on another, and so on. Have at least one group of very large dolls, and another of tinies.

Backgrounds for the smallest dolls can be most interesting. There might be rooms or corners thereof fitted out with wee furnishings, fireplace, pictures, chairs, tables, etc., for one set of figures; outdoor scenes for another. A theatre group with stage setting offers a splendid opportunity for an attractive display. At a Washington exhibition a few years ago, Claire Fawcett arranged a tiny theatre with electric light showing through colored celophane as a background to show off her hand-carved wooden dolls. If you don't have a little theatre, one can be made quite easily with cardboard "columns" from the center of rolls of paper toweling; a cut-out cardboard top fastened over the top and a cardboard backdrop, the whole thing painted to suit. Scenes should be in neutral colors or black to show off brightly colored dresses. Tiny velvet drapes add to the realism of the set-up. Ways to make your props stand will suggest themselves. An effective method is strips of lead (easily cut and bent) to hold the cardboard.

A festive air to the whole exhibition is desirable—lights, color and music help tremendously. A good victrola is one of the best assets of the amateur show. Festoons of brightly colored crepe paper from the middle of the ceiling to the walls help when flowers and ferns are not available.

Guard your tables well. It is human nature to pick up and examine dolls, turn them upside down for minute inspection, and—alas!—there are persons unthinking enough to dig a fingernail in the face of a precious and irreplaceable wax doll. One person at a large table is not enough; there should be at least two. Camp Fire Girls and Girl Scouts are always willing to help, but should be rewarded in some way for their efforts. And the giver usually gets more pleasure than the one who receives. If your church group offers the use of their hall, give them a percentage of the profits, of course.

A simple puppet show, either with hand puppets or marionettes, always attracts. No elaborate setting is necessary. Two persons operating marionettes at a convenient point will suffice, and the hand or fist puppet needs only the back of a chair or table to make him look detached from the operator.

In this connection, a fist puppet fortune teller might be on hand. Have the puppet read a visitor's palm, or the little thing might dive at the back of the table and bring forth a card especially prepared beforehand. Cards appropriate to birth dates or with advice appropriate to anybody are easy to arrange. A book of fortune-telling tricks from your public library will give you all necessary information. The idea was used most successfully a few years ago at a girls' summer camp on Visitors' Day. A hoary puppet witch with streaming grey woollen locks and a wicked eye looked out from the window of a vine-clad cardboard cottage (which hid the puppeteer) and called to passers by, "Hi, there! Want your fortune told? What! You don't believe in such things? Now, by my secret, sacred brew, the things I tell you *will* come true!" And so the witch went on, answering banter with banter and causing a good deal of amusement. On another occasion, puppets at an exhibition of dolls stole the show.

Fist puppets are so easy to make that they are within the reach of all. A simple process is explained herewith. Try it. If time is limited, buy a puppet at your local department or toy shop. Use every trick to attract the crowd, put all you have into the show, and advertise well in advance, and your exhibition can't help but be a success.

*Chapter 20*

# RESTORING THE OLD DOLL

QUITE aside from the thrill of finding the old doll is the satisfaction one receives from restoring it when this is advisable. Perhaps there is nothing fundamentally wrong, just a dangerous tendency, due to incomplete stuffing, for china legs to crack together, wildly flopping arms, or a head too loose on the shoulders. If, after additional stuffing, the "lady" still caves in at the waist, a stick run through the body past the middle will help. When not on exhibition, china legs might be covered with knitted stockings.

Many old dolls are broken at the shoulder. If all the pieces are intact, your problem is simple. Use Major's Cement or Duco, and follow directions implicitly. Mend one piece at a time and allow eleven hours to dry. When all the pieces are firmly mended, reinforce from underneath with adhesive tape.

A more serious problem arises when parts are missing. If your head is valuable, send it to an expert who can match material, who has a kiln, and can do a practically undetectable job. Mrs. Emma C. Clear of Redondo Beach, California, has proven her ability in this direction.

If the doll is not of sufficient value to warrant further expense, a fairly satisfactory job can be done at home by filling in with a mixture of paste and plaster of Paris. (The kind of plaster used by dentists is better than the ordinary kind.) The use of paste rather than water with the plaster enables one to model more easily.

Papier-mâchè should be mended with like material. It may be purchased by the pound from The Papier-Mâché Novelties Co., Reading, Michigan. Mix with wall-paper paste. Experience will show how to do it. Smooth with the flat of a knife blade and dry thoroughly over a hot radiator. The dough is difficult to handle, because it is sticky, but when dry is as tough as wood and extremely light in weight.

If a large part of the shoulder is missing, cut from Scott towelling an outline a little larger than the missing piece, and paste on the doll underneath the part to be filled in. This will not only serve as a guide when filling in, but you will find that the paper adheres more readily to the cloth body than does plaster or papier-mâché.

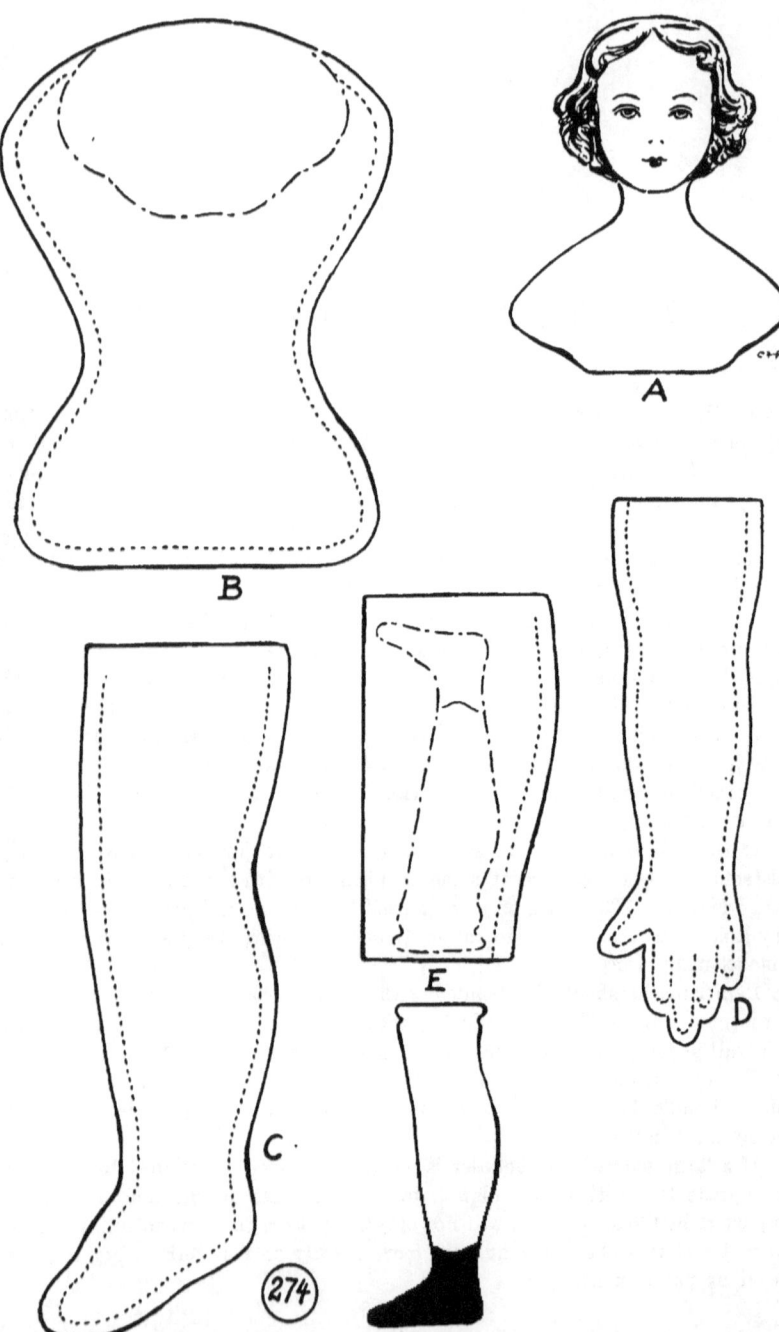

(274) Diagram for reconstructing the old doll body. Pattern No. 1 pre-Civil War period. E shows how the cloth is fastened to the china leg. All pieces should be cut double and stitched together.

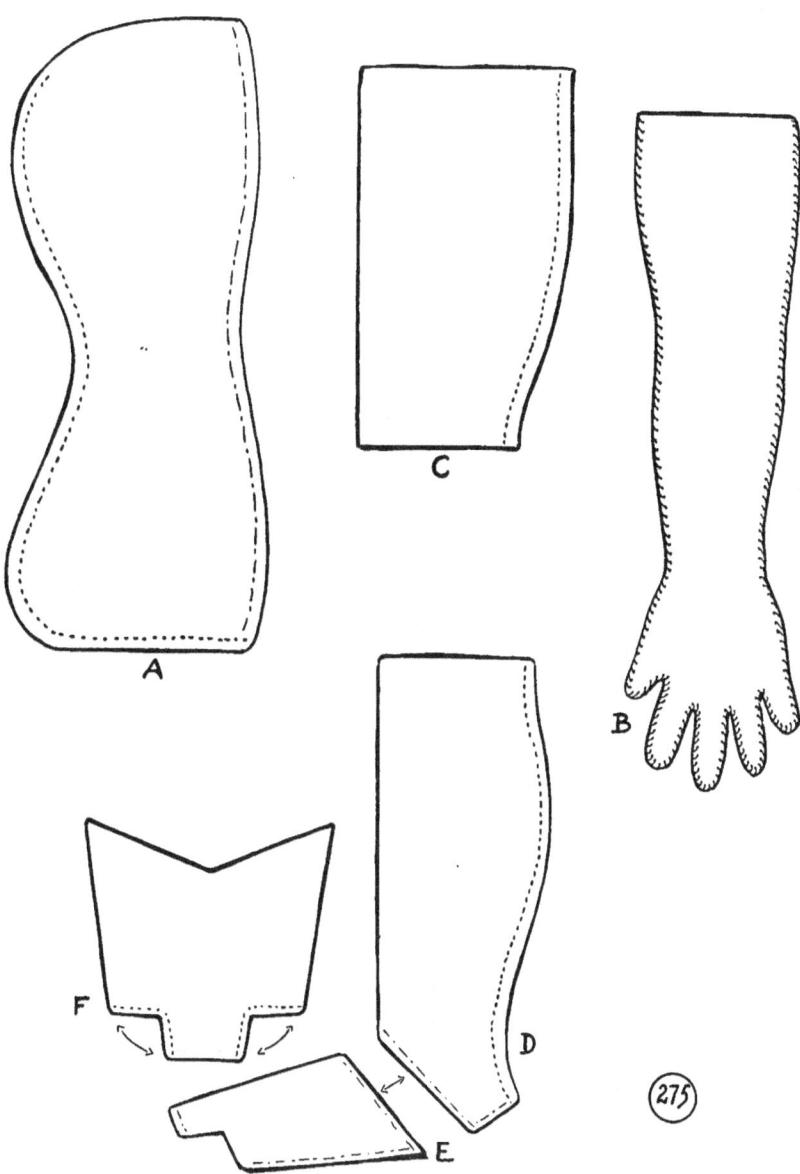

(275) Pattern No. 2. C and D pieces should be folded at right. A is cut double for both front and back, first stitched down the center of body, then flattened and sewn around as indicated in dotted lines. An opening at the top is left to turn the completed body inside out. E, the foot, is sewn to the leg part as indicated by double arrows. The arm, B, might be cut from an old kid glove. It should be cut double and the two pieces sewn together by hand. An overhand stitch is best. This pattern is especially suitable to a large doll.

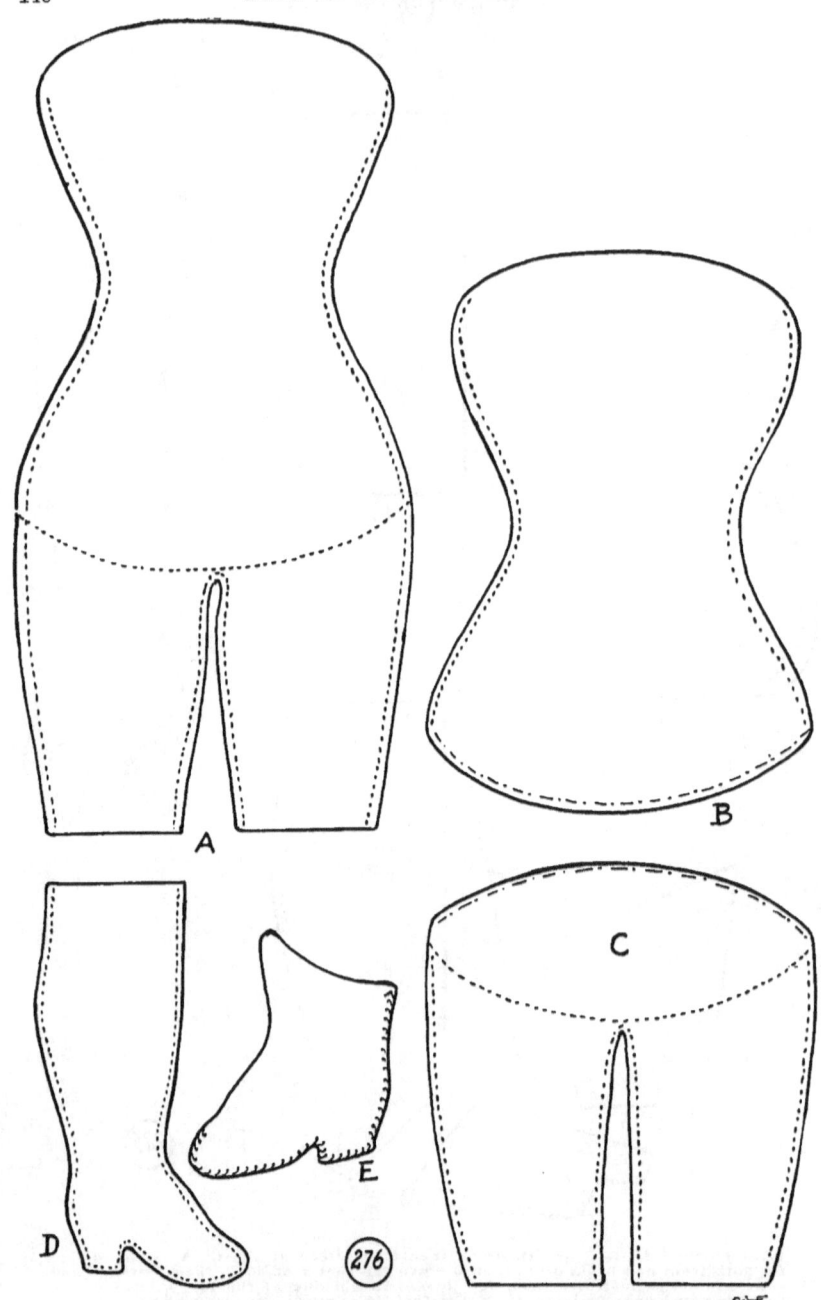

(276) Pattern No. 3 used for late 19th century dolls. B and C are first sewn together, then attached to A as dotted lines indicate. E represents the kid boot which is sewn onto the foot over D. D and E are cut double.

If the complete shoulder is missing, first secure the head to the body by running a stick through the hollow of the head down through the body past the waist line. Paste on a paper outline of the shoulder and build up over it quickly before your plastic begins to dry.

Mended parts may be painted with water color or oils. If this is done, be sure the paint is dry before using china glaze, otherwise it will remain sticky indefinitely.

Re-waxing a doll's head is a most interesting process. While it requires some experimenting to get the wax the right temperature, it is really quite simple. Failure is caused by not having enough wax to completely immerse the part to be covered. When the wax is steaming hot, turn off the heat until cool enough for the wax to adhere to the doll head or whatever you are working with.* Do not attempt to re-wax anything of value until you have first experimented with a stick. If a thin coat is wanted, dip when the wax begins to steam. If a thick coating is desired, wait until the wax is almost ready to form a thin film over the top.

Dip the head quickly into the hot wax bath, taking care that the wax does not run inside the head. This may be achieved by first stuffing it with paper and placing upside down in the bath. Let the head drain for a minute before placing it in an upright position. If a wig is to be used, scrape off the wax from the top of the head before it has cooled; otherwise, your wig will not adhere to the crown. If the head has been re-painted, be sure that the paint is thoroughly dry before dipping. Remember that artists' oils take at least a month to set completely. Paint may be applied over the wax, but a softer blending results from the reverse process.

It is not necessary to go to great expense in purchasing wax. At such places as the Goodwill Industries, the Salvation Army Stores, and the Thrift Shops, ends of candles may be secured at small cost. Use about two quarts of white or cream-colored candle ends with perhaps a three-inch red and a two-inch yellow candle of average width. White wax unmixed with any other shade should be used when the face of the doll is too highly colored. A little practice will give confidence.

---

* Wax becomes plastic enough for the purpose of modelling at 86 degrees Fahr., melts at 155 degrees. It dissolves in small quantities by alcohol or ether.

*Chapter 21*

# COLLECTORS' DOLLS PATENTED IN AMERICA

## Composition or Papier Mache Dolls Patented in the UNITED STATES, 19th Century.

1858—L. Greiner, Philadelphia, Pa.
1866—D. Checkeni, Marion, Conn. (composition under wax).
1872—G. Benda, Coburg, Germany, (composition base).
1874—W. E. Brock, New York, N. Y.
1875—E. S. Judge, Philadelphia, Pa.
1881—Fritz Bartenstein, Huttensteinach, Germany, (composition under wax). All the above used papier mâché in the composition.
1877—Lazarus Reichmann, New York, N. Y., *(first use of sawdust instead of papier mâché in composition for dolls in U. S.)*
1887—Joseph Schon, Reichenbach, Silesia, Prussia, Germany, (heads manufactured of infrangible, the first to be advertised in U. S. as "unbreakable.")
(NOTE: Most of the American-made modelled dolls since this time have been of composition with sawdust instead of papier mâché as the basic substance. Improvements came with the years, and modern composition is at its height.)

## Celluloid Dolls Patented in U. S., 19th Century

1881—M. C. Lefferts & W. B. Carpenter (assigned to Celluloid Mfg. Co., N. Y. In 1880, Celluloid Novelty Co. of N. Y. C., had been coloring features of celluloid dolls).
NOTE: Some dolls made in the United States were not patented. Philip Lerch of Philadelphia is listed (1866) as a maker of doll heads. Some collectors have dolls marked "Lerch & Klagg, 1875."

COLLECTORS' DOLLS PATENTED IN AMERICA 151

## Walking Dolls Patented in This Country, 19th Century

*China heads for these dolls were imported from Germany.*

1862—E. R. Morrison, New York, N. Y., (patent calls for improvement in automatic apparatus for walking dolls.)
One dated 1862 has a beautiful china head with flowers modelled into the hair. This works by clock-work mechanism. Another, circa 1869, propelled by three wooden wheels, has a blonde china head (fine) with flowers.
1866—R. Weir, Cohoes, N. Y., (figure.)
1869—A. W. Nicholson, Brooklyn, N. Y.
1873—H. C. Work, Brooklyn, N. Y.
1875—Arthur E. Hotchkiss, Cheshire, Conn.
1886—Francis W. Peloubet, Newark, N. J.
1896—Henrietta R. Hinckley, Waterbury, Conn.

## Creeping Dolls Patented in America, 19th Century

1871—Robert J. Clay, New York, N. Y.
1871—George P. Clarke, New York, N. Y.

## Crying, Speaking and Singing Dolls, 19th Century (Pat. America)

1877—Wm. A. Harwood, Brooklyn, N. Y. Crying and talking doll.
1886—William J. Lynd, Yreka, Cal. Speaking and singing doll.
1888—W. W. Jacques, Newton, Mass. (Assigned to Edison Phonograph Toy Mfg. Co.) Doll and Phonograph combined.
1893—John P. King, Philadelphia, Pa. Automatic crying doll.

## Wax Dolls Patented in America, 19th Century.

1866—D. Checkini. Four-faced wax doll.
1881—Fritz Bartenstein, Huttensteinach, Germany. Double-faced Wax Doll.
1885—Philip Goldsmith, Covington, Ky. Wax doll (also composition, but most heads were imported.)

## Celluloid Dolls Patented in America, 19th Century

1881—Wm. B. Carpenter (Assigned to Celluloid Novelty Co., N. Y., (celluloid dolls were in use before this date.)

## Metal Pat. Am. 1901

Minerva (in use since 1894) German, sold through A. Vischer & Co., New York, N. Y.

## Collectors' Bisque-Headed European Dolls Patented in America

1888—Emile Jumeau, Paris, France. "Bebe Jumeau" (Jumeau family in the doll business since the early 1840's).
1896—J. D. Kestner, Jr., Waltershausen, Germany. Symbol, a crown with streamers pendant, adopted at this time. Firm much older than 1896. (Kestner-made dolls sold through Borgfeldt & Co., New York, N. Y.)
1902—Steiner, Edmund U., New York, N. Y. "Majestic" (used since 1894.) Also "A scroll with an eagle perched thereon and the word 'Liliput' on the scroll."

## European Felt Dolls Patented in America

1908—Margaret Steiff, Glengen a/Brenz, Germany.

## Cloth Dolls Patented in the United States

1868—G. H. Hawkins (cloth saturated with size and pressed into a mold. Patent for doll head.)
1873—Izannah F. Walker, Central Falls, R. D. "This invention has relation to the manufacture of dolls; and consists mainly, in the secondary or double stuffing next to the external or painted layer, whereby, with a sufficient soft surface, the tendency of the paint to crack or scale off is obviated."
1880—Charles T. Dotter, Brooklyn, N. Y., (body only.)
1883—Sarah G. Robinson, Chicago, Ill., (body only; joints strengthened by the use of buttons.)
1883—Martha L. Wellington, Brookline, Mass. (A wire framework inserted in head and ends of doll under a stockinet exterior kept it in shape.)
1885—Philipp Goldsmith, Covington, Ky., (body only.)
1886—Edward S. Peck Santa Claus Doll, (very unexceptional.)
1893—Ida A. Gutzell, Ithaca, N. Y.
1895—Bernard Wilmsen, Philadelphia, Pa.
 NOTE: The Columbia doll and the Chase Stockinet were not patented. They are secondary collector's items. Many rag dolls were manufactured for advertising purposes during the 1890's and the earlier part of the 20th century. These, with the possible exception of the Palmer Cox Brownies, are hardly collector's items.
1912—Edward I. Horseman, Jr.
1917—James P. Dunne, Chicago, Ill. "Teddy Roosevelt"—a caricature.

## Rubber Dolls Patented in U. S. 19th Century

1851—Goodyear. (Patent refers to material rather than the doll on which patent is recorded.)
1854-1868—Goodyear. Some were marked "I. R. C. Co."

*Chapter 22*

# SHOPS IN AMERICA SELLING ANTIQUE DOLLS

### ARKANSAS

Mrs. Wade H. Orr, 1107 Spring Hill Ave., Mobile, Ala.
Catherine Howard, Hope, Ark.
Marie Russell's Antique Shop, Winslow, Ark.
Hot Springs National Park Shop, 120 Henderson Ave., Hot Springs, Ark.

### CALIFORNIA

Mrs. Emma C. Clear, Redondo Beach, Cal. (makes china heads; restores; sells antiques.)
Porter's Old Curiosity Shop, Berkeley, Cal. ("Almost anything in antiques.")
Mary Maxwell's House, 1464 South Coast Blvd., Laguna Beach, Cal. ("Everything in antiques.")

### COLORADO

Mrs. Albert Punshon, 1024 Lafayette St., Denver. (General line.)
Muehler's Antiques, 5500 E. Colfax, Denver. (General line.)
McBroom, 1211 11th St., Greeley. (Full line.)

### CONNECTICUT

F. Hunter, 2168 Main St., Stratford, Conn.
Maud S. Post, 70 East St., New Milford, Conn.
H. Ginsberg, 763 State St., New Haven.

### DELAWARE

Mrs. Leslie I. March, 103 Kings Highway, Milford.

## DISTRICT OF COLUMBIA

Murray Galleries, 1400 Wisconsin Ave.
Mrs. Laura Waters, 2006 Florida Ave.

## FLORIDA

The Montgomery Sisters, San Carlos House, St. Augustine. (Summer address, Petosky, Mich.)
Wee Lassie Doll Shop, 325 Lincoln Rd., Miami Beach. (Antique and modern.)

## GEORGIA

Violette Hempill, 1156 Lullwater Rd., Atlanta.
Mrs. A. S. Campbell, 964 Park Way Drive, Atlanta.

## ILLINOIS

Richard Smith, Arcola.
Doll Shop, 5212 S. Troy St., Chicago.
Bobbies Hobbies, 4510 Broadway, Chicago.
Soup to Nuts Trading Post, 2233 W. Madison, Chicago.
(NOTE: One of the best districts in Chicago to buy antique dolls is in the vicinity of the Chicago Historical Society Museum.)
Goldie Schneider, 1047 W. Main St., Galesburg, Ill.
Blanche Seltzer, Elmwood.

## INDIANA

Hobbyana, 131 Locust, Evansville, Ind.
Mrs. Tillie Cuisick, 1013 Oakley St., Evansville.
Twolady Shop, Newburgh, (Large general line.)
A. W. Peden, 613 Park Ave., South Bend.
Mrs. W. O. Crawford, 23 N. 10th St., Richmond.
Mary Beauvais, 1320 E. Main St., Richmond.
A. W. Peden, 613 Park Ave., South Bend.
Rose Staley, 431 Middlebury St., Elkhart.

## IOWA

Mrs. Bertha Mangold, 1001 No. 5th St., Burlington.
Virla V. Arnett, Box 532, Nashua.
Mrs. Agnes Koehn, 501 3rd Ave., S. W., Cedar Rapids.
Allien J. Smith, 869 41st St., Des Moines.
Irma Fitzgerald, Box 111, Independence.

*IOWA (Continued)*

>J. J. Sharp, Corydon.
>Mother Barbour's, 933 N. Van Buren, Mason City.
>Della L. Wells, 612 14th St., Ft. Madison.

*KANSAS*

>Dudgeon's Antique Shop, 603 West Kansas Ave., Pittsburgh.
>Mrs. Mary Hoover, 1268 Van Buren, Topeka.
>Mrs. T. E. Foster, 223 E. 16th St., Hutchinson.

*KENTUCKY*

>Mrs. Lena Wallace, Irvine.
>Mrs. W. F. Morris, Route 1, Paducah.
>Antique Shop, Opp. New Castle Hotel, Frankfort.
>Noah's Ark, Church Ave., Louisville.

*MAINE*

>Prudence A. Stickney, Sabbathday Lake.

*MARYLAND*

>Lillian Franklin, Westminster.
>Mrs. E. A. Lewis, 1404 Camden Ave., Salisbury.
>Elsie Clark Krug, 2227 St. Paul St., Baltimore (also sells other collection dolls; issues descriptive pamphlet.)
>Martha G. Stayton, 210 W. Franklin St.
>J. Harris & Sons, 873 N. Howard St.
>S. S. Taylor, 867 N. Howard St.
>(NOTE: Best district to buy antique dolls in Baltimore is North Howard Street.)

*MASSACHUSETTS*

>Norwell Galleries, 299 Cambridge St., Boston.
>Mrs. George Wichelow, 179 Newbury St., Boston.
>Doll Hospital, 37 Temple Place, Boston.
>(NOTE: Best place in Boston to buy antique dolls is Charles St. between Boston Common and the river.)
>Mrs. Harry Garland, Worcester.
>Ox Yoke, West Harwich.
>Harriet McGee, 49 Norman St., Springfield.

## MICHIGAN

Mabelle M. Graves, 1430 Granger Ave., Ann Arbor.
Mrs. McClintock, 1023 N. Front, Marquette.

## MISSOURI

Kimport, Independence.
C. C. Lamb, 929 N. College St., Neosho.
The Sampler, 4459 Olive St., St. Louis.
Miss Tracy's Shop, 12th & Morrison St., St. Louis.
(NOTE: Best district in St. Louis, Olive St.)

## MINNESOTA

Midway Antiques, Kasson.
Colonial Antiques, Box 427, Fairmont.

## NEBRASKA

Myrtle Sunderland, 115 N. 27th St., Lincoln.
Drew's Antique Shop, 101 S. 24th St., Omaha.

## NEW JERSEY

Elizabeth Zenorini, 1144 Buckingham Rd., Palisade. (By appointment only.)
Eileen Bermingham, 211 Elm St., Cranford.

## NEW YORK

Dorothy Nitchman, 1092 Waverly Pl., Schenectady.
Mrs. Z. M. Pollock, 96 W. 169th St., New York City.
(NOTE: Best district in N. Y. C., 3rd Ave. between 20th and 60th Sts.)
Williams Antique Shop, Woodstock. ("Anything Antique.")
Freeman Farms Antiques, Glens Falls. (List, 10 cents.)
Irene M. Lowe, Kirkwood.
Ethol M. Watson, Cornallville.

## OHIO

J. E. Nevil, 4520 Erie Ave., Cincinnati.
Charles and Edith Patrick, 407 N. Main, Marion. (General line.)
Dixie Antique Shop, 4 N. Main St., Mt. Vernon.
Jennie Barton Vaugn, 241 W. Main St., Norwalk.
Mrs. C. A. Robbins, 1215 Hurd Ave., Findlay.

## PENNSYLVANIA

Eugenia Martin, 1001 Broad St., Montoursville.
Ruth V. Ludwig, 1530 Locust St., Philadelphia 2.
Weissman's & Goldberg, 1010 Pine St., Philadelphia.
Irwin Schaffer's Antiques, 1032 Pine St., Phila.
I. Reese, Inc., 928 Pine St., Phila.
Wiener's, 1036 Pine St., Phila.'
(NOTE: Best place to buy antique dolls in Phila., Pine St. between 10th and 20th Sts.)
Dyke's Doll Hospital & Quaker Doll Co., 5210 Cedar Ave., Phila.
Mrs. W. H. Wierman, 314 W. Market St., York.

## SOUTH DAKOTA

Mrs. Florence C. Berven, 5 W. Kemp, Watertown.

## VERMONT

Raymond O. Beaupre, 14 Hickok Pl., Burlington.
White Birches, Rutland.

*Chapter 23*

# MUSEUMS WHERE DOLLS MAY BE SEEN

CALIFORNIA

Los Angeles
    Annex to home of Mrs. George Butler Griffin—2,500 dolls.

Santa Ana
    The Bowers Memorial Museum.

Riverside
    Mission Inn.

DISTRICT OF COLUMBIA

The National Museum.
Trinity College, Catholic University of America.
    Hand-Made Dolls "400 Outstanding Women of the World."—Collection of Minna M. Schmidt.
Trinity College

Smithsonian Institution
    Antique dolls (at present in storage.)
    Ethnological collection of Kachinao god-dolls of Tuysan Indians.

Daughters of the American Revolution
    Antique dolls exhibited periodically.

Department of the Interior
    Indian Dolls.

CONNECTICUT

Hartford
    Children's Museum—Antique and Foreign.

## FLORIDA

*Clearwater*
 Public Library.

## ILLINOIS

*Chicago*
 Historical Society—Costume dolls made by W. P. A.; doll heads rescued from the Great Fire of 1871; figures representing the life story of Abraham Lincoln, and others.
 University of Chicago—Medical dolls.

*Rockford*
 Crotty Hobbies Museum—General Collection.

## INDIANA

*Greenfield*
 JamesWhitcomb Riley Old Home Society.

*Indianapolis*
 Children's Museum.

## IOWA

*Waterloo*
 Wee Lassie Doll House—General collection, very large, seen by appointment.

## KANSAS

*Lawrence*
 Thayer Museum. Creche dolls of the 18th century and general collection.

## MAINE

*Paris Hill*
 Sixteen room doll house of Mary Birchfield.

*Portland*
 Maine Historical Society.

## MARYLAND

*Baltimore*
 Enoch Pratt Free Library.
 Peale Museum.
 Pratt Library.

## MASSACHUSETTS

*Boston*
    Museum of Fine Arts—Egyptian.
    The Harrison Gray Otis House.—Antiques.
    Old State House, Bostonian Society.

*Brocton*
    M. Linwood Fraser.

*Cambridge*
    Museum for Children.

*Duxbury*
    Cook's Antiques.

*Falmouth*
    Historical Society

*Hanson*
    The Trading Post.

*Jamaica Plain*
    The Children's Museum—Antiques.

*Marblehead*
    Lee Mansion Museum—dolls belong to Historical Society

*Northampton*
    Forbes Library.

*Provincetown*
    Historical Museum.

*Plymouth*
    Antiquarian Society

*Quincy*
    Public Library.

*Salem*
    Essex Institute.

*Springfield*
    Museum of Natural History.

*Wenham*
    Historical Society.

*Westfield*
    The Children's Library.

*Worcester*
    Dolls' Paradise Museum—Privately owned.

## MICHIGAN

*Dearborn*
    Edison Institute Museum—antique and foreign dolls.

*Detroit*
    Children's Museum—general collection.
    Institute of Arts—old puppets.

## MINNESOTA

*Duluth*
    Children's Museum.

## NEW HAMPSHIRE

*Manchester*
    The Currier Gallery of Art—small collection antique and foreign.

## NEW JERSEY

*Newark*
    Museum.

## NORTH CAROLINA

*Durham*
    Duke University, Sociology Dept.

## NEW YORK

*Brooklyn*
    Children's Museum.

*Buffalo*
    Historical Society.

*New York City*
    Cooper Union Museum.
    Museum of Natural History.
    Heye Foundation—Indian dolls.
    Metropolitan Museum of Art—Costume dolls.
    Museum of the City of New York—Antique.
    Museum of Science and Industry—R. C. A. Building.
    Historical Society.

## OHIO

*Cincinnati*
    Art Museum.

*Cleveland*
    Cleveland Museum of Art.

*Toledo*
    Costume dolls—Faces all similar; beautiful period costumes from the 10th century to 1915.

## PENNSYLVANIA

*Philadelphia*
    Museum of the University of Pennsylvania—antique, foreign and regional.
    Franklin Institute—writing automaton 200 years old.

*Pittsburgh*
    Carnegie Museum—general collection.

## UTAH

*Salt Lake City*
    Central State Capitol—small collection.

## VERMONT

*Springfield*
    Town Library—general collection.

## VIRGINIA

*Richmond*
    Virginia Historical Society—small collection.
    Confederate Museum—small collection.

## WISCONSIN

*Madison*
    University of Wisconsin.
    Wisconsin State Historical Museum.

*Milwaukee*
    Public Library.

*Chapter 24*

# BIBLIOGRAPHY—DOLLS

THE FASCINATING STORY OF DOLLS—Janet Pagter Johl. H. L. Lindquist, New York, N. Y., 1941.

DOLLS AND PUPPETS—Max von Boehn (translated by Josephine Nicoll). George G. Harrap & Co. Ltd., London, Bombay and Sydney, 1932.

DOLLS—Esther Singleton (out of print). New York, 1927.

THE DOLL BOOK—Laura B. Starr (out of print). New York, 1908.

QUEEN VICTORIA'S DOLLS—Frances H. Low (out of print). George Newnes, Ltd., London, England, 1894.

CHILDREN'S TOYS OF BYGONE DAYS—Karl Grober (translated by Philip Hereford). B. T. Batsford, Ltd., London and New York, 1932.

CHILDREN'S TOYS OF YESTERDAY—edited by C. Geoffrey Holme. The Studio Ltd., London and New York, 1932.

HISTOIRE DES JOUETS—H. R. d'Allemagne, Paris, 1903.

THE STORY OF MY DOLLS—Alice Trimpey. Racine, Wisconsin, 1936.

DOLLS OF MANY LANDS—Mrs. Mary Hazelton Wade (Blanchard). Chicago, 1913.

THE BOOK OF THE QUEEN'S DOLL HOUSE—Laurence D. Weaver. (2 Vols.), London, 1924.

EVERYBODY'S BOOK OF THE QUEEN'S DOLL HOUSE—Arthur C. Benson. London, 1924.

LIBRARY OF THE QUEEN'S DOLL HOUSE—Arthur C. Benson.

DOLLS ON DISPLAY (Japanese Doll Festival)—G. Caiger. New York, 1936.

PEEPS AT THE WORLD'S DOLLS—W. Canning-Wright. New York, 1923.

COLLECTOR'S LUCK—Alice Van Leer Carrick. Garden City Publishing Co., Garden City, N. Y., 1923.

DOLLS OF FRIENDSHIP—Committee on World Friendship Among Children. New York, 1929.

WORLD FRIENDSHIP—Gertrude King. Boston, 1935.

TOYS AND TOY MAKERS—James S. Tippett. New York, 1931.

THE LAND OF THE LOST DOLLS—Fezendie Hector. New York, 1937.

FLOATING ISLAND—Anne Parrish. New York, 1930.

A DOLL'S FAMILY ALBUM—Edna Knowles King. Chicago, 1937.

DOLLS (An Anthology)—Julia Robinson. Wisconsin, 1938.

HITTY—HER FIRST HUNDRED YEARS—Rachel Field. The Macmillan Co., New York, N. Y., first issue, 1929; last issue, 1941.

SANDMAN'S STORIES OF DRUSILLA DOLL—Abbie Phillips Walker. Harper & Bros., U. S. A., 1920.

RACKETTY PACKETTY HOUSE—Frances Hodgson Burnet. New York, 1906.

THE LITTLE WOODEN DOLL—Margery Williams Bianco. New York, 1926.

TWENTY LITTLE MAIDENS—Amy E. Blanchard. Philadelphia, 1893.

THE LONESOMEST DOLL—Abbie Farwell Brown. Houghton Mifflin Co., New York, N. Y., 1901, 1928.

LITTLE JEAN—Helen D. Brown. Boston, 1918.

POLLY COLOGNE—Abby Morton Diaz. Boston, 1930.

MEMOIRS OF A LONDON DOLL—Clara W. Hunt (Editor). The Macmillan Co., New York, 1925. (Copyright, 1922).

DONKEY JOHN OF TOY VALLEY—Margaret Molley. Chicago, 1909.

THE LITTLE RAG DOLL—Ethel Calvert Phillips. New York, 1930.

A DOLL, TWO CHILDREN AND THREE STORKS—Teresah. New York, 1938.

LETTERS DE DEUX POUPÉES—Par Mlle. Julie Gouraud. Paris, 1864. (Out of print.)

AMERICAN MADE DOLLS & FIGURINES—The Doll Collectors of America, Inc., Boston, Mass., 1940; reprint 1944.

SUPPLEMENT TO AMERICAN MADE DOLLS AND FIGURINES—The Doll Collectors of America, Inc., Boston, Mass., 1942.

CAVALCADE OF TOYS—Ruth and Larry Freeman. Century House, N. Y., 1942.

MINIATURIA—Georgene O'Donnell. (Tiny Dolls, pp. 137-140.)

DOLLS THE WORLD OVER—Elizabeth Hooper. Baltimore, Md., 1939.

AMERICAN HISTORICAL DOLLS—Elizabeth Hooper. Baltimore, Md., 1941.

HOBBIES—(a monthly article on dolls; first one, March, 1936.) The Lightner Publishing Co., Chicago, Ill.

DOLL TALK—(published several times a year to advertise dolls for sale.) Kimport, Independence, Mo.

MEXICAN STRAW DOLLS—National Geographic Magazine, Washington, D. C., March, 1934.

DOLLS FOR REMEMBERING—Frances Parkinson Keyes. Good Housekeeping, June, 1936.

AN ASSISTANT TO SANTA CLAUS—Mildred Harrington. Good Housekeeping, Dec., 1933.

WHAT HAPPENED ON THE CHRISTMAS TREE—Georgia Eldredge Hanley. Youth's Companion, Dec. 23, 1926.

WAX DOLLS—Esther G. Veno. The Hobbyist, Sept., 1941.

THE DOLL'S REGATTA—"Aunt Fanny." Our Young Folks, Nov., 1869.

THE STORY OF A FRENCH DOLL—H. L. Palmer. Our Young Folks, Feb., 1870.

DOLLATRY—The Contemporary Review, lxxv, 1899.

LITTLE LADIES FROM TANAGRA—C. F. Talman. The Mentor, Oct., 1923.

INSPIRATION FROM GERMAN TOYS—B. M. Wadsworth. The School Arts Magazine, April, 1929.

AMONG THE PRIMITIVE BATONGO—J. Weeks. 1914.

A PICTURE BOOK OF ANCIENT AND MODERN DOLLS—G. White. 1928.

MANNERS AND CUSTOMS OF THE ANCIENT EGYPTIANS (1837)— J. G. Wilkinson.

THE DOLL-HEAD INDUSTRY—The Literary Digest, Jan., 1915.

DOLL-MAKING IN GERMANY—American Homes, July, 1912.

KATHE KRUSE DOLLS—The International Studio, Jan., 1912.

NEW GERMAN DOLLIES WITH PERSONALITY—The Craftsman, Dec., 1911.

DOLLS IN OLD SILESIAN COSTUME—The International Studio, Dec., 1911.

THE ORIGIN AND USES OF DOLLS—Harper's Weekly, Dec., 1910.

TOY SOLDIERS AND REAL WARS—The World Tomorrow, Feb., 1931.

CZECHOSLOVAKIAN TOYS—The School Arts Magazine, Jan., 1930.

INVENTORS TURN TO TOYS—The Scientific American, Dec., 1928.

FAMOUS DOLLIES AND THEIR HOME—Arts and Decoration, Dec., 1926.

INDIAN DOLLS—Science, Oct., 1923.

TOYS OF AMERICAN INDIANS—Science, Jan., 1923.

DOLLS OF ALL NATIONS—The Mentor, Dec., 1921.

SOME FRENCH TOYS OF TO-DAY—The International Studio, April, 1921.

THE CHILD AND THE TOY—The Spectator, Dec., 1919.

ART IN TOYS—The International Studio, Dec., 1917.

THE NEW ERA IN DOLLS—The World's Work, Dec., 1916.

TOYS BY A RUSSIAN ARTIST—The International Studio, July, 1915.

THE USE OF DOLLS IN CHILD-TRAINING—M. A. Lowe. New York, 1921.

TOYS AND TOY MAKING—J. Lukin. 1881.

TOY-MANUFACTURE—J. T. Makinson. 1921.

OLD DOLLS OF THE ORIENT—A. Matzdorff. The International Studio, Sept., 1923.

TOY-MAKING IN GERMANY—E. Merriam. Harper's Bazaar, Jan., 1911.

SACRED DOLLS OF THE ITALIAN CHRISTMAS—W. Mills. House and Garden, Dec., 1929.

HISTORY OF CHINESE PORCELAIN—W. C. Monkhouse. 1901.

CHARACTER DOLLS—M. W. Mount. Harper's Bazaar, Nov., 1911.

CHRISTMAS DOLLS—M. Munn. The Ladies' Home Journal, Dec., 1929.

LES JEUX DE LA POUPÉE—Paris, 1806.

THE TOY SOLDIER—E. C. Parsons. The Educational Review, June, 1915.

IDOLS IN HOPI WORSHIP—C. S. Pearson. The Mentor, Sept., 1928.

MME. PADEREWSKI'S DOLLS; designed and made by Polish young people to help their native land. The Craftsman, Oct., 1915.

FOLK BELIEFS OF THE SOUTHERN NEGRO—Puckett. New York, 1926.

LOTTE-PRITZEL-PUPPEN—R. M. Rilke. Munich, 1921.

FUNERAL EFFIGIES OF THE KINGS AND QUEENS OF ENGLAND—Robinson. Archaeologia, lx, 1907.

SOME EIGHTEENTH-CENTURY TOYS—M. Robinson. The Connoisseur, Oct., 1926.

TOYS AT THE WHITECHAPEL ART GALLERY—A. W. Seaby. The International Studio, Sept., 1916.

THE EDUCATIONAL VALUE OF DOLL PLAY—F. B. Sherbon. American Childhood, Feb., 1927.

JAPANESE TOYS AND TOY-COLLECTORS—F. Starr. Transactions of the Asiatic Society of Japan, Dec., 1926.

THE EDUCATIONAL VALUE OF DOLLS—L. B. Starr. The Pedagogical Seminary, Dec., 1909.

FOUNDATION FIGURINES AND OFFERINGS—E. D. van Buren. Berlin, 1931.

LES JOUJOUX: LEUR HISTOIRE, LEUR TECHNIQUE—P. Calmettes. Paris, 1924.

LES JOUETS: HISTOIRE-FABRICATION—L. Claretie. Paris, 1894.

ESKIMO TOYS—L. M. Cremeans. Journal of Home Economics, April, 1931.

THE STORY OF A JAPANESE DOLL—S. Culin. Asia, Oct., 1922.

LES STATUES DE TERRE CUITS EN GRECE—W. Deonna. Athens, 1906.

LA RENAISSANCE DE LA POUPEE FRANCAISE—J. Doin. Gazette des Beaux Arts, 1914-16.

JOINTED DOLLS IN ANTIQUITY—K. M. Elderkin. American Journal of Archeology, October, 1930.

A STUDY OF DOLLS—A. C. Ellis and G. S. Hall. Pedagogical Seminary, iv, Worcester, Mass., 1896-97.

DOLLS OF THE TUSAYAN INDIANS—J. W. Fewkes, Internat. Archiv. fur Ethnogr. vii, 1894.

THE STUDY OF DOLLS AMONG POLISH CHILDREN—A. Grudzinska. The Pedagogical Seminary, Sept., 1907.

THE "TRUTH" HISTORY OF DOLLS—M. Harris. 1913.

BUSH NEGRO ART—M. J. Herskovits. Arts Monthly, Oct., 1930.

CHRISTMAS DOLLS FROM RUSSIA—U. N. Hopkins. The Ladies' Home Journal, Dec., 1913.

THE STORY OF DOLLS TELLS THE STORY OF MANKIND—W. Hough. The World Review, Dec., 1927.

INDUSTRIAL ART IN TOYLAND—R. L. Jenkins. Arts Monthly, June, 1923.

THEBAN TOYS—Dorothy Johnson. The Fortnightly Review, July, 1932.

ON DOLLS—P. Kestner. The International Studio, 1923.

PLAYING WITH THE CHRISTMAS DOLL—Kathe Kruse. The Ladies' Home Journal, Jan., 1914.

THE CHILD'S DOLL: ITS ORIGIN, LEGEND, AND FOLK-LORE—E. Lovett. 1915.

ST. NICHOLAS MAGAZINES, Bound Volumes from 1874 into the 20th century. Scribner & Co., New York, N. Y.

DAUGHTERS OF THE AMERICAN REVOLUTION MAGAZINE: Oct., 1933; Sept., 1934; Aug., 1938; Nov., 1942; Dec., 1942:—
  TWO CENTURIES OF AMERICAN COSTUME—Florence Seville Berryman. (papier-maché mannikins by Remo Bufano);
  REVOLUTIONARY FIGURES AND SCENES LIVE AGAIN IN NEW FORM—Thomas M. Johnson (describes the figures made by Dwight Franklin.)
  TREASURES OF OUR MUSEUM—Helen S. Johnson. (describes child and doll in the portrait of Mary Lightfoot by John Wollaston.)

THE ROMANCE OF OLD DOLLS—Helen Siebold Walter.
  TREASURES OF OUR MUSEUM—Rosalind Wright. (describes two early 19th century dolls from the Museum).

TOMB FIGURES OF OLD CHINA—Helen Comstock. International Studio, Jan., 1925.

NINGPO WOOD CARVINGS—Edward G. Day. International Studio, Jan., 1925.

BRIDE DOLLS—Mary Lewis. Pic Magazine, New York, Feb. 27, 1945.

A DOLL HOUSE AND A FAMILY OF PAPER DOLLS—Marian Early Lippincott, Merchantville, N. J.

THE INDEX OF AMERICAN DESIGN—The Metropolitan Museum of Art, New York.

HISTORY OF TOYS—Dorothy Neville.

TOYS OF OTHER DAYS—F. N. Jackson. Scribner's, New York, 1932.

CHILDREN'S BOOKS OF YESTERDAY—P. James. Studio, London, 1933.

GODEYS LADY'S BOOK for November 1859. (paper dolls).

WILSON'S LIBRARY BULLETIN for December, 1943. H. W. Wilson Co., New York, 1908.

HOW TO DRESS A DOLL—Mary H. Morgan. Henry Altemus, Phila., Pa. c. 1908.

LET'S MAKE MORE THINGS—Hary Zarchy. Knopf, New York, 1943.

THE HOME TOP SHOP—Nina R. Jordan. Harcourt Brace, New York, 1941.

HOMEMADE DOLLS IN FOREIGN DRESS—Nina R. Jordan. Harcourt Brace.

AMERICAN DOLLS IN UNIFORM—Nina R. Jordan. Harcourt, Brace & Co., N. Y., 1942.

AMERICAN COSTUME DOLLS: How to Make and Dress Them—Nina R. Jordan. Harcourt Brace.

COSTUMED DOLLS—Florence Huber. (A thesis prepared for Teachers' College, Columbia University, N. Y.)

WOODEN TOY-MAKING—Winifred M. Horton. Manual Arts Press, Peoria, Ill., 1936.

HOME HANDICRAFT FOR GIRLS—Mason, Hall and Neely. Lippincott, 1941.

CRAFT-WORK AND PLAY THINGS—Lippincott, c. 1936.

SUE SEW-AND-SEW—Asta, Delhi and Flavia Gag. Coward-McCann, 1931.

DOLL HOUSE BOOK—Helen D. Fish. Frederick A. Stokes Co., New York. 1940.

ANTIQUES MAGAZINE—SHOP TALK, Aug., 1943;
  THE LITTLE TOY SOLDIER—Rosemary Morse Hopkins, July, 1943;
  PROTEAN FIGURES, ALIAS PAPER DOLLS—Morgan Towne. June, 1943;
  PRIMITIVE PLAYTHINGS. June, 1941;
  EUGENIE IN MINIATURE. March, 1941;
  "LEARN YOUR FORTUNE"—(Fortune Telling Doll). Sept., 1939
  And Others.

PAPER TOY MAKING—M. W. Campbell. Pitman, London, 1937.

PAPER DOLLS—Edith Flack Ackley. Frederick A. Stokes Co. Inc., New York. (handled by J. B. Lippincott Co., Phila., Pa.)

DOLLS TO MAKE FOR FUN AND PROFIT—Edith Flack Ackley. Frederick A. Stokes Co., 1938.

A DOLL SHOP OF YOUR OWN—Edith Flack Ackley. Frederick A. Stokes Co., 1941.

PAPER DOLLS AND OTHER CUT-OUT TOYS—Wilbur Macey Stone. The Newark Museum, Newark, N. J., 1932.

*Chapter 25*

# MUSIC COMPOSED FOR DOLLS

MARIONETTE OPERAS—Haydn.

MARIONETTE OPERAS—W. J. Lawrence. The Musical Quarterly, April, 1924.

THE WALTZING DOLL—Poldini.

THE WEDDING OF THE PAINTED DOLL—Brown.

THE DOLL DANCE—Brown.

THE GOLLIWOG CAKE WALK—Debussy.

SERENADE FOR A DOLL—Debussy.

DANCE OF THE CHINESE DOLLS—Ribkov.

DANCE OF THE RUSSIAN DOLL—Tschaikowsky.

MARCH OF THE TIN SOLDIERS—Tschaikowsky.

MARCH OF THE TOYS—Victor Herbert.

MARCH OF THE LITTLE LEAD SOLDIERS—Pierne.

THE FUNERAL MARCH OF A MARIONETTE—Gounod.

THE DOLL'S DANCE—Bizet.

THE DOLL'S CRADLE SONG—Bizet.

LULLABY TO A DOLL—Frank Black.

DOLL SONG from TALES OF HOFFMAN—Offenbach.

PETROUCHKA SUITE—Stravinsky.

PARADE OF THE WOODEN SOLDIERS—Jessel.

THE TIN GEE GEE—Cope.

TOYMAKER'S DREAM—Ernie Golden.

PINOCCHIO (From the Walt Disney motion picture—see Victor catalog).

MARIONETTES—Glazounow (See Victor Catalog, Marimba Records).

DOLL DANCE—(See Victor Catalog—Nacio "Herb" Brown).

DOLL'S SONG—(See Victor Catalog—Olympia's Aria—Tales of Hoffman).

WALTZ OF A TEENIE DOLL from FIVE MINIATURES—Paul White. (See Victor Catalog).
DOLLY, YOU'RE AN ANGEL (See Decca Catalog. Voice of Sybil Jason, aged 7).
CHINA DOLL PARADE (See Decca Catalog).
RAGGEDY ANN'S SUNNY AND JOYFUL SONGS—Johnny Gruelle; Will Woodin; Charles Miller. Part 1. My Raggedy Ann—Raggedy Ann—Frederika—Little Wooden Willie—Beloved Belindy. (See Decca Catalog).

*Chapter 26*

# LITERATURE ON PUPPETS

ON THE ART OF THE THEATRE; PUPPETS AND POETS; A SET OF PLAYS FOR MARIONETTES; THE THEATRE ADVANCING—Edward Gordon Craig. (Also magazines THE MASK; THE MARIONETTE, published by Mr. Craig in Italy.)

A HANDBOOK OF FIST PUPPETS—Bessie Alexander Ficklen. Frederick A. Stokes Company, New York, N. Y., 1935.

A REPERTORY OF MARIONETTE PLAYS (Also a Year Book on Puppetry published since 1930)—Paul McPharlin. The Puppeteers of America, Detroit, Mich., 1929.

HEROES OF THE PUPPET STATE—Madge Anderson. Harcourt Brace, 1923.

A BOOK OF MARIONETTES—Helen Haiman Joseph. Viking Press, 1920; 1930.

PUPPETS AND SHADOWS: A BIBLIOGRAPHY—Grace Greenleaf Ransome, 1931.

PLAYABLE PUPPET PLAYS—Bruce Inverarity. Mimeographed by University of Washington, Vancouver, 1934.

PUPPET PLAYS—Alfred Kreymborg. French, 1926.

THE SHOW BOOK OF REMO BUFANO—Remo Bufano. Macmillan, 1929.

THE PEEP SHOW, 1927; VAGABONDS AND PUPPETS, 1930; PUPPETS IN YORKSHIRE, 1931; A SUSSEX PEEP SHOW, 1933; HOW TO MAKE A PUPPET SHOW—Walter Wilkinson. Frederick A. Stokes Co.

THE BOOK OF PUPPETS—Munger and Elder. Lothrop, Lee & Shepard Co., Boston, Mass., 1935.

MARIONETTES, EASY TO MAKE, FUN TO USE—Edith Flack Ackley. Frederick A. Stokes Co., 1929.

MARIONETTES, MASKS AND SHADOWS—Mills & Dunn. Paul McPharlin, 1927.

MARIONETTE HOBBY-CRAFT (four booklets)—Helen Fling. Treasure Chest Publications, Inc., New York. N. Y., 1937. (Their book on VENTRILOQUISM also teaches how to make a dummy).

MASTERPIECES—Chikamatsu Monzaimon. Translated by Asataro Miyamori.

KABUKI, THE POPULAR STAGE OF JAPAN—Zoe Kincaid. Macmillan, 1925. Dutton, 1926.

PUNCH & JUDY. London. 1880—Collier and Cruikshank. Cambridge, Mass., 1925.

THE HOME OF THE PUPPET PLAY—Richard Pischel. Translated by M. C. Tawnel, 1902.

A HISTORY OF THE HARLEQUINADE—Maurice Sand, Translated by Babbette & Hughes. 1902.

FAUST, an old German puppet play translated by T. C. H. Hedderwick, London, 1887.

PICTURES FROM ITALY—Charles Dickens, 1846.

HISTOIRE DES MARIONETTES EN EUROPE—Charles Magnin, 1852. (highest authority).

PUNCH AND PUPPETS—The British Standard Hand Books, No. 38 n.d.

PUPPETS—WHAT ARE THEY?—The Literary Digest, Jan., 1931.

RICHARD TESCHNER'S FIGURE THEATRE—The Theatre Arts Monthly, July, 1928.

TELLING THE STORY WITH PUPPETS—The Survey, July, 1928.

BEHIND THE SCENES IN A PUPPET-SHOW—The Popular Mechanics Magazine, June, 1925.

THE VOGUE FOR PUPPET-PLAYS—The Popular Educator, Jan., 1927.

RUBBER ACTORS LEND REALISM TO MOVIES—The Popular Mechanics Magazine, May, 1924.

PORTRAIT PUPPETS—Current Opinion, April, 1923.

GUIGNOL—The National, April, 1923.

LILIAN OWEN'S PORTRAIT PUPPETS—Drama, Oct., 1922.

HOW TONY SARG PERFORMS "MIRACLES" WITH MARIONETTES—Current Opinion, March, 1922.

RESURRECTING CHINESE MOVIES A THOUSAND YEARS OLD—Current Opinion, July, 1921.

PLAY-WRITING FOR THE PUPPET THEATRE—Current Opinion, May, 1921.

ALICE IN PUPPET LAND—The Independent, Feb., 1921.

DRAMA ON STRINGS: TONY SARG'S MARIONETTES IN RIP VAN WINKLE—The Outlook, Dec., 1920.

NEW ANIMATION OF THE INANIMATE THEATRE—Vogue, Aug., 1920.

MOVIES IN THE TIME OF WILLIAM SHAKESPEARE—Current Opinion, May, 1920.

DOLLS KNOCKING AT THE ACTORS' DOOR—The Literary Digest, May, 1919.

INDIAN MARIONETTES AT HASKELL INSTITUTE—Sibyl M. Malm. School Arts, Nov., 1936.

HOW PUPPETS SURPASS OUR HUMAN ACTORS: TONY SARG'S MARIONETTES—Current Opinion, April, 1918.

ARE WE FORGETTING PUNCH AND JUDY?—The Review of Reviews, Jan., 1918.

THE PARADOX OF THE PUPPET: AN EXTINCT AMUSEMENT BORN ANEW—Current Opinion, Jan., 1914.

REVIVAL OF THE PUPPETS—Current Opinion, July, 1916.

PUPPET WARFARE IN FRANCE—The Literary Digest, Nov., 1915.

THE MOST IMMORTAL CHARACTER EVER SEEN ON THE STAGE—Current Opinion, Jan., 1914.

THE RETURN OF THE MARIONETTES—Current Opinion, March, 1913.

THE PARISIAN PUPPET THEATRE—The Scientific American, Oct., 1902

A PUPPET SHOW AT THE PARIS EXHIBITION—The Scientific American, Nov., 1900.

A GREEK PUPPET-SHOW—All The Year Round, March, 1894.

PUPPET-SHOWS—The Saturday Review, March, 1885.

POPULAR PUPPETS—Chambers' Journal, Feb., 1857.

PUPPETS, RELIGIOUS AND ARISTOCRATIC—Chambers' Journal, Dec., 1856.

THE HARLEQUINADE—Chambers' Journal, Nov., 1856.

PUPPETS OF ALL NATIONS—Blackwood's Magazine, April, 1854.

THE PEDIGREE OF PUPPETS—Household Words, Jan., 1852.

THE HISTORY OF PUPPET SHOWS IN ENGLAND—Sharpe's London Journal, July, December, 1851.

CASSETA DE' BURATTINI—The Penny Magazine, March and April, 1845.

PUPPETS, ANCIENT AND MODERN—Harper's Monthly, Dec., 1897.
GUIGNOL—S. G. Young. Lippincott's Magazine, August, 1879.
PUPPETS AND PUPPETEERING—R. K. Wood, The Mentor, April, 1921.
MARIONETTES AT CAMP—E. H. Wood, The Playground, March, 1930.
THE CURIOUS PUPPET-SHOWS OF CHINA—G. Wimsatt. Travel, Dec., 1925.
TEACHING SCHOOL WITH PUPPETS—L. G. Whitmire. The World Review, March, 1928.
ITALY SENDS US MARIONETTES—L. Whipple. The Survey, April, 1927.
EVERYBODY'S THEATRE—H. W. Whanslaw, 1923.
THE MARIONETTE THEATRE OF JAPAN—Our World, April, 1924.
PUPPET-SHOWS—C. F. Wells. The Playground, Nov., 1929.
MARIONETTES, QUAINT FOLK—C. F. Wells. The World Outlook, Oct., 1917.
PUPPET-PLAYS FOR CHILDREN—I. Weed. The Century Magazine, March, 1916.
PUPPET-SHOWS FOR PRIMARY GRADES—M. O. Walters. Primary Education, Sept., 1925.
A NEW FIELD FOR MARIONETTES—G. Underhill. Drama, March, 1924.
MARIONETTE OPERA—W. J. Turner. The New Statesman, May, 1923.
MARIONETTE FURIOSO: A MARIONETTE-SHOW IN THE HOUSE OF MANTEO. The Theatre Arts Monthly, Dec., 1929.
SOME MAGICAL PLAYS FOR SAVAGES—P. A. Talbot. The Strand Magazine, June, 1915.
AN APOLOGY FOR PUPPETS—A. Symons. The Saturday Review, July, 1897.
PUPPET AND CONDUCTOR—H. Straus. The Nation, New York, Feb., 1926.
A BOOK OF MARIONETTE-PLAYS—T. Sarg and A. Stoddart, 1930.
THE RENAISSANCE OF THE PUPPET-PLAY—A. Stoddart. The Century Magazine, June, 1918.
MEMORIES AND PORTRAITS—R. L. Stevenson, 1887.
HOME PLAYS WITH PUPPETS—W. Smith. The Children's Royal, Dec., 1921.
MARIONETTES, THE EVER-POPULAR PUPPET-SHOWS—H. Sibley, Sunset, Nov., 1908.

TEACHING HISTORY BY PUPPETS—J. H. Shults. The Kindergarten Magazine, Sept., 1908.

PUPPETRY AND LIFE—E. Shanks. The Outlook, Nov., 1923.

CZECH PUPPETS WITH A HISTORY—S. Schell. Shadowland, Jan., 1923.

A MARIONETTE-PLAY IN FOUR ACTS—M. J. Saunders. The School Arts Magazine, Jan., 1931.

THE TONY SARG MARIONETTE BOOK—T. Sarg. New York, 1921.

BOOKS ABOUT MARIONETTES—A. Sandford. Library Journal, Nov., 1929.

THE GOOSEBERRY MANDARIN—G. D. Ruthenburg. The Theatre Arts Monthly, July, 1928.

THE MOST POPULAR PLAY IN THE WORLD—E. Russell. Outing Magazine, Jan., 1908.

A PROFILE PUPPET-SHOW—A. Roze. The Scientific American, May, June, 1910.

A PUPPET-PLAY WHICH LASTS TWO MONTHS—V. Rousseau. Harper's Weekly, Oct., 1908.

PULCINELLA—C. Roberts. The Living Age, April, 1922.

KREYMBORG'S MARIONETTES—L. Ridge. The Dial, Jan., 1919.

PLAYS FOR PEOPLE AND PUPPETS—C. Reighard. New York, 1929.

THE PUPPET THEATRE—Peter Quennell. A Superficial Journey Through Tokyo and Peking, London, 1932.

RISE LOUTEK, A PUPPET THEATRE IN PRAGUE—V. M. Powell. The Theatre Arts Monthy, Oct., 1930.

SHADOW-PLAYS—A. E. Poulsson. St. Nicholas, July, 1907.

MARIONETTES—W. H. Pollock. The Saturday Review, Aug., 1902.

PUNCH AND JUDY UP TO DATE—L. F. Pierce. The World Today, March, 1911.

THE TRAIL OF THE LONG-NOSED PRINCESS—E. Petty. Drama, April, 1928.

THE ORIGIN OF PUNCH AND JUDY—J. Pennington. The Mentor, Dec., 1924.

MARIONETTES AND PUPPET SHOWS PAST AND PRESENT—E. C. Peixotto. Scribner's Magazine, March, 1903.

THE PUPPETS ARE COMING TO TOWN—A. Patterson. The Theatre, 1917.

SHADOW ENTERTAINMENTS AND HOW TO WORK THEM—A. Patterson. 1895.

SHADOW PLAYS AND HOW TO PRODUCE THEM—Mills and Dunn. Doubleday, Doran & Co., New York, N. Y., 1938.

PUPPETS—J. G. Park. The School Arts Magazine, May, 1924.

THE PUPPETEER'S LIBRARY—F. Park. The Theatre Arts Monthly, July, 1928.

THE MARIONETTE AS CORRELATOR IN THE PUBLIC SCHOOLS—F. C. Painton. The School Arts Magazine, Dec., 1922.

THE JAPANESE PUPPET THEATRE—Y. Noguchi. Arts and Decoration, Oct., 1920.

A MARIONETTE THEATRE IN NEW YORK—F. H. Nicols. The Century Magazine, March, 1902.

THE DANCING SKELETON OF A MARIONETTE—N. Nelson and J. J. Hayes Drama. May, 1927.

TRICK MARIONETTES—N. Nelson and J. J. Hayes Drama. Oct.-Dec. 1927, April, 1928.

TEACHING DOLLS TO ACT FOR MOVING PICTURES—R. H. Moulton. The Illustrated World, Oct., 1917.

THE MARIONETTES OF TONY SARG—H. K. Moderwell. Boston Transcript, 1918.

PRODUCING THE PUPPET-PLAY—H. L. Mick. The Theatre Arts Monthly. (also articles in Drama on various phases of puppet making from Dec., 1922 to June, 1923).

THE CHILDREN'S THEATRE—R. McQuinn. The Delineator, June, 1919.

THE OLD, OLD STORY IN SHADOW-PICTURES—M. L. McMillan. The Woman's Home Companion, Dec., 1925.

DOLL PLAY IN A DOLL SETTING—N. C. McCloud. The Mentor, Jan., 1928.

A MOVABLE PLAYHOUSE—R. McCain. The Industrial Arts Magazine, Sept., 1919.

THE MARIONETTE REVIVAL—L. R. McCabe. The Theatre Magazine, Sept., 1920.

THE LAMENTABLE TRAGEDY OF PUNCH AND JUDY—B. Matthews. The Bookman, Dec., 1913.

PUPPETS AS PEDAGOGUES—A. Marzials. The World's Children. 1930.

CHILDREN'S PLAYS IN ITALY—C. D. Mackay. Drama, Oct., 1927.

THE FAUST OF THE MARIONETTES—H. S. Macdowall. The Living Age, Feb., 1901.

MARIONETTES AND WAXWORKS—D. MacCarthy. The New Statesman, April, 1923.

EXTER'S MARIONETTES—L. Lozowick. The Theatre Arts Monthly, July, 1928.

THREE PUPPET PLAYS FOR A RURAL SCHOOL—L. S. Lovett. The School Arts Magazine, Jan., 1931.

THE MARIONETTE CONGRESS, 1930, LIEGE, BELGIUM—M. Levin. The Theatre Arts Monthly, Feb., 1931.

THE IMMORTAL MR. PUNCH—W. J. Lawrence. The Living Age, Jan., 1921.

PUPPET-PLAYS—A. Kreymborg, 1923.

WRITING FOR PUPPETS—A. Kreymborg. The Theatre Arts Monthly, Oct., 1923.

A MARIONETTE THEATRE (translation by D. M. McCollester)—H. von Kleist. The Theatre Arts Monthly, July, 1928.

KABUKI—Z. Kincaid, 1925.

PUPPETS IN JAPAN—Z. Kincaid. The Theatre Arts Monthly, March, 1929.

PUPPETS—D. B. Kalb. The School Arts Magazine, Nov., 1925, June, 1927.

ROBINSON CRUSOE IN SHADOW-LAND—D. B. Kalb. The School Arts Magazine, May, 1931.

MARIONETTES EXTRAORDINARY—A. M. Jungmann. The Popular Science Monthly, March, 1918.

A BOOK OF MARIONETTES—H. H. Joseph, 1922 (2nd ed. 1931).

ALI BABA AND OTHER PLAYS FOR YOUNG PEOPLE OR PUPPETS—H. H. Joseph. New York, 1927.

(Articles by Joseph on puppets in the Theatre Arts Monthly, Oct., 1923, Aug. 1924, Aug. 1929).

MARIONETTES OF LITTLE CICILY—L. B. Jerome. New England Magazine, Feb., 1910.

INDUSTRIAL ART IN TOYLAND—R. L. Jenkins. Arts and Decoration, Dec., 1922.

A PRACTICAL PUPPET THEATRE—O. L. Jackson. The School Arts Magazine, May, 1924.

WHERE THE PLAYERS ARE MARIONETTES—A LITTLE ITALIAN THEATRE IN MULBERRY STREET—E. Irwin. The Craftsman, Sept., 1907.

WIDOW POLICHINELLE: OUR FIRST TRAGEDIENNE ADDRESSES HER AUDIENCE—J. Irvine. Lippincott's Magazine, Feb., 1913.

MASTER PETER'S PUPPET-SHOW—D. Hussey. The Saturday Review, Nov.. 1924.

CZECHOSLOVAK PUPPET-SHOWS—S. B. Hrokova. The Theatre Arts Monthly, Jan., 1923.

THE MARIONETTE THEATRE IN ITALY—M. Holroyd. The Nation, Sept., 1922.

PUPPET PERFORMANCES IN GERMANY—G. Hirsch. Harper's Weekly, April, 1916.

THE THEATRE OF ONCE UPON A TIME—M. Hill. Kindergarten and First Grade, Nov., 1921.

THE OLD GERMAN PUPPET PLAY OF DR. FAUST (1887)—T. C. Hedderwick.

THE PUPPET SHOW—C. A. Hammond. Hygeia, June, 1931.

JAVA'S DANCING SHADOWS—M. P. Hall. Overland Monthly, July, 1928.

THE LAST STAND OF THE MARIONETTE—A. H. Gleason. Collier's National Weekly, Oct., 1909.

SHADOW-PLAYS—K. Gibson. The School Arts Magazine, March, 1927.

OPERA ON A TEN-FOOT STAGE—G. W. Gabriel. Arts and Decoration, Dec., 1921.

PUPPETS IN PRAGUE—H. Flanagan. The Theatre Arts Monthly, April, May, 1927.

THE STORY OF MR. PUNCH—O. Feuillet, 1929.

DESIGNING A SIMPLE PUPPET-SHOW—W. Dresbach. The School Arts Magazine, Jan., 1927.

BURATTINI: MARIONETTES THAT ARE NOT MECHANICAL—P. Dilley. Drama, Oct.-Dec., 1923.

AMUSING CHILDREN—L. E. Dew. Harper's Bazaar, Dec., 1910.

STORY-TELLING BY MEANS OF PUPPETS—F. C. Davis. The Playground, Sept., 1926.

A THIRD-GRADE PROJECT: A PUPPET-SHOW—M. V. Cuddy. Primary Education, Oct., 1927.

SCHOOL: AN INTERLUDE FOR MARIONETTES—E. Gordon Craig. The English Review, Jan., 1918.

THE STORY OF PUNCH AND JUDY—S. S. Conant. Harper's Monthly, May, 1871.

PUNCH AND JUDY—J. P. Collier, 1870.

JAPAN'S DOLL THEATRE, THE BUNRAKU-ZA—M. L. Cochrane. Travel, Sept., 1923.

A CHRISTMAS MYSTERY IN THE FIFTEENTH CENTURY—T. Child. Harper's Magazine, Dec., 1888.

TREMENDOUS TRIFLES—G. K. Chesterton, 1909.

WHO WILL COME TO A MARIONETTE CONGRESS?—R. Cheese. The Theatre Arts Monthly, April, 1931.

BALLADS IN BLACK—E. F. Chase. Boston, 1892.

MARIONETTES OF ROME—E. Calvi. The Bellman, Jan., 1917.

AN EVENING WITH MARIONETTES—A. Calthrop. The Theatre, May, 1884.

THE RETURN OF THE MARIONETTES—M. Bully. Current Opinion, March, 1913.

MARIONETTES IN MUNICH—G. Bullett. The Saturday Review, Dec., 1929.

PUPPET ANATOMY—R. Bufano. The Theatre Arts Monthly, July, 1928.

PINOCCHIO FOR THE STAGE—R. Bufano, 1929.

THE MERRIE PLAY OF PUNCH AND JUDY—F. K. Brown. The Playground, July, 1921.

MEMOIRS OF MARIONETTES—G. S. Brook. The Century Magazine, March, 1926.

THE STORY OF PUNCH AND JUDY—A. G. Bowie. The Theatre, Jan., 1884.

THE AMUSEMENTS OF OLD LONDON—W. B. Boulton, 1901.

PUPPETS, THE TEMPEST, AND MR. FAGAN—F. Birrell. The Nation, June, 1923; reply by J. B. Fagan.

MARIONETTES—H. Belloc. The Outlook, June, 1923.

A NEW YEAR'S PUNCH & JUDY SHOW—L. Beard. The Delineator, Jan., 1905.

PUNCH AND JUDY—M. Baring. The London Mercury, July, 1922.

PUNCH AND JUDY—M. Baring. The Living Age, Aug., 1922.

JAVA'S SHADOW-SHOWS AND THE KAWI EPICS—H. S. Banner. The London Mercury, Aug., 1927.

CICILIAN PUPPET-SHOWS—E. Ballantyne. The Theatre, Feb., 1893.

DOLLS THAT COME ALIVE—S. Baldwin. The Woman's Home Companion, Dec., 1922.

THE LESSON OF THE PUPPET—A. Bakshy. The Theatre Arts Monthly, July, 1928.

CINDERELLA CASTS A SHADOW—H. R. Abels. The School Arts Magazine, Feb., 1931.

BIB PUPPETS—Ruth H. Kemp. The Guardian, a Camp Fire Girls Publication, June, 1942.

MITTEN PUPPETS—Ruth H. Kemp. The Guardian, June, 1938.

PUNCH'S PROGRESS—Forman Brown, New York, 1936.

RAG BAG ALLEY PUPPETS—Weaver Dallas. Woman's Home Companion, Sept., 1930.

DANCING DOLLS—Hamburg Puppet Guild. New York, 1937.

A TREASURE OF PLAYS FOR CHILDREN—Montrose Moses. Boston, 1932.

HANS BULOW'S LAST PUPPET—Grace Ruthenberg. New York, 1931.

MASKS AND MARIONETTES—Joseph Spencer Kennard. Macmillan Co., 1935.

# INDEX

| | |
|---|---|
| Ackley, Edith Flack | 84, 92 |
| Ackley, Telca | 92 |
| Adams, Miss Emma E. | 91, 92 |
| Advertising dolls | 92, 128 |
| Advertising dolls (sketches) | 129 |
| Africa | 24 |
| Alaska | 117 |
| Alaskan doll, ancient (example) | 12 |
| Alcott, Louisa M. | 83 |
| "Alice in Wonderland" | 135 |
| "Alice in Wonderland" (sketch) | 83 |
| Alexander doll | 78 |
| Alexander Doll Co. | 32, 78 |
| Alexander, Mme. | 75 |
| Alexandrowicz, Mme. | 97, 98 |
| Ameera | 117 |
| America | 26, 76 |
| American | 90 |
| American Potteries | 40, 44, 84 |
| American potteries (examples from) | 85 |
| American-designed Gibson Girl | 66 |
| American rag dolls (sketches) | 93 |
| Anderson, Imogene | 100 |
| Andrews, Mrs. Earle E. | 131 |
| Ann | 97 |
| Ann, Queen | 100 |
| Ann, Queen (sketches) | 15 |
| Antiques, an encyclopedia of | 40 |
| Antiquity, dolls in (sketches) | 11, 12, 13 |
| Antiques, finding | 50 |
| Antoinette, Marie | 16 |
| Aphrodite | 34 |
| "Apollo and Marpessa" | 108 |
| Arabia | 32 |
| Armond Marseille | 62, 66, 67, 68 |
| Armond Marseille dolls (sketches) | 59 |
| Army | 132 |
| Asia | 21 |
| Association, l'des Petits Fabricants | 96 |
| Audubon | 116 |
| Aulnoy, d'Mme. | 97 |
| Austin, Erma Fiske | 83 |
| Automata | 32 |
| Averill, Georgene | 57 |
| Baby dolls, early (sketches) | 14 |
| "Baltimore, Lady" | 65 |
| Bambola Regina | 94 |
| Bambola Regina (sketch) | 95 |
| Barbour's Irish Flax Thread | 128 |
| Barnum's American Museum | 126 |
| Bavaria, Duchess of | 16 |
| Beauharnais, Josephine | 110 |
| Beery, Wallace | 77 |
| Belton, Messieurs | 60 |
| Berlin, Irving | 77 |
| Bienville | 116 |
| Billiken | 79 |
| Billiken (sketch) | 78 |
| Bisque doll, French-made | 66 |
| Bisque doll, French mechanical | 28 |
| Bisque dolls, kinds, where made | 55 |
| Bisque, early | 58 |
| Bisque, French | 64 |
| Bisque dolls, small (sketches) | 65 |
| Bisque dolls, tiny | 26 |
| Bisque, Dresden | 65 |

## 184 INDEX

|  |  |
|---|---|
| Bisque-headed dolls (sketches) | 56, 57, 58 |
| Bisque, late | 58 |
| Bisque, stone (sketches) | 65, 67, 68, 69 |
| Bisque, sugar | 58, 68 |
| Bisque, whiteware | 58, 68 |
| Blouse, molded | 61 |
| Blouse, shirred | 53, 65 |
| Blossom Creation, a (sketch) | 93 |
| Blue Fairy | 77 |
| Blue Scarf Doll | 62 |
| Bode, Dr. | 107 |
| Body, cloth | 23 |
| Boehm, Max von | 89 |
| Boltz-Massé | 58 |
| "Bon, Mme. le" | 62 |
| Bonnet, Betty | 128 |
| Bonnet dolls | 68 |
| Bonnet dolls (illustrations) | 67 |
| Books, English picture | 26 |
| Borgfeldt, Geo., Corp. | 66 |
| Bottger | 42 |
| Boulogne-sur-mer | 96 |
| Bourbon, Mademoiselle de | 16 |
| Boyer, Mrs. D. L. | 82 |
| Boyer, Mrs. D. L. (sketch of doll) | 83 |
| Boy, Parian (sketch) | 62 |
| Boy, tiny (sketch) | 62 |
| Bread-kneader dolls (sketches) | 13 |
| Bretonnes | 98 |
| Britannica, Encyclopaedia | 106 |
| British South Africa | 104 |
| British toys (sketch of symbol) | 69 |
| Brown-eyed doll (sketch) | 23 |
| Brownie dolls (sketches) | 93 |
| Brouiliet, M. | 60 |
| Browning, Elizabeth | 83 |
| Bru, Jeune | 60, 63, 64, 65 |
| Bru, M. | 34, 56, 65, 114, 118 |
| Bruyere, Mrs. Muriel Atkins | 82 |
| Bruyere, Mrs. (sketch of doll) | 83 |
| Burlington Magazine | 107 |
| "Butch" | 78 |
| Buying antique dolls | 6 |
| Bye-lo doll | 57, 66, 79 |
| Byzantine | 32 |
| Calvert, Mrs. Jennie | 124, 125 |
| Cameo Doll Co. | 79 |
| Campbell Kid | 79 |
| Canadian | 76 |
| Carlton moule | 72 |
| Camp Fire Girls | 95, 133, 144 |
| Carpenter, W. B. | 121 |
| Celluloid | 120, 121, 122, 123 |
| Century Dictionary | 1, 2, 71 |
| Ceramics | 35 |
| Ceylon | 104 |
| Chad Valley Co. | 94 |
| Chaffer's "Marks and Monograms" | 53 |
| "Chamber of Horrors" | 111 |
| Chandler, John Greene | 130 |
| Chaplin, Charlie | 83 |
| Character dolls | 76 |
| Chase | 90, 91 |
| *Charlot* | 97 |
| Charlotte, Frozen | 51 |
| "Charm" doll | 112 |
| "Charm" doll (sketch) | 113 |
| Checkini, Domino | 34 |
| Checkino, Domino (sketch) | 109 |

## INDEX

| | |
|---|---|
| Chelsea | 37, 53 |
| "Child" doll vs. "adult" | 17 |
| China | 22, 71, 104 |
| China busts with inscriptions | 53 |
| China, definition | 35 |
| China, discovery of hard paste | 39, 40, 42 |
| China dolls, price of | 29 |
| China dolls, diminishing popularity | 29 |
| China head, rare | 50 |
| China heads | 27 |
| China-heads, common (sketches) | 36, 37, 42, 43 |
| China heads, dated | 45, 46 |
| China heads, examples, 1850's-1860's | 45, 46, 47, 49 |
| China heads, examples, 1860's-1870's | 44 |
| China-heads less common (sketches) | 38, 39 |
| China heads, marked | 53 |
| China heads, numbered | 54 |
| China heads, rare (sketches) | 43 |
| China-heads, tiny (sketches) | 51 |
| China heads, unusual | 42 |
| China-heads, variety | 35 |
| China-heads, where made | 43 |
| China, soft paste vs. hard paste | 40, 41 |
| China teeth inset | 50 |
| Chinese features (sketch) | 59 |
| Chinese doll (sketch) | 103 |
| Chinese theatre dolls | 71 |
| Chittenden, Mrs. Horace | 109 |
| Christmas Crib | 130 |
| Cinderella sitting doll | 20 |
| Cita | 97 |
| Civil War "benefit" dolls | 84 |
| Civil War "benefit" doll (sketch) | 109 |
| Civil War doll (sketch) | 75 |
| Clarabel | 97 |
| Clark's O. N. T. | 128 |
| Clay dolls (sketches) | 14 |
| Clear, Emma C. | 44, 56, 65, 67, 119, 145 |
| Cloth dolls | 90-96 |
| Clothespin dolls | 85-86 |
| Cochran, Dewes | 77 |
| Cochran, Dewes (sketch of doll) | 75 |
| Coleman, Harry H. | 32 |
| Columbian | 90, 91 |
| Composition | 71-80 |
| Composition (examples) | 75, 76 |
| Composition, modern | 77 |
| Compton's Pictured Encyclopedia | 21 |
| Controller | 138, 139, 140 |
| Coptic "stuff" dolls (sketches) | 13 |
| Corday | 110 |
| Cordova | 128 |
| Cottrell, G. W. | 131 |
| Costume dolls | 79 |
| Cox, Palmer | 92 |
| Cox, Palmer (sketches) | 93 |
| Créche figures | 3, 87 |
| Créche figures (sketches) | 88 |
| Creeping dolls | 30, 32 |
| Crying dolls | 29 |
| Curtius, John Christopher | 110 |
| Daddy Long Legs, U. S. Toy Corp. | 131 |
| Daffonds, Mme. | 96 |
| "Dagmar" (sketch) | 46, 64 |
| Damaras | 24 |
| Damerval, Maison | 96 |
| da Vinci, Leonardo | 107 |
| Davis, Mrs. Franklin Hill | 33, 42, 47, 56, 57, 65, 112, 113 |

# 186  INDEX

| | |
|---|---|
| Davis, Winnie | 42 |
| Dean's Rag Book Co. | 94 |
| DeBaine, Madeleine | 78 |
| Deb-U | 79 |
| de Grange, Miss Lenore | 126 |
| Dennison's | 128 |
| Desaubliaux, Mlle. | 97 |
| Dhomont, Mme. | 98 |
| Diamond Dyes | 128 |
| Diamont, Mrs. Henry A. | 33 |
| Dionne | 78 |
| Doble, Mrs. Frank C. | 64, 131 |
| Doebrich, George | 76 |
| Dolls, bonnet | 68 |
| Dolls, bonnet (sketch) | 67 |
| Dolls, "child" vs. "adult" | 48 |
| Dolls' ages | 47 |
| Dolls, dated | 45, 46, 53, 68 |
| Doll House dolls | 58, 66, 120, 122 |
| "Doll Talk" | 84 |
| Doin, Jeanne | 94 |
| Dotter | 20, 38 |
| Dotter (sketch of doll) | 53 |
| Dresden | 39, 42, 65 |
| Dressed dolls | 39 |
| Dressler, Marie | 83 |
| Durbin, Deanna | 77 |
| Durnbaugh, Evelyn | 82 |
| Durnbaugh, Evelyn (sketch of doll) | 88 |
| Duvall, Mlle. | 97, 98 |
| Early toy dolls (sketches) | 14, 15 |
| Early toys | 10 |
| Earthenware | 41, 42 |
| East Indian wooden doll | 104 |
| East Indian wooden doll (sketch) | 101 |
| Ee-Gee Co. | 32 |
| Effanbee | 77, 78 |
| Egypt | 16, 21, 100 |
| Egyptian | 106 |
| Egyptian doll, ancient | 11 |
| Eichthal, d', Mme. | 97 |
| Eisenhower | 80 |
| Eisfeld | 96 |
| Elizabethan | 100 |
| Eissler, Fanny | 131 |
| Ellicott, H. W. | 26 |
| Ellis, Joel | 104, 105 |
| Ellis, Joel (sketch of doll) | 103 |
| England | 21, 25, 34, 55 |
| England (sketch of doll) | 101 |
| English doll | 130 |
| English toy book paper dolls | 131 |
| Essex Institute | 125 |
| Eskimo | 27 |
| Eugenie | 16, 47, 81, 90 |
| Europe | 24 |
| Eva | 126 |
| Eva (sketch) | 127 |
| Eyes | 25, 35 |
| Eyes, blown glass | 21, 63, 64, 65 |
| Eyes, brown vs. blue | 23 |
| Eye, flirting | 32 |
| Eyes, glass | 50 |
| Eyes, "jewel" | 66 |
| Eyes, inset | 59, 61, 62, 63 |
| Eyes, inset (sketch) | 65 |
| Eyes, luminous | 58 |
| Eyes, sleeping | 67 |
| Excavations | 11 |

# INDEX

| | | | |
|---|---|---|---|
| Fabrics, old | 6 | Gallea, Bébé | 97 |
| "Family" dolls | 58, 66, 120 | Garland, Judy | 77 |
| "Fashion" dolls | 71, 79, 106, 131 | Garrison, Mrs. William | 45, 67, 108, 109 |
| Fawcett, Claire | 82, 83, 102 | Gautier | 60 |
| Fawcett, Clara | 73, 74, 108 | Gavroche | 97 |
| Feast of Dolls | 22 | *Gazette des beaux Arts* | 94 |
| Feast of Flags | 22 | Gebruder Heubach | 59 |
| Fields, Lew | 77 | Genius, Little | 78 |
| Figure, figurines | 2, 3, 71, 106 | Georgene Novelties Co., Inc. | 92, 93 |
| Figures, animated | 88 | "Geraldine" | 108 |
| Figure vs. doll | 3 | "Geraldine" (sketch) | 109 |
| Fiszerowna | 96 | Georgenthal | 96 |
| "Flanders' Babies" | 34, 102 | German, ancient (sketches) | 11, 13, 14 |
| Flapper Girl | 66 | German, bisque-headed (sketch) | 33 |
| Flaxman | 107 | German symbols | 69 |
| Flaxman, John | 108 | Germany | 24, 27, 34, 36, 38, 55 |
| Fleischaker & Baum | 77 | Gib on girl | 66 |
| Fleischmann & Bloede' | 95 | Gibson doll (sketch) | 57 |
| Flirting eye (sketches) | 76 | Gibson, Irene | 20 |
| Floradora | 67 | Girl Scouts | 144 |
| Florian, Gertrude | 82 | Gilles | 98 |
| Florian, Gertrude (sketch of doll) | 83 | Glass | 21 |
| Foreign dolls | 84 | "Glitter Girl" | 79 |
| Francai, Petite | 63 | Godey's Lady's Book | 128 |
| France | 25, 34, 55 | Goldsmith dolls (sketches) | 38, 56 |
| France, Madeleine de | 16 | Goldsmith, Philipp | 20, 53, 74 |
| *Francia, La* | 98 | "Gone With The Wind" | 126 |
| "Freddie" (sketch) | 62 | Goodyear dolls (sketches) | 119 |
| French | 94 | Goodyear, Charles | 118 |
| French dolls (sketches) | 33, 56, 99 | Goujon, Mme. Pierre | 98 |
| French "fashion" doll, early | 15 | Greece | 94 |
| French Revolution | 71 | Greek ancient clay dolls (sketches) | 11, 14 |
| French symbols | 69 | Greeks | 106, 107 |
| | | Grafley, Charles | 105 |
| | | Greenaway, Kate | 49, 97, 121 |

## INDEX

| | |
|---|---|
| Greiffier, M. | 60 |
| Greiner | 46, 47, 73 |
| Greiner, Improved | 74 |
| Greiner, Ludwig L. | 74 |
| Greiner patent | 74 |
| Greiner, unusual | 74 |
| Gresholtz, Marie | 110 |
| Guardian, The | 85, 133 |
| Guimp, molded | 50, 62 |
| Gum tragacanth | 71 |
| Gutmann & Schiffnie | 95 |
| Gruelle, Johnny | 92 |
| Gruelle, Johnny (sketch of dolls) | 93 |
| Hairdo | 45, 49 |
| Hairdress, unusual | 48 |
| Hair, natural | 71 |
| Hands, china (sketches) | 18 |
| Handwerck-Halbig | 68 |
| Hanska | 98 |
| Hall, Mrs. Virgil Wilson | 49 |
| Hapsburg | 124 |
| Haroun-al-Raschids | 97 |
| Harris, Mrs. Aileen (sketch of doll) | 83 |
| Hart, William H., Jr. | 131 |
| Harwood, W. A. | 29 |
| Hawkins | 90 |
| Heels, high | 43 |
| "Heil" | 104 |
| "Heil" (sketch of doll) | 101 |
| Heizer, Dorothy | 81, 90 |
| Heizer, Dorothy (sketch of doll) | 91 |
| Henie, Sonja | 78 |
| Henry VIII | 141 |
| Heubach | 68 |
| Heubach, Gebruder (sketch of doll) | 59 |
| Heubach Koppelsdorf | 68 |
| Hildburghausen, M. Voit de | 60 |
| Hobby-Craft | 140 |
| Hoffman, Soloman E. | 76 |
| Hopi (sketch of doll) | 81 |
| Holland | 34, 118 |
| Holland (sketch of doll) | 119 |
| Horse-shoe symbol (sketch) | 68 |
| Hosmer, Herbert H. | 130, 131 |
| Howard, Hope | 38 |
| Hunt, Mrs. George R. | 46, 60, 63 |
| Hurd, Miss Lydia | 126 |
| Huret, Mlle. Calixto | 118 |
| Hyatt, John Wesley | 121 |
| Ideal Novelty and Toy Co. | 77 |
| Images | 106, 107 |
| India | 21 |
| Indian children | 26 |
| Indian doll (sketch) | 85 |
| Indians, North American | 84 |
| Irish peasant | 82 |
| Isabella, Queen | 126 |
| Isabella, Queen (sketch) | 127 |
| Jachowski, Mrs. Elsie | 56, 64 |
| Jacques, Wm. J. | 30 |
| Jan | 98 |
| Japan | 22, 23, 55, 70 |
| Japanese | 96 |
| Japanese symbol (sketch) | 69 |
| Jedrek | 98 |
| Juggler | 133 |
| Johnson, C. C. | 105 |
| Jointed, ball | 75 |
| Juno | 112, 113 |

| | | | |
|---|---|---|---|
| *Journal der Moden* | 130 | Lefferts, M. C. | 121 |
| Jumeau | 58, 59, 60, 62, 67, 95 | Legs, China (sketches) | 18 |
| Jumeau dolls (sketches) | 33, 55, 56 | Legs, cotton (sketch) | 19 |
| | | Lenci | 93, 94 |
| Kansas, University of | 89 | Lenci (sketch of doll) | 95 |
| Kaffir | 24 | Lepape | 98 |
| Katchina | 84 | Lerch and Klagg | 74 |
| Kestner dolls (sketches) | 57 | Liberius, Pope | 87 |
| Kestner, J. D. | 66 | Library of Congress | 100 |
| Kestner symbol (sketch) | 69 | Limoges | 96 |
| Kewpie | 57, 66, 79 | Lincoln, Mary Todd | 44, 48, 49 |
| Kimport | 82, 83, 84, 98, 104, 116, 117, 123, 126 | Lind, Jenny | 46, 48, 49, 118, 125, 131 |
| King, J. P. | 29 | Lind, Jenny (sketch) | 119 |
| King's Porcelain Manufactories | 52 | Lines Bros., Ltd. | 76 |
| Kiwanis, Camp | 135 | Lion | 128 |
| Kleninger, Johann | 89 | "Little Women" | 83 |
| Knobloch, Mrs. Wm. | 28, 31, 82, 83, 84, 85, 116, 117 | Lloyd, Mlle. | 98 |
| Knot, Miss | 104 | London doll | 25 |
| Knot, Miss (sketch of doll) | 101 | Louis XIII | 16 |
| Koenig, Mlle. | 98 | Louis XIV | 16 |
| "Koko" | 117 | Low, Frances H. | 104 |
| Koran | 117 | Lucas, Richard Cockle | 107 |
| K. R. | 68 | | |
| Krug, Mrs. Elsie Clark | 82, 98 | Mademoiselle | 121 |
| Kruse, Kathie | 92, 93, 114 | Madison, Dolly | 53, 122 |
| Kruse, Kathe (sketch of doll) | 95 | "Magic-skin baby" | 120 |
| | | Magnin, I. & Co. | 94 |
| "Ladies" | 59 | Maine, battleship | 57 |
| Ladies' Home Journal | 128 | Manson, Mme. | 97 |
| Lamballe, Princesse de | 110 | Marat | 110 |
| Lane, Letty | 128 | Marion | 98 |
| Laumont, Mme. de | 98 | Marionette | 133, 134, 135, 138 |
| Laumont, Mme. la Baronne | 96 | Marionette, how made | 133, 142 |
| Lazarska | 96 | Marionette (philology of word) | 2 |
| Leather dolls | 24 | Marionette (sketches) | 136 |

| | | | |
|---|---|---|---|
| Marionette vs. Puppet | 141 | Minton, Thomas | 53 |
| Marks Bros. | 123 | Mohammed | 21 |
| Marks, china doll | 52, 53 | Mohammedans | 117 |
| Marks, old china (sketches) | 52 | Monica Doll | 79 |
| *Marlborough s'en va t'en guerre* | 97 | Monica Studios | 79 |
| Martin's Book, John | 128 | Montanari | 79, 108, 109, 111 |
| Martin, F. D. | 104 | Monroe, Ansil W. | 118 |
| Marks and Monograms, Chaffer's | 53 | Monroe (sketch of doll) | 118 |
| Masks | 106 | Morocco | 117 |
| Mauger | 60 | Moroccan dolls (sketches) | 116, 117 |
| McCall Fashion Model | 75 | Morrison, E. R. | 31 |
| McCarthy, Charlie | 77 | Morrison family | 107 |
| McFlimsey, Flora | 78 | Model dolls | 120 |
| McGuffey, Anna | 78 | Mother Goose | 135 |
| McKim, Mrs. | 82 | Multi-faced dolls | 34, 65 |
| McLaughlin's | 128 | Museums: | |
| McLoughlin Bros. | 126 | Barnum's American | 126 |
| McLoughlin Bros. (sketch of paper doll) | 127 | British | 12 |
| | | City of New York | 46, 124, 125, 128, 129 |
| | | Confederate | 75 |
| | | Confederate Museum doll | 42 |
| McPharlin, Paul | 141 | Freidrich, Kaiser (Berlin) | 107 |
| "Meat baby" | 26 | Hillcrest, The Little | 11, 122 |
| Mechanical toys | 27 | Los Angeles | 82 |
| | | Maryland Historical Society | 56 |
| Medal | 69, 98 | Metropolitan | 11, 89 |
| | | New York Historical Society | 46 |
| Medal (Polish Victim's Relief) | 99 | Ontario, Royal | 90 |
| Medici, Katherine de | 16 | Red Cross, Washington | 109 |
| | | Smithsonian | 125 |
| Meissen | 42 | Wenham | 92 |
| Metal | 112, 113 | Naples, king of | 98 |
| Metman, M. | 96 | Napoleon | 107, 110 |
| Michele | 98 | Navy | 132 |
| Miller, Miss Grace Stanley | 82 | Negro | 96, 97 |
| Miller, Wesley | 118 | Neustadt | 96 |
| Miller, Wesley (sketch of doll) | 119 | New England Mincemeat Co. | 128 |
| Mimi | 98 | New Zealand | 24 |
| Minerva | 112 | Nicholson, A. W. | 31 |
| Minerva (sketch of doll) | 113 | Nightingale, Florence | 83 |

## INDEX

| | | | |
|---|---|---|---|
| Nilsen, Margit | 79, 118 | Paris, doll population | 38 |
| Nilsen (sketch of doll) | 119 | Parmentier | 98 |
| "Nina" (sketch) | 75 | Parsons-Jackson "baby" (sketch) | 78 |
| Nippon | 70 | Patterns | 147, 148 |
| Noufflard, Mme. Berthe | 98 | Patti, Adelini | 45 |
| Novelty dolls | 29 | Partsch, Josef | 89 |
| Nowes, Mrs. Frank B. | 90 | Peck, E. S. | 92 |
| Nuremburg | 24, 96, 102 | Peddler dolls | 3, 27, 28 |
| Nuremberg doll, early | 14 | Peddler doll (sketch) | 33 |
| Nursing doll | 30 | Peepshow | 130 |
| Nutt, Commodore | 126 | Peggity doll | 103 |
| | | Peggy (McCall doll) | 75 |
| Oberammergau | 89, 102 | Peg-jointed | 104 |
| Oberly, Miss Portia M. | 122 | Pennsylvania Potteries | 84 |
| O'Hara, Scarlett | 78 | Pennsylvania Potteries (sketch of doll) | 85 |
| Oil Paint, Devoe's | 86 | Penn, William | 100 |
| Old, Miss | 104 | Perkins, Marion L. | 103 |
| Old, Miss (sketch of doll) | 101 | Perrault | 97 |
| O'Neill, Rose | 57, 70, 79, 92 | Persia | 83 |
| Ouvre, Mme. Vera | 97 | Phonograph doll | 30 |
| Ozarks | 104 | Pierce, Franklin | 62 |
| | | Pink lustre | 35, 36 |
| Paderewski, Madame | 98 | Pinky | 78 |
| *Pantins* | 129 | Pisano | 107 |
| Paper dolls | 124-130 | Playthings | 10-13, 21-27 |
| Papier maché | 71-75 | "Plushie" | 79 |
| Papier maché dolls | 75 | Plastolite, La | 62 |
| Papier maché dolls (sketches) | 72, 73 | Pliny | 21 |
| Papier Maché Novelties Co. | 135, 145 | Pocahontas | 84 |
| Pat-a-Pat | 78 | Polish | 96, 98 |
| Patsy | 78 | Polish Victim's Relief Fund doll (sketch) | 99 |
| Parian aristocrat | 65 | Polo, Marco | 128 |
| Parian bisque | 49, 69 | Pomona | 76, 94 |
| Parian bisque (sketches) | 60, 61, 62, 63, 64 | Pomona dolls (sketches) | 85 |
| Parian, Elizabeth | 65 | | |
| "Parian, Princess" | 64 | | |

## INDEX

| | | | |
|---|---|---|---|
| Pompeii | 21 | "Raleigh, Lady" (sketch) | 101 |
| Pontalba, Baroness | 116 | Raleigh, Sir Walter Expedition | 100 |
| "Pop-up" books | 130 | Raphael | 107 |
| Potteries, English | 37 | Raphael Tuck & Sons Co., Ltd. | 126 |
| Pottery defined | 35 | Raphael Tuck (sketch of paper doll) | 127 |
| Pottery, early | 35 | Ravca, Bernard | 84 |
| *Poupee Travelleuse, La* | 28 | Ravca, Bernard (sketch of doll) | 85 |
| Powell, Violet M. | 82 | Regina, Bambola | 94 |
| Prialythe, La | 62, 63, 69 | Regina, Bambola (sketch) | 95 |
| Price of old dolls | 6-8 | Robinson (sketch) | 20 |
| Prince Charming | 77 | Robespierre | 110 |
| Puck's Workshop | 135 | Rodgers, Kathryn | 65, 82 |
| Pumpkinhead" (sketch) | 25 | Rodgers, Kathryn (sketch of doll) | 88 |
| Punch | 98 | Roig, Mme. | 97 |
| Punch and Judy | 141 | Romans | 106, 107 |
| Puppet, fist (sketch) | 140 | Ronmer, Isaac A. | 118 |
| Puppet, fist (how made) | 142 | Roosevelt, "Teddy" | 92 |
| Puppet (philology of word) | 1-2 | Ross, Betsy | 83 |
| *Puppetry* | 141 | Rosellino, Antonio | 89 |
| Puppets | 133-142 | Ross, Walter | 121 |
| Puppets, how made | 133, 142 | "Round-about" paper doll | 130 |
| Puppets, shadow | 141 | Roussel, Cadet | 97 |
| Puppet vs. marionette | 141 | Royal | 16, 94 |
| Putnam, Grace S. | 57 | Rozmann, Mlle. | 98 |
| Pyro | 62 | Rubber | 118-120 |
| | | Rubber dolls | 65 |
| Queen Anne doll | 90 | Rubber toys | 26 |
| Queen Anne dolls (illustrations) | 15, 93 | Ruff, molded | 65 |
| | | Russian | 94 |
| Rag baby | 25 | Russian (sketches of dolls) | 98 |
| Rag doll, old French (sketch) | 93 | *St. Nicholas* | 10, 13, 21, 38 |
| Rag doll, Roman | 90 | Sanders, George W. | 104 |
| Rag doll, Roman (sketch) | 91 | Sanders, George W. (sketch of doll) | 103 |
| Rag dolls, Indian | 21 | Sappho | 34 |
| Rag dolls (sketches) | 93 | | |
| Raggedy Andy, Raggedy Ann | 92 | | |

# INDEX

| | | | |
|---|---|---|---|
| Sargent, Miss Georgiana | 124 | Steiff (sketch of doll) | 95 |
| Sarg, Tony | 141 | Steiner, E. U. | 32 |
| Scavini, Di E. | 93 | Steiner, Rudolph | 30 |
| Schoenhut | 32, 102, 105 | Steuber | 20 |
| Schoenhut, Albert | 105 | "Story Book Dolls" | 56 |
| Schoenhut, Harry E. | 105 | Stowe, Harriet Beecher | 126 |
| Schoenhut (sketch of doll) | 103 | Stone bisque | 68 |
| Schon, Joseph | 76 | Stockinet | 90, 92 |
| Schonbein, Christian Frederick | 121 | Stuffing | 20 |
| Schultz Bros. | 122 | Sugar bisque | 58, 68 |
| Scootles | 70, 79 | Sun Rubber Co. | 118 |
| Scott towelling | 145 | Superior | 74 |
| Seven Dwarfs | 77 | Superstition | 107 |
| Sevres dolls | 53 | *Surprise books* | 130 |
| Shoes, dolls' | 26, 43 | Swedish wooden doll (sketch) | 14 |
| Shoulder head | 35 | Swiecka, Mlle. | 97 |
| Shoulder head of common doll | 42 | Swiss doll | 112 |
| Sigilarii | 106 | Swis doll (sketch) | 113 |
| Simon & Halbig | 57, 58, 59, 67 | Switzerland | 104 |
| Singing doll | 29 | Switzerland (sketch of doll) | 101 |
| Singleton, Esther | 94 | Swivel neck | 35, 50, 58, 59, 65, 66, 67 |
| Sleeping doll | 29 | Syria | 21, 83 |
| Smith, Captain John | 100 | Tanagra figurine | 3 |
| Smith, John | 84 | *Tatler* | 108 |
| Snood doll | 63 | Tastled tiara doll | 63 |
| Snow White | 77 | Taylor, Luke W. | 105 |
| Sonneberg | 95, 102 | Temple, Shirley | 77 |
| Sophie | 97 | Temple, Shirley (sketch of doll) | 75 |
| South America | 24 | Thayer collection | 88 |
| Spain | 126 | Theatre dolls, Chinese | 71 |
| Speaking doll | 29 | Theatres, cardboard | 131 |
| Staffordshire | 37, 53 | Theatres, mimic | 26 |
| Statuettes | 106 | Thorne, Olive | 10, 21 |
| Steele | 108 | Thrift Shops | 77, 141 |
| Steiff, Margaret | 93 | | |

## INDEX

| | |
|---|---|
| Thumb, Mrs. Tom | 126 |
| Thumb, Mrs. Tom (sketch of doll) | 127 |
| Tiny old dolls | 26 |
| Tiny old dolls (sketches) | 26 |
| Tin soldier | 112 |
| Tongren, Mrs. Adel | 32 |
| Topsy | 126 |
| Topsy (paper doll sketched) | 127 |
| Treasure Chest Publications, Inc. | 140 |
| Triptych doll | 28 |
| Tugboat Annie | 83 |
| Tussaud, Madame | 108, 110 |
| "Uncle Tom's Cabin" | 126 |
| Uneeda Biscuit Doll | 79 |
| "Valentine, Lady" | 62 |
| Valissa the Fair | 25 |
| Venice | 25 |
| Verita, Mlle. | 97 |
| Vernon, Viola | 82 |
| "Vickie" | 104 |
| "Vickie" (sketch) | 101 |
| Victoria, Princess | 71, 104 |
| Victoria (sketch of dolls) | 103 |
| Victoria, Queen | 48, 49, 52, 126 |
| "Vie" | 82 |
| W A C | 132 |
| "Waifs of Cracow" | 98 |
| Walker, Dolly | 32 |
| Walker, Isannah F. | 90 |
| Walker, Jeannie | 32, 78 |
| Walking doll | 29, 50 |
| Walking doll, patents for | 32 |
| Walking doll (sketches) | 28, 30, 31, 32 |
| Walking paper doll | 131 |
| Walterhausen | 96 |
| Warren, Lavinia | 126 |
| Warren, Minnie | 126 |
| W A V E | 132 |
| Wax | 25, 26, 106-110, 113, 149 |
| Waxing, re- | 149 |
| Webber doll | 29 |
| Wedgwood, Josiah | 107 |
| Weigel, Christoph | 106 |
| Welles, Mrs. Benjamin | 126 |
| Wellings, Norah | 94 |
| Wellings, Norah (sketch of dolls) | 95 |
| Wellington, Martha L. | 92 |
| Wezee | 24 |
| Whichelow, Mrs. George | 50, 63, 72 |
| White bisque doll | 63 |
| White House Ladies | 79 |
| Whiteware | 58, 68 |
| Wicar | 107 |
| Wiener, D. | 121 |
| Winnebago | 117 |
| "Willoby" | 59 |
| Wilmsen, B. | 92 |
| Wilmsen, Bernard (sketch of doll) | 93 |
| Wooden doll (sketch) | 12 |
| Wooden dolls | 100-105 |
| Wooden dolls (sketches) | 101 |
| Work, Henry C. | 31 |
| Working doll | 28 |
| Working doll (sketch) | 33 |
| Wright, Alan | 104 |
| Yves, Bébé | 97 |
| Zobeides | 97 |

www.ingramcontent.com/pod-product-compliance
Lightning Source LLC
Chambersburg PA
CBHW020231170426
43201CB00007B/391